THE FASCINATION
OF THE ABOMINATION

THE FASCINATION

OF THE ABOMINATION

POEMS, STORIES, AND ESSAYS

by REED WHITTEMORE

The Macmillan Company, New York
Collier-Macmillan Limited, London

The Macmillan Company, New York
Collier-Macmillan Canada, Ltd., Toronto, Ontario
Divisions of The Crowell-Collier Publishing Company

Printed in the United States of America

Library of Congress catalog card number 63-14186

To Peg and Larry Gould

Acknowledgments

Poems, stories and essays in this volume appeared in various magazines, as indicated below. My thanks to the publishers involved.

In the *Sewanee Review,* "Literature as Persuasion," "English Bards and a Hot Reviewer," "MacLeish and Democratic Pastoral," and "The Principles of Louise Bogan and Yvor Winters."

In *Poetry,* "Childe Byron," "Three Reasons," "A Letter to Karl Shapiro"

In *Furioso,* "Fragments from Major Martin's Proceedings"

In *The Carleton Miscellany,* "The Virtues of Vulgarity," "But Seriously," "The Alienated Poet Insists," "Ebenezer and his Eight-Man Rocket," "Our Ruins," and "The Cultural Conference"

In *The New Republic,* "Three Political Poems"

In *Esquire,* "Nice Fireplace, Good Beach"

In *The Western Review,* "The Stutz and the Tub"

In *The Carleton Drama Review,* "Shakespeare at 3 o'Clock in the Morning"

In *The Virginia Quarterly Review,* "The Music of Driftwood" and "The Sacred Way"

Author's Note

Like its predecessor, *The Boy from Iowa* (Macmillan, 1962), this volume is a miscellaneous collection of writings which have, with a few exceptions, appeared in various magazines over a period of years. Appropriate acknowledgments are made below, but of the essay, "The Fascination of the Abomination," I should say that, while it has never before been printed, some of my comments in it on Shaw appeared in the *Tulane Drama Review* in an essay entitled "Shaw's Abstract Clarity"; and I also wish to acknowledge my debt, in the essay on Browning, to Elvan Kintner of the Carleton College English Department and to Howard Nemerov of Bennington College for their suggestions and advice, as well as to Betty Miller for her biography of Browning, and to William Clyde DeVane for various works on Browning, particularly *A Browning Handbook*.

Table of Contents

POETRY

STORIES

ESSAYS

MISCELLANEOUS REVIEWS

POETRY

The Music of Driftwood

The music of driftwood? Yes. It comes from deep water
And floats with the wind in the foam and is beached and
    bleached,
Lying still for a movement or two, then floating farther
To enter the mind's many chambers,
                        as Wagner perhaps,
Or Bach, or whatever—it changes,
But always I like it.
I think, I hope without arrogance, it is the music
Of poetry,
                true to the temper and pulse
Of each flutelike, bassoonlike image that pads or flutters
Within in the midnight recesses, yet true too

To its own poor selfless self, bare, bearing
From way, way over yonder its theme of old blossomings:
Temples in orchards, rites, supplications,
                            art.

Our Ruins

Our ruins are not ambitious yet, mostly.
Except for a couple of Williamsburgs they age
In the grass and thistle of waste country
Where nobody who would rebuild or tear down comes to rage
At what is unsafe, un-American, unsightly.

The small silent mills are the solemnest—squat, square,
With a thickness of wall and an air of social stability
That the fishermen in their hook-and-fly hats from the city
Take to be clear
Evidence that the Greeks or Romans have been here.

But in death the square-eyed farms have their dignity too,
Where the myth of the fixed point, the still center
In all this surge and wash, this flux and flow
Has been gelded again and again, over and over,
As each agrarian buries his deathless hoe.

And now, as the country's thoroughfares widen and stiffen,
Soft little cultures with country store, gas pump, crossway,
Depot (long-closed) and a weedy, rusted siding
Display some of the virtues of long-term decay
Without the agrarians even moving away.

4

Antiquity doesn't matter. In but a decade
An empty house can gain centuries, and old mills
Can lure the bright trout and slim pike for miles and miles
To swim in the depths by their old walls by falls
Or lurk in their rotten wheelways, savoring the shade.

The Run

The run
From Piltdown to Paddington
Is done.
End of the line.

The satchels stand in the station under the clock.

The four-coupled, three-axle engine with bogey truck
Steamless sits in the shed, its wagons empty
As Pompeii.

End of the line.

The Sacred Way

"Homer was the first to demonstrate the independent power of
the human spirit. He alone showed that by facing his inescapable
destiny, man might escape his bondage to it."
                    —from *The Loom of History*, Herbert J. Muller

I.

A cold coming we had of it—
Ice and an unscheduled landing
At Gander, followed, in Athens,
By a week of rain and the flu during which our delegate
For the Philippines and the smaller island groups
Took ill and was bedded, forbidden the pilgrimage.
Then the potholes, mud and slop, and fanatic drivers,
And the shrill gusts from Helicon and Parnassus,
These too played a part in the pathos, so that:

Hang it all, Apollo!

And the oak was silent.
And the sacred fish in the silver tank were motionless.
And the serpents, twined, of the Pythoness, would not eat.
And the entrails, burned, of the Pylaeic-Delphic fishhawk

Were curled to no clear divulgence, Western anyway.
And it rained, the halls dripped, the columns glistened,
And the oracle (on the omphalos), dimly amplified
By an antiquated loudspeaker loaned by the Embassy,
Said little.

How to survive?

—No secrets.
—None?
—None, having all been spoke for
By the better tragic poets
And the lesser lyric poets
And the students of civilizations, Spengler, Toynbee,
And is the name Muller?

II.

I had hives myself, on my arms. My ulcer troubled me.
I drank mostly canned milk and avoided the "teas."
In private the Pythoness spoke to me brusquely, saying,
"Poet, why are you here? why did you come?"
And I had no reply and my wit failed and we walked
Down the Sacred Way to the Argive Kings.

III.

Deep in the temple.
I drank from my can of milk. "To be right,"
She said, "is all hope to blight." I nodded.

And the sungod beamed.
The delegations enplaned with their memoranda.

The temple warmed and the owls stirred in the olives,
And we lurked in the glade alone by the Rock of Sibyl,
Gay, reverent.

My Nation's Hero

He is sad, my nation's hero,
Who weathers in his study, armed and ready,
With all his gear about him, logos, lotions,
Sad in the wind and wet,
Waiting at his window, wistful, watching
The pelting of his culture,
The leaves' elegiac drooping
And a house cat rampant in the rhubarb.

Waiting.
It is all a waiting.
It is all a dressing, folding, packing,
A lacing, strapping, filling, snapping,
For the unexpected call that will not come,
A waiting,
As the rain comes,
And the leaves pay tribute,
And the hero, faithful, weathers by his window,
Thinking of cats, culture and of his
Poor nation.

No Retreat

"I am in earnest. I will not equivocate. I will not excuse. I will not retreat a single inch. I will be heard."—Pres. Kennedy, quoting William Lloyd Garrison.

We who must write GM a stinging letter
About the defective fuel tank on our Buick,
Who must purchase for baby a lightweight, foldable,
    washable,
Nylon-mesh-with-aluminum-buttons playpen,
And spread on our lawn a nontoxic lawn-food miracle;

Who've just been considering renting a Tuckaway cottage
Complete with a fiberglas cruiser sleeping four
For July, and possibly August, on the North Shore,
Where the nights are cool and the Club has a weekly
    smorgasbord;

Who plan to subscribe next fall to the Kiplinger Newsletter
And to take a week off for a cultural fling at Christmas
At the theaters (off Broadway) and the U.N. (maybe) —

In earnest are we
In Geneva, Seoul, Jakarta, Karachi, Macao and (of course)
    West Germany;

Nor equivocate nor excuse will
In Amoy, Saigon, Llasa, Lambeth, Laos and Leopoldville;

Nor retreat
(If a case should arise) from Lemnos, Nexos, Chios, Sicily,
    Pantellaria, Malta or Crete;

But will heard be
From London, Paris, Rome, Athens, Vienna, Warsaw,
    Budapest, Prague, Moscow, Omsk and New Delhi
To ultima Thule.

It Is Not Clear

It is not clear
Where we go from here,
Or, for that matter,
Who we're.

More Heroics

It was time, was it not? for sacrifice. But what kind?
Cigarettes, butter, fuel were in ample supply,
As were advice, polemic.
The government and the larger corporations
Had already made the arrangements for critical items
Like brains,
And though these arrangements were faulty, no human
    agency,
No matter how honest and earnest and sacrificial,
Could change them till after the Flood and the Holy
Holocaust (those were the rules). So what could be done?

What about *self*-sacrifice? He
Took to sleeping on boards and scorching his feet,
Tried fasts and trances and walking to work and not drinking;
But these only served to toughen, firm up, better
His battered selfdom. This was discouraging,
For he was one wishing to spend, not gain, always mumbling
About how we must take from the one for the many.
    Somehow.
What then?

It came to him in a flash as he read the *Times:*
By God he would read

The *Times,* cover to cover, daily and Sunday,
And the weeklies,
And *L'Express, China Pictorial, Manchester Guardian,*
Neue Zürcher Zeitung, Przeglad Kulturalny, Plamak,
L'Osservatore Politico Letterario, Pravda,
And above all, of course, all the *Congressional Record*
—Would read and read and take notes and make charts, as in
    clinics,
Of the fevers, pulses, excretions, injections, pills
Of nations and heads of nations and generals of armies
And workers in mills and housewives in kitchens and
    stockbrokers,
In the process becoming
A paradigm on his own of enlightened citizenry,
To whom other lesser heroes with lives on their hands
Could look to for solace and comfort as they, like him,
Sat in their studies silent,
Reading,
Waiting.

Few Are the Fiends

Few are the fiends but many the dreamers who dream fiends
After spice and everything nice when innocence simmers
In hot blood and seed in pastoral gardens. Gardens?
Few are the gardens also but many the Hades
Weedy and dry, empty lots in the suburbs.

Hell goes a-withering, shrinking, shriveling,
Fires banked with bored clinkers from burned-out lakes.
Yet the golden girls in their beds and the boys in their beds,
Dreaming of pendulent buds and prune-faced fagans,
Take drippings from all the old churches for all their cute
    caches:

Wax for the faded petals, the shrunken rhetoric.

Adam and Eve

On the salt flats, in the scrub and the dour draws,
Randy as grass,
Stroking the limbs and loins, spiking the nectar,
They lie in the sun in the pretty, pretty seedtime, and slither.

Old, old that flab, that flagrance, cold,
Cold that bawdry,
Pure, pure those sores, those creases, swag
From a swatch of waned moons with the seven deadly.

Rinsed and sanded, bleached and blown, sifted
Like shells, seeds, humped shores,
They're dragged, foul-mouthed with souls new-swollen, back
At last to the garden.

Cover

There's a section, with sketches and text, in an Army field
    manual,
About it: how to take cover. Some basic refuges—
Cellars, foxholes, ditches, trees, bushes—
Are first described at some length in good Army prose,
Then judged and rated,
For the purpose perhaps of firming up frightened recruits
Who else might be stirred to stand bare amid flak and bullets
Weighing their options.
At the end of the rating attention is given, briefly,
To what those recruits should do when nothing's in view—
No ditch,
No bush—
And the planes or machine-gun squads or snipers have got
    them
Fixed in delicate gunsights,
Caught between breath and brine in a marvelous still shot—
Gaunt, nightmarish shapes in the wastes of the moon
With maybe a second left them of God's free will—
At which time, the Army advises, they should be sure to
Hit the deck smartly, lie flat, try to look like Nature.

Of course.
Here is the basic cover, the self. If that is

Fat or unduly long, or addicted to wearing
Gaudy coats and sweat socks, it may not be much;
And indeed no human form is as happily suited
To meet this critical test as the lower forms,
Like lizards, spiders, many small birds and fish.
But to make do, get along with the little provided
Is to have learned
About cover.

The Dawn Walker

When he wakes to it,
Which is seldom,
He expects a good bit of the dawn. The dawn is evidence
Of creation,
Of the possibilities inherent
In a world uncommitted as yet except to weather,
Birds, milkmen.
                    The dawn in fact
Is just about all he has left of the pastoral in him.
What, he wonders,
Became of the rest, the soft days
When he strode to beach or bar and sat
Fawning o'er Amaryllis under an awning?

Whatever happened, it's gone, gone,
Except at dawn,
When he ventures forth maybe once a month to the graveyard
Pleasantly strewn with pines, pillars, plaques,
And a few open patches of grass with the dew upon it,
And the dead under foot,
And the plots neatly tended with flowers fresh in old vases

To renew
His sense
Of beginnings.

I.
The Sand Dollar

The sand dollar lies in deep water, feeds on plankton,
And busies itself in engraving itself with a picture
Not of a statesman or flag or somebody's house
But a five-petaled flower.

Simple, childish, lined with the greatest delicacy
From an image out of some ten-fathom dream of finance,
It serves its tiny economy (plankton for dollars)
For its term, and then passes on

To its own fancied heaven ashore where the higher powers
Make, it has heard, millions of dollars with flowers.

II.
The Starfish

"... the humble starfishes and sea urchins are our nearest invertebrate cousins ..."
— *A Guide to Earth History*, Richard Carrington

The starfish is not gentile.
Slurps and sticks his stomach out.
Makes, really, a barbarous thing of a meal.

That rube. Is also a clinger,
Gladly giving his right arms, or his left,
Rather than leaving a party of him bereft.

Is spineless too, yet a species climber,
Endlessly agitating
To better his station in life by vertebrating.

III.
Bacteria

"After fifteen hours about a thousand million bacteria will have been produced from a single parent, and in double that period these will have so increased that their bulk will occupy about 4,500 cubic yards, which is about the capacity of a goods train of a hundred wagons."
　　　　　　　—A Guide to Earth History, Richard Carrington

Bacteria provoke at least one all-purpose homily:
It's much too easy begetting too large a family.

Another?—*Lebensraum* was a conceptual fraud
After that first week of our busy Lawd.

A third?
No man is an island—but that one you've heard.

Fetishes

Our grass fetish, and games fetish, and cleanliness fetish—
    these
In themselves are enough to begin a study
 (For one with a study fetish)
Of our cultural links with primitive peoples and monkeys.
But if you dislike studies? Then, presumably,
You brush your teeth nightly and mow the grass Sundays and
    play
Your poor life away and thank the good Lord
 (With your deity fetish)
For all the possible fetishes fetish-you
Has missed thus far,
                  if there are
Any—like the fetish fetish perhaps?
                         No, you have that too.

The Bishop Elias

"A Bishop Elias of Phrygia who attended the Council of Constantinople in 448, to help make the subtle verbal distinctions in dogma that had become necessary for eternal salvation, was unable to sign his name."

—Muller, *The Loom of History*

"Who has not bias
For Bishop Elias,
To rise as high as
He did, and to try as
He could,

Yet not write 'Elias'?
Elias, alas."

"I know the Bishop
And with him I worship
And gladly would hush up
The case if I could.

But pious Elias
Who can't write 'Elias'
(Elias, alas)
Can and doth gas."

25

I.

Monk Bede

If as a child I was dropped in a bowl by a bishop,
Or was otherwise handled with thumbs by godly authority,
I don't know it. The best of my memory informs me that my
    soul suffered
Little from churches and tracts, and grew into puberty
Without any provocation other than reason
For all of the malice it bears saints and heavens now.

Starting with Bede, whom I can't read,
And extending right through to the newspaper of my diocese,
The history of the West (the East is impossible)
Has been watered and muddled for me by prominent persons
Doing whatever they did for His sake or Hers,
For the glory of God or the Church or Saint so-or-such,
As if all that blood in those ancient heads and genitals
Passed through some twilit chapel before it pulsed.

I like history. History
Is my soul's wisdom, such as it is.
But Church History?
If one could cut it out, cut out the parts
Where "the Pope wrote to Queen Ethelberga as follows"
    (see Bede),
The history of the West would have been, for one thing,

Shorter, and for another would have omitted, completely,
    Bede.

I know that the Culture involved is massively Xian,
And that Chaucer and Shakespeare and all (I'll not mention
    Milton)
Would be hard to get on with without X (about whom,
    indeed,
I have only minor complaints) .—I mean to have said
That I'd not destroy the whole Culture, only the part-Bede.

Oh Bede! you have made me
One of the West's great admirers of crooks and renegades,
From the Pardoner to Fra Lippo Lippi, and of each happy
Sinner within the Faith and fool without, who sits at our table
Sighing and making a face at the grits and old grease,
But then pitching in with good grace—that is, with no Grace.

II.

Tomatoes

It is common among our moralists of either the saintly
Or secular arm to tell us with fervor,
From pulpit, rostrum or back of horse, to *take stock*.
Now to *take stock*—meaning, presumably,
"To make an estimate of; set a value upon,"
Having taken
"An inventory of stock or goods on hand"—
Is an old commercial phrase of no modern distinction
That wouldn't trouble at all if it weren't so typical
Of the gentlemen who employ it.
                                    They imagine
A store full of such commodities as sinners,
Reds, Americans, Christians, poets,
Which,
Being the kind of canned items canned items are,
Have a certain stability; that is, they stay
Put.

              And all that the diligent moralist (who is a stern
Old paternal entrepreneur in disguise)
Has to do to straighten things out in his troubled store
Is to ascertain that his clerks ascertain how many
Of what. Thus, to convert,
To know thyself is to know if thou hast the tomatoes

Daddy thinks should be sitting wherever he put them.

—God help the clerks of the world with the world's
stocktakers.

III.

The Cultural Conference

The author, critic and cultural messenger (me)
Comes to the cultural conference with snap-on tie,
Two shirts and a briefcase; and in between drinks
Holds forth for a week on the state of the state
Of letters—
                    that is, takes stock.
He finds science doing its best and wishes that artists
Would pay some attention to thermodynamics.
He doubts that our age will go down in the books for its
        verse,
But hopes for the novel. He thinks there is room
For a new vital form of some sort—the novella?—
And wonders if any mass culture, even our own,
Can really sustain a high art, thinking that paperbacks
Help. Lastly he knows it is late and the room is stuffy,
But if anyone really wishes to, he would be more than.
        Thereupon,
Asked if he thinks that the modern poets are difficult,
Or that writers should be depressing, defeatist or dirty,
He smiles, looks at his watch, hunches over the lectern
And recites (for another half hour) (with lengthy asides)
Passages out of the Great Tradition from Chaucer
To (with suitably deprecatory sniffles) himself, *simply to
        show*

—Uh, would the lady repeat the question? Thereupon
She does and he firmly agrees and everyone breaks up
And the week goes insanely on and he leaves at the end of it
Alone on a plane for home where, arriving, he'll take

Another week, of a cultural silence profound,
Getting used to the hardship of having himself (me) around.

Our Napoleons

Our Napoleons now are bores, own chains of stores,
Die old in large houses, complaining of tax and tooth,
Foreign entanglements, unions, loss of youth,
And go to their graves in convoys, highly regarded
By heirs, old flames and friends, the departures guarded
By friendly sergeants in squad cars, keeping the skit
As solemn as weather and traffic conditions permit.

So Little Time

There is so little time, really,
To write poems about how little time there is
(And spread them all over the place—say two copies in
    Washington,
Five in New York and an indeterminate number in San
    Francisco),
That the poet's a desperater man than most. He must
Get it all down for the ages before the ages
Are up, which,
As any poet will tell you, is a bitch.

In and out of the world, with little sobriety,
He weaves, then, vexed that the world does not worry
As he has to do about its poor battered posterity.

Passions?

You want passions? I've got passions,
The best,
With hot blood, spleen, raw nerves, clenched teeth, old coals
With or without controls
For use on poets, Buicks, pets, nations.

But for myself? To anger slow,
I keep myself in hand, saving the *e*
And mc^2
Up, to spend them wisely
Once or twice a month in one big blow
On wife and family.

A Horror

A horror? Oh yes, a staple,
A salt-and-pepper thing,
A three-times-daily rack that one mistook
For a Toastmaster, maybe, if one didn't look,

And who had mind to?—
With all the screaming, pounding, all the minor
Spock, Gesell allowables, plus the hoarding,
Storing, shoring up of flotsam
From the fat Sears, Roebuck dreams and drugstore rages;
And the scholarship thereof,
The reading
Of ads, instructions, warnings, the taking in
Of spooned-out truths from buxom social sages,—

Yes, who had mind
Or time or spirit to observe
That gothic joker in his cauldron corner
Vaporizing something,
Someone—
Who?

Questions and Answers About Mazurkas

I.

—What is the basket for,
The large cylindrical basket beneath the piano?
A basket for laundry, toys, old teddy bears?
Beneath the piano?

—No,
It is for Mommy's funny old
Surplus mazurkas.

II.

—And are the mazurkas,
The oval mazurkas with filters,
The blended Turkish mazurkas carelessly scattered
Within the open piano
True mazurkas?

—Loyal and true.

Ebenezer and His Eight-Man Rocket

CANTO I

And the dawn.
And Ebenezer arose and paced the lawn;
Checked multitudinous instruments and dials;
Jotted top secret stuff for hist'ry's files;
Stared at the dewy sky, hands on hips;
Took out a golden bugle; raised to lips;
Puffed up cheeks, took breath, and (leaning heavily
On warmed and waiting mouthpiece) rendered *reveille.*

> *And Ebenezer was sixty and straight as a tree,*
> *And a scientist with honors from M.I.T.*

Instant from all seven of seven doors,
Dressed in space-age sweatshirts and plus-fours,
Emerged his cohorts, ready for ascension,
And fell in ranks before him at attention
"All present, sir," the sergeant cried, and smartly
Saluted Ebenezer, who then tartly
Said if Mars or Russia they would trouble,
Damn quick should they learn to live on double;
Then marched them off, hip hip, to rocket gleaming
In sun's first rosy fingers, banners streaming.

For Eben knew the elements and man
And made them tremble lightning quicker than.

Thus, on a morn in June, while mortals slept,
Science and its minions forward stepped,
And soon were fast aboard and locked in place,
All facing forward, grim-lipped, into space.
Meanwhile Eben, midships, button fingering
That'd send them heavenward with no malingering
(This was in rockets the very last word, flown
From inside like an astro jet or St. Joan),
Began the countdown: "NINETY; EIGHTY-NINE;
EIGHTY-EIGHT"; and so forth—which, though fine
For tales that take their fans by storm,
I'll leave out here in deference to my form,
Which is too grand to be a slave of time,
Serving instead th' eternal and sublime;
And while he counts I'll prate for p'r'aps a page
Of Science in the large, its Golden Age,
Of what it's done for mankind, and of how
Without it we would not be where we're now.

OH Science! Science! Science! now victorious—
With pill and noble pile thou makest glorious
Music in the world's laboratories
And turn'st men's thoughts to brighter territories
Than poor base man himself, whose faults notorious
(Harped on by sick moralists censorious)
Are soon forgot in Science's flirtation
With viruses, equations, radiation,
Fruitflies, rats, test-tubal procreation,
Solid fuels, soft water, sanitation,
Thrust, torque, boost, lift, blast, acceleration,
Teller, Von Braun and atoms for salvation.
OH Science what a hot shot you've become.

In praising you I'm stricken deaf and dumb,
And need a muse to help me briefly peer
In th' heaven reserved for you (not me) this year.

Muse, are you there?
Are you there, Muse?
Do I hear thee, old thing?
Are those your footsteps in the corridor,
Crunch crunch,
As you tiptoe toward me wearing your old Apollonian
Slippers?

OH Science! Science! Science! now victorious—
With pill and noble pile thou makest glorious—

Well!
I guess old Muse has been here all the time.
I hadn't noticed her metronome about,
Or her calipers, tuning forks, red pencils, scissors, Scotch
    tape,
But I guess she's here all the same, which is good to
    know—
For without her I'm insecure, and what I have written
Never seems *right* somehow, as, for example . . .

"FIVE; FOUR; THREE; TWO; ONE!"
—A quavering voice (aft) cried, "The trip's begun!"
Seven thin mouths trembled ope together,
Fourteen fists curled round the arm-rest leather,
And all brains framed as one the one great query,
"Whither steer we?"—
All, that is, but he who was pronounced,
From Princeton to Argonne, prince of long counts,
Old Ebeneze,
Who, as the count ran out, began to freeze
 (As ne'er before in all his years three-score)

With his long, lank, button finger poised before
Its fatal object, like that child
Of rotten Denmark, who with wild,
Wild eyes on Claudius, 'n' all black-biled
Found that to plunge the dagger one brief foot
Was more than he could plunge; he couldn't do't;
AND SO like the lion poised 'fore Daniel's throat
With his tendons tensed, his steep brown tail afloat—
But I lose touch.
I mean that Ebenezer, in the clutch,
Would not, could not, did not push the button.
And so, what happened?
                        For the moment, nuttin.
Instead, from the bucket seats where they sat faint,
The others, 'mazed, heard Eb begin complaynt:
"Alas, what boots it with incessant care
To spend the money of the poor taxpayer?
Were it not better done to stay at home
And keep not Mars but Rome from sacking Rome?
Science is the spur that patriots raise
To scorn the alien, live pure button days;
Then comes the Summit and the empty chairs,
The various abasements, Cuban scares,
And slits the thin-spun scheme; AND all the praise.
And then, alas! . . ."
                        —but at that soulful phrase
The wrinkled hand and finger that had hung
O'erdue o'er those many lives was flung
 (Oh, was it a dramatic Byronism
or unmeant cataclysmic paroxysm?) —
Was flung far out and down, ah down, to where
The button lurked and waited, red and bare,
And fell hard upon it. OH! from stews
Of Vera Cruz to avenues
Of Moscow, Reykjavik and Syracuse,
Mortals heard the noise and shook in shoes.

40

For Ebenezer he was a scientist,
And, in the old phrase, what he kissed stayed kissed

CANTO II

At the tender age of ten
When his father Sid was mixing two parts of hydrogen
With something or other
(In the basement where he could seldom hear Eben's
    mother),
Eben decided that he, like his father, would follow
In the footsteps neither of Mercury nor Apollo,
But nature, nature in test tubes, clouds and rocks,
Nature divorced from the thousand natural shocks
That flesh (upstairs) was heir to.
He'd prepare to
Conquer the air, the sea, the earth and the atom
By keeping at 'em
The way his mother did
With her Sid.
At fifteen
He designed a perpetual motion machine.
Three years later
He got scholarships from Harvard, Caltech, Chicago, Carle-
    ton, Bennington, Coe and his father's alma mater,
M.I.T.,
The last of which took him in and gave him quick mastery
Of chemistry, physics and all inhuman relations,
Including those between nations,
SO THAT
At the time of his graduation he knew whereat
All villainy lay (overseas where it was begat);
AND resolved
That he'd sleep but three hours a night until he'd evolved

Such wonders as'd make the arrogant heathen abroad
Awed.
AND so he went at it;
AND for twenty or thirty stern years he consistently batted
Six or eight hundred percent with the Army and Navy,
SO THAT most of their basic-research cut was, for him,
    gravy;
AND testified
(For every committee of Congress that could funds provide)
To the urgency of his plan to keep the world petrified;
AND won so many medals for serving the Pentagon
That somebody said he needed a suit to hang them on;
SO made him a Colonel,
AND appointed him to lead the first of our space platoons to
    regions supernal.
Does this not bring you-all up-to-date on ol' Ebeneze?
I think so; and so in a flash I'll return to his tragic freeze,
Merely observing here briefly that he, in his time,
Managed to make more enemies than Fagan or Frankenstein.

CANTO III

It is perhaps not generally understood
(Except by those like myself who have withstood
All tales of smooth sailing for Man when he gets to the space
    age)
That the second stage of a rocket should follow the first stage,
And thus take place
When the rocket's up in the vasty, not at the Base.
Now whether or not Eb's bilious delay contributed to
The subsequent double-firing and resultant to-do
Is a matter that will be discussed down the ages by sages,
Some of them taking the line that of sin the wages
Is what they has always been, others complaining
That rockets are strictly a-moral, still others claiming

That evidence and not argument should decide
(Which is fine except that the first, in this case, took a ride).
The one fact agreed on by all amidst the debate
Is that both stages *did* blow as one, and the rocket, late,
Then left so fast that observers (those not cremated)
Thought that it left not at all but evaporated,
And reported this news to the Pentagon, which quick let soar
One of its best cover stories, writ weeks before,
About a large meteor falling in Utah's lands bad
And digging a crater exactly the size of a launching pad.
The story had just hit the wires when another came in
Of a strange object blundering by the towers of the Kremlin;
And this tale in turn had just crazed the nation's press
When Washington saw a like object swiftly progress
By the White House at tree height, and to the left slightly
Of the Washington Monument, glowering brightly.
(A technical note: the skin
Of this rocket was capped with a marvelous fin
That deflected the heat caused by friction of air and smog
To the rear, where the metal glowed like an old log
But left the occupants coolly drinking their grog.)
What was it? Well, radio's prominent big and quick thinkers
Mentioned saucers, sunspots, airport blinkers,
Optical tricks played by light on humid June days,
And a new model U-2 flown low on account of the haze.
But they'd little air time to be thinking, alas, so deep,
Before the Kremlin reported another alien peep
Trespassing like its sire but somewhat higher—
To avoid, the Kremlin asserted, deadly anti-peep fire;
And shortly thereafter the President, out on his lawn,
Missed a mere four-inch putt and was swiftly withdrawn
To the wine cellar by six secret-service scrubs,
Five of whom ran with him and one with his clubs,
When an object passed at the same height and vanished at
    treeline
Beyond the Potomac's banks, like the Cheshire feline.

43

(Could any two perogees be thought worse luck
Than Washington and Moscow, horror-struck?)
Between each of the four "attacks," two here and two there,
Precisely one hour had passed, which meant the affair
Was taking on order; it would be in the hair
Again, at four-ten, of the Muscovite Bear;
At five-ten again of the Eagle; and so forth. But where,
Where had it come from? And was it an "it?"
The newscasters pondered this question and what it would
    hit,
While the populace popped in its cars and blocked all the
    bridges
Leading to safety in Md. and Va.'s blue ridges,
And the Air Force's pundits in secret listened unnerved
To the jibberish coming from space on the channel reserved
For the ill-fated bird.
All in all things were blurred.
And at four-ten plus one, when Moscow bragged with delight
That the bestial invader had passed at a cowardly height,
Those few yet strolling the Mall took panic and flight,
While the President, who in a lull had been whisked away
To a very deep hole in Maryland where he could play
Miniature golf and at leisure direct the armed forces
With all the most modern communications resources,
Announced that whatever it was it was under surveillance
By the Army and Navy, who'd act against foreign assailants—
By which (in six thousand words) he seemed to imply
That everyone should stay calm till the Fourth of July.

CANTO IV

"Friends!
Followers of the sun and the warm earth
And evenings cool and love soft in the orchards!

44

Sharers!
Free and equal partners in the proud promise
Of earth and sky and government by and for men,
Men who know the feel of the earth in the darkness,
And how in the darkness a man by the white of a birch tree
And the odor of lilacs sifting into his nostrils
May pick out the path to the promise and pack his belongings
And head up the hill with no compass, sure-footed wanderer!
Companions!
You in the faded denims and dusty brogans,
You . . ."
    Thus
Did a poet of note (not me) begin to discuss
The incident of the rocket in his most piteous
Vein.
He was standing in front of a microphone in the rain
By the marge of the pool on the Mall between Abe and
    George
Where tourists alight to commemorate Valley Forge,
The Alamo, Custer, The *Maine,* Pearl Harbor, Bataan,
Payola, the D. A. R., and the Rights of Man;
And had only six or eight pages remaining of "you's"
(To whom he was bringing his message of praise and abuse)
Before he would get to the message itself which, in brief,
Would say that YOU should have faith (OH BELIEVE!) in
    belief.
Indeed he was well wound up, well on his way
To making one of the bravest talks of the day,
When the rocket passed with such speed that the backwash
    o' it
Poolward directed microphone, speech and poet,
Two of whom shortly were rescued, wet but unhurt.
But the speech, alas, like the lock of Pope's beauteous flirt,
Vanished amid the tumult, and thereby was greeted
With huzzahs louder by far than for those e'er completed.

Meanwhile, across the salt water, statesmen and seers
Of all creeds and nations simmered and shifted their gears
To accommodate their best convictions, accounts and White
    Papers
To the tiny new force in the sky that gave them the vapours.
Its source was still secret (save to the top-secret few
Who trembled at thought of that time when more than they
    knew) ;
So blame could be dealt out freely to both East and West,
Or even to Venus or Mars if't served dealer best.
And was.
Switzerland in the high tariff found the true cause.
Ireland sniffled, 'twas Downing Street's menopause.
Spain looked on France with disdain; France couldn't refrain
From blaming it all again on Alsace-Lorraine.
In Moscow, where the Thing's passage was now scarcely
    visible,
The anti-American screech mounted decible by decible:
"The war-monger of the West, the Capitalist Pig,
Has launched his ultimate weapon, but't zags when't should
    zig"—
(A statement which'd been funnier, said in secret some brass,
If't had not had a truth bedded in it, alas) .
Such items lurked in *The Times* on page fifty or so,
Since the first heavy section was taken by Reston & Co.
(Plus a pre-summer sale at Gimbels of calico
And the text of a pact with a hot archipelago) ;
For you may be sure that the pundits found just magnifico
The task of revising the whole world's balance of power
Each hour on the hour.
So they did.
Most of them thought the thing Russian, a Russian bid
To get concessions in Cuba, Berlin, Pakistan,
The Congo, Korea, Hong Kong and/or Iran,
Seeing it as a change in the party line

From unpleasant to medium-nasty, or bad to malign,
And predicting that since world reactions were much more
    severe
Than *they* could have possibly wanted, the rocket's career
Would stop in a moment, the thing would vanish someplace
If *we'd* find a way for *them* somehow to somewhere save face,
Adding that what was needed from *us,* however,
Was firmness, above all firmness, firmness forever.
Only one of *The Times'* correspondents had the audacity
To insist that the rocket was ours; for that he was acidly
Jumped on by fellow scribes from L.A. to East Lynne
For taking his cue from Moscow or Peking or gin.
They said that if it were ours we'd have shot it down
Before it went off its course and buzzed Washington town;
FURTHER, that clearly the orbit was *not* a mistake,
For what rocket would e'er do thus on its own, for pete's sake.
THEREFORE, its orbit was just as some mastermind planned
In Russia or Mars or some other unfriendly land.
IF Russia, surely the early accounts from the Kremlin
(That the thing had whizzed by the tombs of Stalin and
    Lenin)
Had been fabrications to hide where its true seeds were sown
And suggest that its target was not the White House alone.
—With wise words like these escaping like germs by the hour
Was Error enthroned on high, mighty Error whose power
On this hapless globe would I gladly tweak
For a canto or two if I were but tragic and Greek.
MEANWHILE from quarters official a silence profound
Lasted while Eb and his troops went twelve times around,
And might have continued, indeed, right up to this minute
If Eben, brave Eben, had not put his foot again in it.
But when the rude rocket first zoomed off into its odd
Orbit 'twixt heroes here and villains abroad,
Eben, brave Eben, a scientist foremost he,
Quite lost his reason and espoused the soft repartee

Of a funny old sentimentalist, lover of birds,
Trees, Christmas, mothers and words.
He could not contain himself, could not be wise and make do
In his vivid reports with the weather, the food, the view,
The instruments' readings and what-all astronauts brew,
But had to launch forth on some woolly poetic chatter
That made the Pentagon quiver like pancake batter,
Matter so brief that 'twill pack but one canto more,
But so dread that the mem'ry will last long as rockets soar.

CANTO V

"Amigos!
You who have seen the lightning strike, and the panther,
Who have fared through the desert, paddled the swollen
        tributary,
Who have measured the winters with frozen fingers, the
        summers
With sweat I speak to you.
I come to you out of the sadness of loss and leavetaking,
Out of the terrors of wreckage and wastage and whirlwind,
And I say to you . . ."
—At this point the static increased and the strained voice
        faded,
Giving me time to explain, if the verse seems jaded,
That this was Eben himself, not my earlier poet
(For Eb had picked up the lingo, and could now "oh woe"
        it),
And was speaking not on a secret wavelength in code
But on an open and popular frequency which flowed
Straight to the horrified heart of old NBC,
Which rebroadcast it at once, scoop of century—
Was speaking against the commands of the highest brass
Ever assembled in one sad cellar *en masse*
In bitter Maryland. "Amigos" indeed!

The brass had been cast off, betrayed by its own mad seed,
Who went on:
"I say to you
That the world is round and green and the orchards are green
And the oceans are blue and their waters lie in their beds
And the air is soft in Turkestan and Havana
And the wind blows like an old *chanson* through Louisville,
And there is peace there.
And I say to you,
Where there is peace there is love and a man can walk out
In his orchard and lie there under the apples
And a woman can come to him there and soon it is later,
And all this is good, amigos, good! as I tell you!
But how do you lose it?"
—For an answer Eben returned to the fall of Rome
And staggered manfully forward on his way home
To his point, which was that he wished to resign from his
     duties
And take all scientists with him back to the beauties
Of the aforesaid roundness and greenness, leaving behind
Rockets and atoms as too much for human kind.
He therefore proposed to plunge his infernal machine
On the first nation's capitol whose summitry failed to convene
At once on the Rue de la Paix in Paris, France,
For the purpose of ending all this, for Christ's sake and man's,
Concluding:
"Hear me, amigos!
This is your chance to take, to take it and hold it,
For if you not take it now you will mourn the not taking,
Mourn the knowledge and strength lying waste in the desert,
Mourn the good faith drained off into empty basins,
Mourn without solace your losses, lost in the causes
Of empty rooms in the capitols, eternal vacancies
Of minds that know not the greenness and roundness and
     speak
Without singing, think without feeling, create

49

What though created is not a creating
But a burning, emptying, wearing down, sapping, destroying,
Since no life cometh forth out of it, stone
Only, stone and abstraction, stone and rhetoric, vacancy,
Vacancy, vacancy, in which the greenness
And roundness green be and round be no more
And the lovers under the apple trees touch no more
And the wind is not in the branches, nor softness in
      Turkestan,
And need I explicate further this drabness, amigos?
Amigos!"
A moment of silence fell o'er the green sward.
For Eben had spoken; Eben once more had scored.
Eben! thy words so touched me I found I could scarce
Put my pen to paper and peddle my wares.
With this thou showed me thou shouldst be shrined with the
      saints
Of hist'ry and other recorded quaints.
With this thou mastered each of my lingering doubts.
With this thou won me—and oh! if thou'd but won the louts
In high office who listened a-feared to your plea
(*They* will be smit by a two-handed engine, pardee,
But not yours, as you now know, to your misery),
And would perhaps, given time, have taken a dose
Of some of the sense of it hidden midst your "amigos."
And then, ah then, would the orchards apples have grown;
Then, then would this globe have your true science known.
But alas!
None of your green round hopes were to come to pass.
Remember?
Remember that e'en as you spoke your machine's grim *third*
      phase
Went off with a roar and ruckus the world did amaze?
And you rocketed skyward, your voice growing thinner and
      thinner

Like conversation after a seven-course dinner?
Ah this, wherever you are, you well must remember,
As we down here do too, we who now render
Our praises to you and your troops who, though now thus
    sped,
Will not, we hope, be forgot in the dark years ahead.
Oh Eben, praise be to you and to your career,
To which we daily pay homage and sing loud and clear
—Thou without whom or your ilk of the hard-knocks school
We'd never have learned the now golden—though of thumb
    —rule:

If scientist, making world better, mendeth his ways,
Mendeth he must before the very first phase.

FINAL NOTE TO THE READER

Reader, dear reader, I want you to know
That this was a fiction, a fantasy show.
No one named Ebeneze *I've* ever met
Ever has rocketed anywhere yet.
I mention this lest you be fearful and pious
And start to pop off like six Jeremiahs.
You know, as I, that science each day
Shortens the way to a world *toujours gai.*
You know, as I, that men of clear think
Never would put the world on the brink.
The whole tale's a fraud, as am I; truth abides
Alone on the good gray Potomac's sides.

STORIES

Fragments from Major Martin's Proceedings

I understand perfectly that I *might* have held him suspect from the first (do you *know* that I did not?) for some trivial irregularity in his appearance perhaps, or because his slang was shot through with anachronisms, like "floozy." But, you say, I did not; so I defend myself. Is civilization so systematized in this century of standardization that no deviations may be permitted, much less pass unnoticed? I admit that in the army fewer deviations are imaginable than elsewhere—one does not go about in bright neckties—but he wore no bright necktie. And surely a middle-aged man (he was a middle-aged man) must be allowed an occasional lapse, must be tolerated when he conjures up a "floozy" out of his salad days. Surely even in the army—and heaven knows I do not presume, I do not permit myself to dream that the army is in any respect anything other than it is—surely I am not expected to expect nothing but sheer khaki, as it were, twenty-four hours a day.

But I am in Intelligence. Yes. And what the common soldier or officer is allowed not to see—because he is a common soldier or officer and has therefore delegated his responsibilities as a patriot with eyes and ears to the nearest chap in Intelligence—the chap in Intelligence is *not* allowed not to see, even if he must toddle through cocktail parties looking like a plainclothesman from the stationhouse in the seventeenth precinct, the man who always gets his man, an animated divining rod, Holmes himself. And therefore—because I am in Intelligence and did not (as you think; but do you know?) *see*—you put me down as an ass, or a traitor, or both. Tell me, why don't you? that the people of The United States are disappointed in me. I didn't get my man.

In all fairness, however—not to me; I am nobody; I am simply the fall guy for the occasion—but to the cause of justice or whatever you choose to call the cause—in all fairness to whatever it is let me point out that I didn't join the army to *get my man;* that I wasn't dumped in Intelligence to *get my man;* that nobody ever told me to *get my man;* and that *my man* was in no sense *my man* until I failed (as *you* say) to *get* him.

All this is irrelevant? Of course. When I was first inducted, an officer, whose rank I did not know at that time, who impressed me hugely with his importance, and who turned out, naturally, to be a second lieutenant, told me in the most aggressive manner that a soldier in time of war is on duty at all times, and that there is no job (mean, difficult, absurd, wasteful, idiotic, dangerous) for which he is not subject to call at any time of the day or night. Furthermore—and frankly this lieutenant got on my nerves—he told me that a soldier must use his head at all times and never, never be caught simply sitting around on his big, fat—but all this is irrelevant. I didn't get my man. Off with my head. Very well.

But you want a report. It is not sufficient to condemn me; you must also work me to fill your files with nonsense about an incident which though not, obviously, forgotten is after all irrevocably past. Can we retrieve it? And can you suggest uses major or minor to which this report may be put? Is The Intelligence School interested—yes, I suppose it is—in teaching its bright young things how they will *not* get their man? Very well . . .

56

My man met me at the boat in Oran. I should have grabbed him there and then, of course, and put an end to this business. I could have. He came up to me and saluted. He said, "Major Martin?" "Yes," I said. "Will you please load your men on these trucks?" "Certainly, Captain," I said, and loaded my men on the trucks. How stupid of me. But at that time, I remember, he looked very much like a Transportation Officer (which, indeed, at that time he was) responsible for the un-loading of American troops on the docks of Mers-el-Kebir. I remember also that he was dressed as an American Captain (which, indeed, at that time he was). The fact remains—let me tell *you*—that I could have surrounded him on the spot. I *could* have had my man there and then.

And there were clues too; I will not deceive you. In the first place he looked German. In the second place his name was German. In the third place he was German. But he said he was from Ohio (which, as it happened, he was) thus cleverly trying to lead me off the scent. And it must be recalled that at that time I had not been advised that I should have been *on* the scent, and that I was extraordinarily busy loading my men on the trucks. Also in my favor I must say that I loaded the trucks with a minimum of confusion and delay; with, I might even add, Intelligence. But that is of course irrelevant.

Or is it? I hate to trouble you with side issues when as I know you are anxious to have my report over and done with and to have me promptly excommunicated or shot or repri-manded or given a medal for disservice (there really should be a medal for disservice, you know, worn above the left breast pocket in conjunction with battle stars and The Con-gressional Medal of Honor) but I believe that this matter of irrelevancy has to be settled before I can go on. Intelligence demands, first of all, all. No stones are to be left unturned, no leads not followed, no facts, hints, asides ignored. Nothing— as I am sure all good detectives and bad detectives have at one time or another said—is irrelevant until proved so. So is what I say irrelevant? Or even if it is, is it irrelevant that what

I say is irrelevant? Very well. I loaded the bloody trucks with extreme efficiency.

Indeed it is possible (I am not, mind you, saying that it is so) that the fact that I loaded the trucks in the presence of *my man,* as he turned out to be, with extreme efficiency is *most* relevant. I suggest—I do not affirm—that had I—I do not say I did—recognized *my man* as *my man* at the instant when he came up to me and said, "Major Martin?" I would have acted in precisely the same fashion as in reality I did act; that is: I would have loaded my trucks with extraordinary efficiency. I would not have surrounded my man there and then—for the simple reason that he had not at that time *done* anything—even if I had known (and I do not say that I did) that he *would* do something. No. I would have watched and waited, gathering incriminating evidence, dragging his life story from him over a bottle, trailing him at night. And I would have hidden from him—as I did, by loading my trucks with tremendous efficiency—the fact that I was not primarily an Officer in Charge of Troops, but an Officer in Intelligence.

You will point out that I was *not,* at the time, primarily an Officer in Intelligence; you are quite right. But I might have foreseen—mind you, I do not say that I did—that after I had finished loading my men on the trucks and leading them out to The Replacement Depot, I would *become* an Officer in Intelligence and would then be able to use this admirable truck-loading job as a blind. I admit nothing. I merely point out the possible relevancies of the case.

We met again two days later in the waiting room of The Commanding General of the__ _____ __. And we waited. From your seat it is of course incomparably easy to imagine how, in those two days, I might have gathered together the evidence which was lacking at our first meeting and have accosted him there, in the waiting room of The Commanding General, with, "Sir, it is my duty to inform you that you are under arrest. I must warn you that anything you say may be used against you." But for reasons which will appear if you will only *listen*, I said no such thing. He spoke to me first. He said, "you are Major Martin, are you not?" "Yes," I said, "and you are the Captain who unloaded me two days ago, are you not?" "Rossbach is the name," he said; and he added, "yes, I am the man, though you found me at other than my normal duties." "So?" I said. "Yes," he said. "You see, I'm in Intelligence."

Well! *Now* what was I to do? Let us suppose for an instant that I *knew* he did not mean American Intelligence (although, of course, he meant that too) but meant German Intelligence. If I had known this, what would I have done? I would have done exactly what I did. I said, "well, well, I'm in Intelligence too." After all, I was fully aware of the fact, by then, that within two hours I would be sitting in that very same building in an office over the door of which would be hung "G-2," and that he would then be able to walk to and fro in front of my door, reading my name carefully inscribed thereon and notice that I was not With Troops. I even suspected, instantly, in the waiting room of The Commanding General, that he, in Intelligence, would have dealings with me, also in Intelligence, in the same building. So I do not see that my actions until this moment were in any respect actions I would not have taken if I had—and I am not saying I had —suspected him as a spy. In fact I rather pride myself on the cleverness with which I intruded upon his friendship. I said, "well, well, now isn't that a coincidence. I hope we'll see something of each other."

"Oh, we shall!" he cried. "I'll be working for you."

I can see by your faces that you are torn between the desire to give me a full opportunity to defend myself, as you say, and the impulse to shut me up because I am wasting what you are so egotistical as to call your time. You did not believe, did you, that what I said a moment or so ago about irrelevancy was *really* relevant, and you do not believe, do you, *really,* that anything I may say here will affect in even the least important way the outcome of the Case of Major Martin. You are sitting there suffering, chafing at what appears to be a necessary delay in the proceedings of justice, and you are not —yes, I accuse you—giving me justice.

Do you not see that mere patience is not enough? Can you not understand that to understand me you must stand vicariously in my shoes as I tell my story and make each decision with me as I make it? Only by so doing will you be able to give me a fair trial. Only by doing so will you be able to pass your judgment on with a clear conscience to the reviewing authority, whoever in this instance he may be, who—because this is the army—sits above us both in his silent Majesty. And so I recommend that you mark attentively, gentlemen, these "irrelevancies" of mine.

Is it, for example, irrelevant that thus far my actions have been completely correct in respect to this Captain Rossbach, this German agent who was thrust upon me the moment I landed in Africa—correct whether or not I knew his "status"? Mmmmmm. I see that you are saying to yourselves about me, "this man is very clever. I must not let him pull the wool over my eyes." You see!

Mind you, I am not trying to make you uncomfortable. Surely not. But I am now entering upon the *most important* phase of my relations with this Rossbach . . .

He was pushed upon me as my associate, or pushed himself upon me, in my most secret work. His credentials were in order. He passed completely as "one of us," gentlemen, and made no significant slips of which I have knowledge before he made away, as you have been told, with the goods. In other words the doubts which I might have entertained about him could only in any case have been acted upon with the greatest circumspection. Had I recognized him as *my man,* and had I

60

been out to *get* him, I could not have done other than that which I did; that is: make the goods available to him so that he would, in due time, give himself away. Had I not made these goods available he would have been *unable* to give himself away. I therefore had no choice but to treat him as a confidant—or to appear to treat him so—and to permit him to believe he was not being watched and could, at any time, walk out of the office with the goods. This I did.

But it probably occurs to you, as it has of couse to me, that a limit, unrecognized by him, might have been placed upon our confidences to prevent, in the event of his escape, the transmission of important facts to the enemy. In a normal situation this would have been S.O.P. I would have planted false papers or papers of no importance in my safe and have led him to believe they were true papers and papers of great importance. Why, you ask, did I not do this?

Do you know that I did not do this? Are you not, as a court can never do, jumping to conclusions? Have you proof that Rossbach has in his possession copy 33 of the Top Secret papers pertaining to Operation B_____ _____? How do you know Rossbach is not carrying proudly in his possession at this moment a complete set of false instructions? How do you know I will not pull from a secret pocket in my blouse the real, the true, the genuine copy 33 which you have supposed up to this moment to have been whisked away to the enemy? You do not know, do you! Furthermore you are thinking, dreaming that perhaps after Operation B_____ _____ has been miraculously saved . . .

And if it is true that copy 33 now rests in the secret pocket of my blouse, you may wish to withdraw—I will permit it—these absurd accusations you have leveled against me for having failed, as you say, to *get my man*. Now possibly you understand that it is not always either expedient or wise to get one's man, and that there are occasions when *letting one's man go* is an entirely commendable, indeed brilliant deception. Now, possibly, some of you are even privately wishing Captain Rossbach godspeed.

But if you are willing to admit *this* subtlety, you must in all fairness admit another. You do not know Rossbach as I do and therefore cannot determine—as I may have done—the lengths to which a deception must be carried to be effective with him. Rossbach, for all you know, is by far the craftiest agent the Germans have, and cannot, therefore, possibly be taken in by an obvious ruse, a simple substitution of the false for the true. Think of the boldness of the man, walking right into my office and sitting down as my assistant! And think of the absurdity of trying to pawn off on a man like this—a man who daily for a month observed the development in detail of the plans for Operation B_____ _____ (or at least believed he did so)—patent falsehoods.

No, gentlemen, it would not have done. He would never have flown with simple misinformation. And if indeed I now were to pull from the secret pocket of my blouse the complete copy 33, you would be justified in accusing me of playing my cards clumsily.

I might, however, pull from the secret pocket of my blouse a *portion* of copy 33, the Secret X Secret section which, as you all know, gives the precise date, time and places of landing. And I might tell you Rossbach walked out with all but this, for which I provided a masterfully incorrect substitute. Surely, if I had made such a substitution properly, he could not have distinguished the wheat from the chaff; and, as you must admit, part truths are frequently more misleading than outright lies.

But no again, gentlemen. I agree that this plan *also* would have been unsatisfactory. For even without completely accurate information the enemy, knowing the size of the assault and the nature of it, the disposition of troops, the air cover, the approximate whereabouts and time, could have prepared an impressive defense. Even without the Secret X Secret section, copy 33 is a dead giveaway.

Were there then any other reasonable lines of action open to me? I know you are anxious to discover what if anything I have in the secret pocket of my blouse; and I am fully aware of the importance you attach to the missing copy 33, particularly at this time (am I correct in assuming that the assault is *still* scheduled for tomorrow?) . But I do not wish to scant any possibility that might have been open to me, and I do not think the one remaining possibility—which I will now broach —is irrelevant to the case at hand.

I wish to suggest a paradox, gentlemen. We are *men of the world.* We have been, as it is so frequently put, *through the mill.* And we pride ourselves on knowing *what side our bread is buttered on.* We should not, then, be upset by strange *fortunes of war* even when they are, as in the case before us, contrary to what we would wish for and, indeed, expect if we were *not* men of the world and had *not* been through the mill. I wish to suggest—and I depend upon your broad experience to verify my suggestion—that the simple and the complex, the wise and the foolish, the planned and the unplanned, the chance and the mischance, in fact all the opposites all of us can name are frequently (and perhaps always, though I will not insist upon it) identical. And I suggest that what you have until now taken to be negligence on my part, or stupidity on my part or, if you rate me differently than I have supposed, evil on my part—I suggest that you may with equal justice take to be oppositely otherwise.

For example. Let us now suppose (for we are still entertaining possibilities) that I have nothing in the secret pocket of my blouse, and that (it is not impossible) I do not *have* a secret pocket in my blouse. Let us suppose that the whole of copy 33, including the Secret X Secret section, has been turned over by me, but deliberately (!) , to Captain Rossbach who is now, to the best of our knowledge, in conference in Berlin. See it with your mind's eye, gentlemen: the Generals are quizzing him. "How," they are asking, "did you get it?" What can he reply, but, "I got it from the safe." "How?"

"Major Martin gave me the key." "But why?" "He trusted me." "Trusted YOU?!!"

You see, don't you, gentlemen, in what an embarrassing predicament Captain Rossbach may very well be at this moment. He finds himself telling the Generals, who also know what side their bread is buttered on, in all seriousness that the papers were given to him *as a trust;* and he finds the Generals laughing because, so obviously, they think (and what general in what army under what circumstances would not?) that the trust was all Captain Rossbach's! . . . But Captain Rossbach protests . . .

"Show me," he cries, "in what respect this information is false. Check it against all the other information you now have, from your agents in Algiers, Bizerte, Bone, Casablanca, Tunis, Constantine, Mostaganem, Dakar and Sousse. Check it!" But the Generals smile blandly and say, "we *have,* Rossbach, we *have*. Everything tallies perfectly. If only everything *didn't* tally; if only there were one false lead, one unaccountable discrepancy, contradiction, yes, irrelevancy—your life might be spared, Rossbach. You played your cards too well . . ."

Gentlemen! Do you want me to pull copy 33 from the secret pocket of my blouse, *now?* Do you want to know that Rossbach has reached Berlin with partial information which may do great damage to our cause, or that he has reached Berlin with complete information which will do no harm whatsoever? Do you want him to be received as a German hero, or shot as an American agent?

And yet, if I do *not* produce copy 33 . . .

Gentlemen, the defense rests.

O Destiny That May Not Be Eschewed!

It was a dream boat, not because it was big, high-powered or romantic, but because it was in his dream. He was on it and he was making a lecture tour to a number of towns most of which he didn't get the name of—Charleston, West Virginia, for example. The boat was small but noisy; its motor sounded like the wind through a window vent. The sea was calm mostly, but the boat pitched anyway—or swayed as if it were dizzy—so that when he got up to lecture in all the towns he swayed too, either because he hadn't got his sea legs yet when he went on land, or because he remained on the boat and harangued his audience from a point somewhere off Sandy Hook. The lecturing went on and on, while the audience sat and sat. There were no symptoms of discomfort in the audience, no squeaking of chairs, no coughing, whispering, doodling, ogling, passing of notes. And on his side there was no tension either; he just talked.

Not that he was not eloquent. He waved his arms, walked up and down the platform (or deck). He said "Friends!" and "I do not come to praise (bury?) Caesar." For emphasis he sometimes let his voice sink to a whisper, paused for effect on critical words like "life" and "levels of meaning," and drew diagrams on the blackboard. But no one who appreciated such things was there. The audience sat, and sat. Where were their minds? What did one do to wake them up? How did one *get* to them? If there were only somebody there who would—and he thought he saw a freckled girl who might—raise her hand or shake her head or leave the assemblage or wink or do something suggesting approval, disapproval, enthusiasm, boredom, then it wouldn't be so bad to be out there by Sandy Hook. But there was no response at all from anyone except an old drummer in the back (sometimes the front) who beat irregularly on his kettledrum and then dozed off. No one gestured, no one moved, no one grimaced, no one smiled, until it became almost more than he could do to talk at all, though he knew he must, and almost more than he could do to keep his feet, though he knew he must, as the boat swayed from one side to the other, farther, farther. . . .

Cynthia was asleep, so he got out of bed quietly, removed his clothes from the chair and went into the bathroom to shave and dress. It was barely dawn; through the window a tracery of winter branches was just visible against a deep gray backdrop. The wind was up (that had been in the dream) and was banging the door to the garage gently but persistently (that had been in the dream too). Shaving he cut himself, and putting his newly starched white shirt on before the blood had stopped, he managed to spot the collar. He went downstairs and served himself corn flakes, a piece of toast and instant coffee. He gathered together his books, put on his overcoat and his cap with the earflaps, pushed out-of-doors into the wind, opened the garage door that was banging, got in the car, started it, backed out, got out of the car, closed the garage door (but it would still bang), got back in the car, backed out the driveway and drove off to his eight o'clock class.

Each one of them that came to him was very young and very nice, a kind of yes-sir, no-sir and I-agree-with-you niceness that was also soft, like the edges of a television screen. They came and sat at the end of his very large desk (it *did*

66

seem to have grown) and they held their themes in their hands and they nodded their heads, or shook their heads, whenever he appeared to tell them to. He did not in fact even have to say anything, *actually* say anything to them to get them to nod (or shake) their heads; all he had to do was to open his mouth *as if* he were going to say, for example: "But you do want to improve your writing, don't you?" (for nods) or "But you wouldn't want to fail the exam, would you?" (for shakes) and they would know, though it was admittedly remarkable, which way their heads should go before any words were spoken. This meant simply that no words were spoken. He kept opening his mouth and licking his lips and looking intelligent, and they kept nodding and shaking and holding out their papers over the big desk.

It was really a very nice relationship. The trouble was that they kept coming in one by one and thus replacing each other for the nodding and shaking, but he sat at his end of the desk stimulating each one of them in turn and unable to get out of his chair to get out of the room to get out of the cycle before the *next* one entered and sat down, held out the paper, nodded, shook and was nice. Hours and hours. It was apparent that he would have to do something, but what he would do, and how he would do what he would do, when they were always coming in or going out or sitting there expecting that he would stay and tell them what was wrong with their papers, was a problem. Hours and hours. And what made the hours worse was that he had a number of really rather more urgent matters than the papers to get at, such as, for example, getting out of the room. He desperately wanted to do that. Every muscle in his body was straining to lift his great turgid body out of that chair behind that desk, come hell or high water. And if only one muscle were to take the initiative— that is, if only one finger or hand or toe or foot or lip or ear or eyelash or shoulder were simply to take it upon itself to *move, then* there would be an immediate insurrection of all the muscles and the body *would* move and the chair in which the body sat *would* be pushed back and the student who was sitting at the far end of the desk holding the paper and nodding and shaking *would* be swept aside, as would all the others waiting in the hall for their turn; and the whole operation, which for some reason seemed impossible to consummate, *would* come off, and *would* come off in a twinkling, a flash, a mere blink of an eye that had blinked for years, would probably continue to blink for years, and certainly, even at this perpetual unblinking moment, had all the force, the power, the potentiality of blinking, but *wasn't*. Blinking.

That was the trouble.

And it was really quite an extraordinary trouble if one were in it. That is, one could stand both inside and outside the trouble at the same time and see, therefore, simultaneously, that the trouble was both ridiculous and tragic. And therefore sublime? Perhaps sublime, but at any rate trouble. One could stand both inside and outside and say, therefore, simultaneously, that there was nothing and yet everything to leaving; one could say simultaneously that the difficulties were insurmountable and zero. One could in short say a number of things, and the impression he had of himself, sitting there in his chair as the line moved in, paused with its papers and moved out—the impression he had of himself was that he was on a boat and the boat was like a desk and the boat-desk was moving gently up and down in one place as it met the waves (which were students?) and considered the possibility of starting its motors. The motors were down below. To get to the motors one had to take the forward stairs (because the back stairs were out of order) (or perhaps there were no back stairs), and the forward stairs were unfortunately crowded with some of the very same students who were standing in line waiting to come in to sit at the desk with their papers, and nod and shake. What it amounted to, if one analyzed it, was that the students who were in the way, physically, on the stairs, were the students whom he was obligated to see, and wanted to see, so that they blocked each other and him, these students, in their own quiet way while he blocked himself behind his boat-desk by failing to recognize that the students—at least some of them—were terribly anxious to let him get away (although they were blocking his way) because they felt very embarrassed and humble and studentlike and nice about getting in his way, although they knew both that it was their right to and that they were supposed to get in his way, and so they *looked* anxious about it all and they tried very hard both on the stairs and at the desk to persuade him that really he *could* get up from the desk and walk down the stairs and go to the bathroom or wherever he wanted to go (and as a matter of fact he did want to go to the bathroom) without their interfering at all. Indeed they were, he observed, crushing themselves against the wall of the stairs and hanging precariously over the bannisters to open a way for his exit. But they were also coming in in their usual manner, nodding and shaking and holding out their papers.

So he concluded that there was nothing that he could do. He could not move an eyelash. And yet he also concluded that something ought to be done. What? Should he shout at them, tell them all to go away? In the first place that was impossible because he could not move an eyelash, much less his mouth, to open it, to shout at them. And in the second place, if he were able to shout he might shout too loud and thereby create a panic among the students some of whom, hanging on the bannisters, would then be hurt. Therefore he had better not shout. And it had already been established that he could not move. Was there any solution at all? No. And this fact was so depressing to him that if he had been able to get up he would have rushed out and drowned himself. For it became apparent to him that drowning would be very easy. The ocean was there. The ocean was available. The boat was rocking uncomfortably. The boat was not really seaworthy

69

what with its low gunwale (so that the big ones could be slithered aboard) and its high mast that rocked, sickeningly, with the ground swell; but it was after all the only boat that one had and it wasn't a bad boat; one could stand on the low gunwales, so long as one had one's lectern, and feel comfortable and not totally exposed to the elements, or at least not exposed to them in the way that made it elemental. No, it was more like being, as previously stated, behind an enormous desk with the confronter (wanting to go to the bathroom) at one end and the confrontee (nodding and shaking) at the other and a paper, a perfectly unintelligible 300-word paper in between with its failures primarily of COH (coherence) and PARAL (Parallelism-unfulfilled) staring him in the face and demanding that he write respectively COH and PARAL so that the student, nodding and shaking, would get what he came to get. And so between the boat and the desk, or the teacher and student, or the gunwale and mast there remained always the gap which he felt to be less a gap than a pause or perhaps a musical interlude but which remained nonetheless a kind of a hole or vacancy that had to be filled, had to be accounted for, had to be *loved* if one were ever either to remove one's self from the desk or push one's way down the stairs or even lift a finger, hand, toe, foot, lip, ear, eyelash, or shoulder.

. . . and so Cynthia, being up, got the breakfast while he shaved and the children watched Captain Kangaroo. This morning he had eggs and bacon, and when breakfast was over he gathered together his books, put on his overcoat and his cap, went out, opened the garage door, got in the car, started it, backed it out, got out of the car, closed the garage door, got back in the car and drove off to his nine o'clock and ten o'clock classes, after which he settled down to his 300-word themes of which there were 102.

We will take the Thunderbird, they said. We will take

that car which one sees in the popular magazines parked at beaches with the top down and the girl in the silk shawl or the bag bikini leaning against the cordovan fender and talking to the boy wearing the eight-foot blue-and-white scarf and nothing else except a light meter and a sheaf of packages from Burpee for seeding the 100-acre plot behind the Thunderbird and of course a pair of trunks—we will take that car and put it on a boat. And so they did. And when the car was on the boat and the boat had put off and was lying off shore in a light haze near Sandy Hook, on a Sunday, with the sails nodding and shaking and the anchor firmly enmeshed in the themes and the ropes all carefully stacked away in the trunk, they set sail. The weatherman had promised them a day of light breezes and intermittent sun, and as usual the weatherman was wrong for they had scarcely cleared the bell buoy, the breakwater, the lighthouse, the desk and the bannister when the clouds climbed in from the south and they knew they were in for it. Scudding, the clouds were. And the wind was battering the garage door furiously, so that he knew that before the summer was out the garage door would have to have a new latch and probably the house would have to have a new roof and the cellar crevices would have to be sealed. At least, however, the Thunderbird was there, shining, on the forward hatch; it had a rattle in the radio speaker and the automatic choke stayed open after the engine was warm and the back deck stuck when one pushed the button that was supposed to open it and the Cruis-o-matic cruis-o-maticked up to thirty without shifting out of first, but one could get a hundred out of the thing in a short burst and what did one want out of a Thunderbird?

Very little. He got used to the elements as he grew older. The wind was howling in the halyards and lanyards and window vents, but he faced that fact. He sat at the desk as the procession moved in and out; he talked from Sandy Hook (over the big desk) over the heads of the whitecaps, through the teeth of the gale, to the nodders and shakers; and mostly the messages got through. Modern science triumphed; the radio, radar, omnirange, complete frozen dinners, the Point-Count-System and all that tamed the tempest effectively, and if he were out in his Thunderbird he need only, ultimately, put the top up. It was just that simple.

But because it was so very simple it was very hard to understand why, with the wind blowing the jib to shreds and the salt sea shipping its weight over the port bow with every plunge of the Thunderbird's prow and the bilge water slopping up on the seats and the deck tipping precariously in the green water as it slid tumultuously along the side—it was hard to understand why he did not put the top up unless it was because he had to get out of the car to do it and this was more than he could do. The button for putting the top up was under the back deck, and to get there he would have to get the themes out of the way and clear the stairway, in addition to walking into the teeth of the gale. Clearly he could not do it; and yet with the wind blowing as it was, and with the sheets so twisted and the comforter fallen from the bed and the wind blowing the curtain out so that it flapped against the dresser, he could not but feel that perhaps he *might* be able to do it. The finger would rise. Or perhaps the hand. Or maybe the toe. Or foot? Or lip? And with the one motion, if it should occur, quite suddenly the sea or desk or bathroom would be as smooth as glass and he would go to the button and thereby get the top up and go to the class, off Sandy Hook, without further incident.

Would it be the toe?

Yes, it was the toe.

. . . Cynthia was still asleep, so he dressed in the bathroom, padded downstairs, got his breakfast, put on his overcoat and his cap, went out, opened the garage door, got out the car, closed the garage door and drove off to his eight o'clock class. Immediately after class he went to the Superintendent of Grounds' office (a moving of the toe), and knocked, and

72

went in, and said to the Superintendent—a small man standing behind a rake—that he was resigning (a moving of the finger) as of June, and he hoped that he would understand.

The Superintendent looked at him sharply (he was trying to get out of his office with his rake) and said, "Sam, you don't look well. Have you been sleeping?"

And the haze on the Sound rose before his eyes, and the Thunderbird, and he said to the Superintendent, "Frank, you've got this all wrong. You want to make out that I'm sick, don't you. I know you. You want to make out that it's all in my mind. Well, I tell you that it's not all in my mind. There are factors here, forces. You don't understand. I don't ask you to understand, I ask you merely, yes, to empathize."

"I think you should go down to the clinic. I'll call Chuck."

"Chuck Schmuck."

"You've been under a strain."

And the Thunderbird slipped on the desk, and the themes blew in the wind, and the students lined up aft nodding and shaking, and all through the lanyards was to be heard the sound of a polished public speaker saying, "Friends! I do not come to praise (bury?) Caesar."

"You've just got to take yourself in hand, Sam," the Superintendent said. "You drink too much and you don't get enough sleep, and then you get in these terrific depressions and you go to somebody and say you don't think you have any future here. You know that's nonsense if you will only take yourself in hand. Courage, man."

"That's what Pertelote said."

"What?"

"Nothing."

"Pertelote?"

"The trouble with all you people," Sam said, "is that—"

"What people?"

"—you administrators, disciplinarians, 8-to-5 gods that we have to put up with—"

"Who are we?"

"You wouldn't even know, would you? You think that everyone must be like you, and you know that if you were sick you would be sick because you had eaten too much or drunk too much or not slept enough, *not* because of anything outside of you that was sick, sick unto death, dying in the classrooms, on the stairs, at the desks in the little offices."

"What are you talking about? I'll call Chuck."

"Don't call Chuck. *Don't* do anything. Because anything that you would do would be done to treat, to cure *me*. You don't see that I'm not the one to be treated."

"Who, then? Me? Have *I* done anything? Have *I* said I wanted to resign? And what are you resigning to me for anyway? Why don't you go see the Chairman, the Dean, the President, the Head Cook, anybody, not me. I'm just the Superintendent of Grounds."

And the Thunderbird rolled on the bridge and the stairwell filled, and the Superintendent's face looked like a kind face. "No," Sam said, "I'm not blaming you." And he left the Superintendent's office and walked down the stairs and walked out on the campus and past the library which was rocking and past a small pile of raked themes, and got in his Hudson and drove off.

The Stutz and The Tub

They went to a restaurant built on a pier out over the water, which was low (it is always low tide at Savin Rock). They sat in a dark corner from which the sea was not visible but where the smell of the mud-flats was particularly strong, and they waited a very long time to be served a bad meal. They talked about those who fitted their pasts together in that weak pattern they were obliged to make the most of for the evening—about Johnny Clark who was now working for the bank, and Peggy Brown who eloped with a soldier and went off somewhere—New Mexico? Georgia?—in the middle of the night. They sipped their watery coffee and were reminded of an evening when Alec spilt a whole pot of coffee on Mrs. Clark's Airedale. They worked the past over and over, and then they went out and walked around the park, with the smell of cheap candy, hot dogs and gunpowder in their heads—past The Whip, which he remembered as enormously fast and frightening and which now looked like an obsolete invention for upsetting the stomach, past the motorboats no longer sleek and bright, floating, heavily, in apple-core and orange-peel sewer water, past the Mystery House, boarded up, the signs fading, the façade leaning precariously out over the street, and past the stalls of shooting galleries, dart games and *wheels* where without exception the same cheap prizes of ashtrays and grotesque china figures that he remembered from twenty years ago were lined up in rows, as if in all that time either nobody had won a prize or nobody, having won a prize, had accepted it but had gone home, raging mad, to say, "I punctured three balloons with three throws and what did they offer me but a goddam ashtray which said on it 'Souvenir of Savin Rock.'" And the girl, Esther, said to Alec in front of the Virginia Reel, "It hasn't changed much, has it?"

She was impossible. All that good breeding in private schools in Pennsylvania, all those dancing lessons at the Lawn Club, all that broadening travel to France and California and the Caribbean and Mexico, and all those parties at Yale and Princeton and maybe for practice Williams—all of that for years and years and she stood in front of the Virginia Reel and said, "It hasn't changed much, has it?"

The Stutz was parked in front of the Virginia Reel. It had been converted into a kind of gross pickup and the back end had been sliced off and a boxlike affair inserted for carrying, say, bricks. It might have been blue once, like Alec's mother's, but now it was that withered black all really old cars achieve. The channel in the front fender for the spare tire was empty; the front bumper was held up on the right side by a rope; two of the windows, broken, were backed up by boards. Not only had the distinguished lady who formerly mounted the radiator cap vanished, but the radiator cap had vanished too, and steam rose from the rusty aperture.

"Heavens, that can't be a Stutz," Esther said.

"Do you remember our Stutz?"

Of course she remembered. How could she forget?

"That might even be it."

"That? Oh no, Alec, *really.*"

But the man in the ticket box of the Virginia Reel thought that it might be. "I couldn't help overhearing," he said, and he allowed as how he was the owner of the Stutz and had bought it in New Haven—did Alec live in New Haven and did Alec remember where his mother had sold it? It wasn't, he admitted, the best car he had ever owned but wouldn't Alec like to buy it as a souvenir of the old days?

"Alec, let's get out of here," Esther said.

But Alec went over to the Stutz, with Esther in tow saying this was too silly really; and the man from the Virginia Reel came out of the ticket booth to show them what he called the fine points. He was sorry that the car was so dirty and he hoped that they would overlook the dirt and the dents, the rope on the bumper, the missing radiator cap and the broken door handles because, if they did, they would see what a fine piece of machinery it was *basically* though it wasn't, he would tell them frankly, the most reliable machinery any more and did Alec want to make an offer.

Alec opened the back door. The rear section had been left almost intact when the car had been converted into a truck; the box had been inserted from the back and pushed in until it rested against the front seat (in the other direction it extended about three feet outside the car). The carpet on the floor in the rear had never been removed but it was covered, except at the edges, by the box as well as a thick layer of dirt.

Esther wanted to know what he was doing. He lifted the box about three inches on the right side and scraped at the dirt with the first thing he found in his pockets, his key ring. The dirt was thick and dry and swirled up in his face; twice he sneezed and had to let the box down and stand away from the dust cloud, but in two or three minutes he had uncovered it—it was still there, though the charred material on the edges had worn away leaving a much larger hole than he remembered.

"I never would have believed it," Esther said. "You mean you *remember* burning a hole in a carpet twenty years ago?" She was standing outside the car at a considerable distance from the owner who said it was really wonderful what people remembered sometimes and Alec would be surprised how

77

little he would have to pay for the burned rug, if he wanted it.

"Now Alec, don't be an idiot," Esther said from her distance; but Alec opened the front door and slipped in behind the wheel. Everything was right; the deep grooves for the fingers on the underside of the wheel, the speedometer that went up to one hundred and ten, the sharp bend, halfway up the shaft, in the gearshift lever and, especially, the horizontal lines of piano wire embedded in the windshield. In the garage at home he had sat for hours behind this wheel, going through all the motions. At first he had had trouble reaching the accelerator and the clutch even with his mother's pillow behind him, but by the time he was eleven he could do it. He had sat there shifting and shifting, making motor noises with his lips and steering through the Connecticut countryside at precisely one hundred and ten. When his mother drove downtown he had sat beside her and begged her not to let the other cars—none of which, surely, could go one hundred and ten —pass her. He was disgusted because all that power indicated by the speedometer was being left untapped, unexplored, unused. Once when she parked, near Malley's Department Store, she left him in the car and left the key in the ignition switch. He started the motor, pushed in the clutch, shifted into first; and when he let out the clutch somehow the car lurched forward more quickly than he had expected. He forgot all about the brake and banged into the car fortunately parked only three or four feet in front of him. When his mother came back she was angry because the car in front had backed into her, but he didn't say anything.

"What would you say if I bought it?" he asked Esther.

"Oh, Alec, not really."

But the man from the Virginia Reel knew that Alec would be surprised how low he would go. "Just make an offer, that's all."

Alec asked if it ran at all.

The man said it ran like a dream. Smooth as silk, with that big-car feeling.

78

"How are the tires?"

"Tires? You want tires too?" The man was prepared to be perfectly frank; the tires were not so good, he couldn't guarantee the tires, but how did Alec like the gearshift knob?

"Alec, really," Esther said. "You've got a car."

The man had an answer for this. "This isn't exactly a car, lady. This is an heirloom." And he admitted that he was prepared to let it go, though it was a steal at the price, for fifty dollars.

Alec's mother had packed the eight of them in the Stutz and taken them to Savin Rock for the afternoon, paying all their expenses on the scooters, in the Tunnel of Love, in the Mystery House and then back, again and again, on the Scooters. She had not let them go on the Thunderbolt or the Virginia Reel because she "had to draw a line somewhere," and when she insisted that they ride on the merry-go-round they were all bored and disgusted until they found out about the rings they could reach for as the merry-go-round went around; and then she had to draw another line. Johnny Clark got lost for fifteen minutes in the Mystery House, and when Alec's mother got the management stirred up to look for him he appeared, mumbling about a big hole in the floor with ogres with horns. Johnny Clark also ran head-on into Billy Altman with his scooter and knocked Billy out on the floor on his head. The party cost more than twenty-five dollars. They went on the scooters six times, and the last time Johnny shouted, "Jesus, another dollar-forty." They were all sick when they got home and Alec's mother declared frequently for fifteen years thereafter that she had learned the absolute limits of her endurance there and then. Alec went to lunch at Johnny's house the next day and Mrs. Clark thanked him ostentatiously for the wonderful birthday party and said, "But you must remember, Alec, that most of us cannot afford that sort of thing." Alec reported this to his mother and the next week she doubled his allowance.

But the man at the Virginia Reel thought that fifty dollars

was as low as he could go, even for such a special customer as Alec. "You think it over," he said. "You can't lose." And he went back in his ticket box.

Alec got out of the car. Esther said she was very glad he had not gone completely out of his mind. They walked slowly down a side street lined with stalls out of which fat men in bright vests and women with bright shawls draped over their shoulders leaned and called to them to take three throws for ten cents, to take a chance on winning a beautiful clock for their mantel, to spin the wheel and win a prize every time. They came to the new Ferris wheel but Esther said that she did not like high places. They came to the Rocket but Esther did not want to be turned upside down. They came to the scooters; Alec went in while Esther stood outside, but Alec's scooter was in bad repair and wouldn't steer properly, so after bumping into the side and getting caught in a corner he came out and they walked toward the parking lot.

Separate from the other concessions, near the dark area where Savin Rock trolleys let passengers off and the conductors pull down the front pole and let up the rear pole for the trip back to New Haven, was The Tub. It was an ordinary washtub about three feet in diameter and half full of water, set back six feet from the rail. Alec bought three rings for fifteen cents and tossed them carefully into the tub. One of them hit a stick (set in a round, floating base) and sent it bobbing up and down, but the ring slipped off into the water. The others weren't even close.

"Really, Alec," Esther said as he bought three more rings. In the back of the tent, on shelves behind the tub, were the ashtrays and clocks and china figures. Alec tossed the three rings rapidly, carelessly; one stayed on a stick.

"There you are," said the fat concessionaire in the bright vest, producing an ashtray on which was written "Souvenir of Savin Rock." He pointed out that Alec could keep this or try for a better prize, such as a beautiful china figure for his mantel at home, or a genuine Waterbury clock, or even a radio. But Alec said he wanted to keep the ashtray, and he put down fifteen cents more.

"You're *not* going to do it again?" Esther said.

Alec bought five more rounds of rings, and with each set he tried a different technique. He found that he was most successful when he shot quickly without looking. It seemed as if the flat, accurate shots were the shots that knocked the sticks over while the flukes caught the sticks, as it were, by surprise. When he had finished the five rounds Esther said he had spent a dollar five, just thrown it into that tub for three of those damned ashtrays. The concessionaire said he could trade in the ashtrays for a china figure, but Alec decided to keep the ashtrays. He bought five more rounds.

By the time he had spent four-fifty he had twelve ashtrays. Then Esther disappeared for about ten rounds and when she came back she told him in no uncertain terms that there was a trolley in twenty minutes and she would be on it unless he gave up this foolishness.

Alec said he would be through pretty soon.

"Really, Alec," she said. But he bought some more rounds, the trolley came and went, and Esther was still there, standing about six feet from Alec and lighting one cigarette after another.

When he had spent nine-ninety and had sixty-four ashtrays, the concessionaire said he was very happy that Alec liked both The Tub and the ashtrays, but that he had no more ashtrays and wouldn't Alec like to trade some of them in for, say, a nice clock for the mantel?

Alec said he would prefer to keep the ashtrays.

"Nine dollars and ninety cents," Esther said, "and sixty-four ashtrays."

"These aren't exactly ashtrays," Alec said. "They're . . ." but he didn't know what they were. He asked the concessionaire to do him a favor and let him have the last three rings he

81

was going to shoot for ten cents rather than fifteen cents. This would make an even ten dollars and, he said, he wanted it to come out that way. Furthermore, would the concessionaire mind very much getting him another ashtray—or two, or three—if he should win one—or two, or three—on his last three shots since, surely, though The Tub was out of ash-trays, there were plenty of ashtrays still to be had in Savin Rock.

The concessionaire agreed, though he really thought that perhaps a clock . . .

Alec took the three rings and closed his eyes and turned his back on the tub. With a careless gesture like that of tossing salt over his shoulder he threw the first ring backwards in a high arc toward the tub.

"Made it," said the concessionaire.

Then Alec carefully measured five paces from the rail and made a mark at that point in the dirt. He sat down with his buttocks up to the line, his back still to the tub, and closing his eyes again he tossed the second ring over his shoulder in an arc even higher than the first.

This also caught on a stick.

He measured an additional five paces out from the rail, drew another line, and, with his back to the tub and his eyes closed and his legs spread wide apart, he bent over and flipped the third ring through his legs in the highest arc of all.

"Really, Alec," Esther said, "really!"

The concessionaire said he'd get those ashtrays and be back in a minute.

The Ocean Cottage

The big birds were there in all seasons, and the fish, but not the people. The people were migratory, in Cadillacs and cruisers. They were two-house people (but they said "homes") who sniffed the air in the north suspiciously in the late fall, the air in the south suspiciously in the late spring. And when the cold in the north or the heat in the south got to be simply *too* much they went off in their Cadillacs and cruisers to their other houses (homes).

But when they moved (in either direction) they always made sure that when they got to their new homes the homes would have been cleaned and aired and made comfortable—and also made indistinguishable from the old. When it was all done properly they could move sedately fifteen hundred miles south or fifteen hundred miles north without feeling the tiniest physical or spiritual jar. Without, indeed, feeling anything. They could go right on reading the same magazines even, and talking about the same people, and drinking the same two cocktails before the same dinner, and shopping for the same things in different branches of the same stores.

They thought about this, when they thought at all, as a very advanced sort of living.

But there was one woman (who had a husband) who said no. She said no, it was not right, it was primitive, it was bourgeois. Why should people who had everything they could possibly want in the world, and who could buy what they wanted when they didn't—why should such people be so unimaginative, so fuddy-duddy, so stupid as to devote all their time and energy and money to making themselves narrow, not broad?

"Daddums," this woman said. "I am going to do something. I am going to expand our horizons."

"How, my dear? Start a shell collection?" (Daddums was himself interested in shell collecting.)

"No," she said, "I'm going to start a gift shoppe."

"Yes, my dear."

So she did. She bought a going gift shoppe with a big stock and the best connections on a traffic circle right near the most fashionable beach, and she went at it hammer and tong one winter. She had a natural flair for it. A woman would come into the store looking for a gift for a relative, and Maddums would be unobtrusive (she never hovered), patient (she hurried no one) and sympathetic (nodding her head as the woman explained all the difficulties of getting a gift for Gumbo or Bimbo). Without pushing the woman at all, without even seeming to suggest things, Maddums would lead the woman to exactly what she wanted (even though the woman didn't know what she wanted) and the woman would give a regular little shriek of delight, buy it and become a regular customer. Maddums could analyze the customers as they entered the store. Just by the clothes they wore and the way they sniffed around the counters. She would know how much money they wanted to spend, whether they wanted something ornamental like a china giraffe for atop the TV set, or functional like a man's barbecue apron, and how they felt about things being frilly, plain, gaudy, written-on, austere. Daddums couldn't do this sort of thing at all, but Maddums was just great at it and she would give Daddums goose pimples as she walked around the store with a customer saying that such-and-such an item was darling, cute, clever, different, quaint, cuddly, charming, devilish, risqué, intime, gauche, daring or demure. Oh yes, she did just fine.

But after one season, despite her success, she said to Daddums, "No, I'm not going to do this any more."

"Why, my dear?"

"It's really so vulgar, you know, vulgar."

"I agree, my dear. Why don't you take up shell collecting? Or pelicans?" (Daddums was himself interested in stuffing pelicans.)

"No, houses."

"Houses, my dear?"

"Homes."

"Very well, my dear."

"More challenging. More opportunities. The concept of living space, all that. I'll change people's lives, make them less narrow, more broad."

"Yes, my dear."

So the very next winter when they came south to Florida Maddums began to buy and sell houses. She bought and sold beach houses and town houses, small houses and houses with swimming pools. She advocated kitchens with glass refrigerators, living rooms with glass fireplaces, bathrooms with glass showers, porches with glass sliding doors. She liked glass—more living space; and she persuaded a great many other people to like glass too. She also liked tile roofs and split-shingle roofs, redwood paneling and wormy cypress paneling. And she liked Rustic and Modern and Spanish and Norman. And her customers soon did too. She did just fine.

Daddums went on with his shell collecting. He also began to preserve pelicans in the deep freeze for mounting.

Maddums thrived on her houses all winter, but at the end of the winter she began to notice that despite the glass refrigerators and the wormy cypress paneling, and despite the new, modern, bugproof, nonscuff, nonstain floors, and despite the genuine cold-rolled duo-therm safety-glass picture windows

85

and the four-unit blower-ventilator systems in the fully insulated half attics and the dandy walled-in, imitation Spanish patios with real orange trees—despite all this there was a great drawback in the buying and selling of houses in a modern, industrialized, unionized place like Florida: the houses were all badly made.

The doors didn't hang right, the windows didn't fit, the floors warped, the ceilings leaked, the sewage backed up, the rats got in, the wall plaster cracked and the cement driveway didn't drain. It was just no good buying and selling houses designed and constructed by others, by persons who didn't *care* about anything except *money*. Next winter, she decided, she would buy and sell no more houses, but she would *build* a house, a dream house just for herself. And of course Daddums.

"Yes, my dear."

So she did. The very next winter she built the most different (Southern) (ocean-cottage-type) home. It was in the architectural magazines, described as wholly new, a radical departure. It was built fifty yards off shore on the Gulf of Mexico (sea breezes from all sides). Built on pilings like a bridge. Protected from the open sea by a retractable steel wall.

It had a dock right off the south porch. It had an aerial cart on wires for getting to and fro. It had pelican roosts.

"Different!" the magazines cried. "New from the ocean up!" One of the articles began: "Mrs. Ronald (Maddums to her friends) Carrothers, of the iron foundry Carrothers—nee Esther Killigrew, of the mining Killigrews—has spirit, drive, imagination and a boyish bob. Now fifty, she has at last eminently achieved her lifelong ambition of setting the pace—and what a pace!—in contemporary ocean-cottage design." Then followed pictures of the house, pelicans, Maddums.

"Bully, my dear," Daddums said.

Maddums was really gratified by the magazines. She had

been in the public eye before, when she had come out at New-port in the twenties, and then again during the war when she had helped sponsor "Culture for England." But that had been social. Nothing had been said then, as was being said now, about her imagination, her flair for the striking, the novel. She felt justified in her life at last. "Who was it," she asked Daddums, "who said, 'All things come to him who waits'?"

"I don't know, my dear," Daddums said.

"It was Milton," Maddums said. And so she had the maga-zine pieces framed. She sat in her pace-setting living room and looked alternately at the sea and the magazine pieces. She even felt *almost* content, and she knew that she would have been absolutely content (and Daddums too) if it hadn't been for the weather.

Oh, but the weather. The weather that winter, by the time they got moved in, was simply frightful. Coldest winter in Florida's history. And stormiest. The northern papers were full of it—"damage running in millions," "citrus crop de-stroyed," "snow hits orange orchards," and so on. Indeed the weather was so bad that a good many of the Cadillacs and cruisers just didn't come south at all. Sales tax proceeds dropped sharply; beaches were deserted; hotels were half empty; Nassau and the Virgin Islands were jammed. And as for Maddums and Daddums, well, life for them fifty yards off shore in the Gulf of Mexico wasn't as charming and gracious as the magazines said, even though Maddums had carried through her construction with consummate skill and energy, and even though Daddums stayed hard at work with his peli-can mounting. The wind, the waves, the dampness, the gray sky, the cold and the isolation sometimes made it just plain difficult. They just weren't as *happy* as they should have been in "the perfect southern ocean cottage."

The wind was the worst. It howled through the pelican roosts, whistled through the wires of the house-to-shore cart, battered and salted the ocean-side picture windows.

And the retractable steel wall was no blessing. It should have had three, not two stops. When it was down the cottage floor leaked. When it was up the waves hit its exposed surface with a great whack. If it could have been stopped just below the surface—but no, it hadn't been designed that way. So whack! whack! whack! went the waves. Poor Maddums found it frightfully hard to think creatively.

And when the waves went whack! the spray was driven by the wind against the house like a lash. Th-th-thurrrr-wh-wh-whack! Th-th-thurrr-wh-wh-whack! Daddums said it was like living in a glass suit under fifty toilets.

"Daddums!" said Maddums.

And there were no pelicans. They all flew inland and fished in the sheltered bays.

And it was damp, damp. Matches wouldn't light. Clothes wouldn't stay dry even in their drawers. For someone with less character than Maddums it might have been a winter of giving in, giving up, saying that after all it didn't do any *good* to fight the narrow and constricted ways of the world with imagination and energy. But Maddums was bound and determined that *she* was not one who was going to give in. Indeed, she said to Daddums, adversity gave her a kind of push, put her on her toes, made her want to develop herself and her talent further, not just vegetate out there in the midst of the wind and spray. She would not, simply not let down; no, she was hard at work on a *new* plan.

No, not shells.

A different, a really different *northern* house.

What had been done, she asked Daddums, what had really been done in the last hundred years for city living? Elevators and bathrooms. More elevators, more bathrooms. Not that there was anything wrong with elevators and bathrooms, but heavens.

"Absolutely, my dear," Daddums said.

She bought herself a high stool, a slant desk and all the paraphernalia, and put it all in the sunroom opposite the pelican roosts. There, in February, she sat herself down and began to try to visualize (with her imagination) some positive alternatives to the present hidebound trends in city living. She drew sketch after sketch, some detailed, some fragmentary, day after day, day after day, as the wind howled and the waves went th-th-thurwh-wh-whack! Sometimes she got very discouraged. She would sit for hours at the desk, fighting the hypnotic effect of the wind, telling herself that she would never be able to produce a northern city house with anything like the flair of her southern house if she let her thoughts get in a *rut*—and then she would sketch maybe fifty different designs for a living room bathtub or a kitchen bed and find that she *was* in a rut, all the sketches were *exactly* the same. It was terribly discouraging and sometimes she could hardly keep her temper.

"Daddums!"

"Yes, my dear."

"I wish you wouldn't make such an infernal racket out there with your electric razor."

"Yes, my dear."

"It is hard enough to think around here anyway with the wind and the waves. You could at least spare us that buzzing while I am working."

"Yes, my dear."

Poor Daddums lost his interest in pelican-mounting and went back to his shell-collecting. Unshaved, he would take the aerial cart off about ten, walk up and down the beach in a couple of sweaters and his mackintosh, and come back to the cottage at noon for the market reports. In a few weeks he collected many whelks, limpets, coquina, boat shells, pen shells and measled cowries, all of which he arranged neatly in boxes beside his bed.

He studied the habits of bivalves, univalves and starfish. He thought it bully how the starfish suffocated the clam, how the whelk battered everybody with its shell.

And Maddums struggled with her kitchen beds. Sometimes

she just had to take hold of herself physically, grasping her own shoulders and squeezing them till they hurt, to remind herself to be fanciful, mentally sprightly, not hidebound. And sometimes it didn't do any good even to do that; there were a few really dark days when she couldn't do anything at all. She would lie on her bed with her seagreen Venetian blinds down and her sketches covering her head and she would listen to the th-th-thurwh-wh-whack th-th-thurwh-wh-whack! and she would tell herself that what she was doing was just nonsense. Who wanted to live in New York or Boston in a house with a built-in beach? a kitchen bed? For that matter who wanted to live fifty yards out in the Gulf of Mexico? It was wrong, all of it; she could kick herself. She was an idle, stupid old woman whose values had gotten all mixed up. Why did she have to waste her talents on material possessions, a house, a kitchen bed, a retractable steel wall? Better to live in a two-bedroom rambler or one of those horrible old brownstone things uptown. Better to live *anywhere* so long as where one was living did not make a slave of one's free mind and spirit. There was too much of that in America, too much slavery to things built of metal and stone, wood and polyethylene.

Once when she was like this Daddums came in and said, "Dear?"

"Stop it, Daddums, stop it! Can't you leave me alone even for an instant?"

But Maddums was not a stupid old woman. She was a strong woman. Even in the depths of her depressions she had enough presence of mind, enough control of herself not to tear up the sketches. She locked them in a drawer and put the key in the Cadillac on shore. For she knew how to fight sloth, despair, despondency; it was not for nothing that she had carried the burden of a weak-willed husband and managed the affairs of "Culture for England" and run a gift shoppe and a real estate business and now become an architect, builder, maker. So it came as no surprise either to her or Daddums that when her depressions passed she was again the same old Maddums, seated at her drawing board imagining, creating, projecting the life of a Family Unit in a truly different northern city home.

And Daddums' shells progressed admirably. He had fine specimens of nearly all the prominent local shells, and bushelsful of colorful coquina.

But there was just one shell that he simply yearned to find and couldn't: the junonia. "A rare and majestic shell," it said in his shell book. "A prized shell among collectors." He walked up and down, up and down every day on the lonely, windswept beach. He took off his shoes and waded in the freezing water to where the waves broke and the shells first gathered. He got sand in his trousers cuffs. He got wet and cold. He got the snuffles. He got *very* discouraged, for in all his searching he could never even find a recognizable fragment of what the book described as "creamy white, with rounded spots of reddish or brown; lip thin, lined with white, the spots showing through faintly." But he was not one to give up.

Neither of them gave up. And they were rewarded.

April 15 dawned, a beautiful warm day, the first in three months. The wind died down, the retractable steel wall was lowered, the pelicans returned flapping their great wings, and the Cadillacs and cruisers reappeared as if by magic.

The change was so startling that it was impossible not to take it as a sign, a symbol, a prophecy. Daddums celebrated by getting up an hour earlier, catching and killing and putting in the deep freeze a rare pinkish pelican, and driving into town and buying himself a junonia at a shell shop for seven dollars. Maddums sat down early at her desk and discovered that suddenly everything was realizing itself right before her eyes. In less than two hours she sketched in all the most difficult sections of her living areas—the sections in and around

91

the living room-bathroom that had driven her to despair for weeks—and she could see immediately that now the whole city-home project had been thoroughly achieved, consummated. By noon she was done, and Daddums was back with his shell, and both of them sat out by the noisy pelican roosts with a wonderful sense of fulfillment and completion.

If they had been of a communicative nature (but they were not) they would have said to each other that they had each in their own fields succeeded: they had broadened their horizons; they had beautifully sublimated their pathogenic wishes. But they didn't say it that way.

"We'll go north early," Maddums said.

"No sooner said than done, my dear," said Daddums.

They closed up the house about 2 P.M., took the aerial cart ashore, strapped it down firmly, got in their Cadillac (just a teeny bit rusted underneath from the salt spray) and drove away (stopping at the Railway Express Office to mail the pinkish pelican) —drove up Gulf of Mexico Drive past the conventional houses just opening to greet the warm weather, past the narrow, uncreative millionaires standing on their lawns with their rakes muttering, "*There* go the Carrothers —where the hell are *they* going?—what are they going to do *now?*" and past the motel owners in consultation with their lawyers about the new threat to private beach rights presented by the Carrothers' ocean-cottage-type home.

They drove fast. They drove triumphantly. They drove in silence. They were thinking.

Maddums was thinking there was too much talk about the evil effects of money. It was not the money that was evil. The money was inanimate. The money didn't do anything. It was the people *with* the money, who didn't use it right.

Daddums was thinking that he would have a glass case built for his pink pelican, and the pelican would hold the junonia in its beak.

At last, in rare good spirits, Maddums said, "About the New York house."

"Yes, my dear?"

"It will float in air. Moored by nylon cord. Steadied by gyroscopes."

"Fascinating, my dear."

"And what will you do, Daddums?"

"Don't you worry about me, dear." He patted her knee.

Nice Fireplace, Good Beach

Alec settled back in his chair, lighted his pipe laboriously in the great tradition of storytellers, and informed them that this evening he was going to tell them a story about youth and innocence. But he wanted them to understand that only the extenuating circumstances of this particular story persuaded him to undertake such a harebrained venture.

One of the listeners, stretched out before the roaring fire as the wintry wind growled and barked outside, said that he had heard about extenuating circumstances before, and did Alec have another story?

Alec smiled tolerantly and said he was sure nobody in the room had heard this one because he hadn't either. Further, he had nothing but contempt for youth and innocence, and besides there was a catch to this story.

Another listener said he certainly hoped so; he hadn't driven forty miles over icy roads in the middle of January to hear some simple and straightforward anecdote; and would Alec please get on?

Alec said that the problem, or catch, or extenuating circumstance which most interested him about the story could probably be best described as a basic misunderstanding between the protagonists. . . .

Hoity, toity, another listener said.

. . . a basic misunderstanding between the protagonists about who, exactly, was young and innocent.

Very well, another listener said. And would Alec *please get on?*

Both girls were late of course (Alec began) when we arrived in town from Princeton, and so we stood in the hall of their rooming house for an hour, talking of the lateness of women and wondering why a place where so many men spent so much time waiting for so many girls didn't sport a waiting room with ash trays and comfortable chairs and copies of books on the Sane Sex Life. It was a hall converted to electric light by putting the bulbs where the gas jets had been; and through it in both directions, pounding up and down the stairs at one end, opening and slamming the glass doors at the other, was a steady procession of girls, single and in pairs. They were all in a hurry. They arrived in short skirts, disheveled, with packages under their arms, and they left in longer skirts, immaculate, perfumed, demure and taller. Ralph and I flattened ourselves against the wall and waited. And waited. When they arrived at six-twenty (we had come at five) they rushed in, out of breath and distraught, protesting that they were terribly, terribly sorry. They had tried all afternoon to reach us by phone at Princeton; they had even called the Dean's office, but we had gone and there was nothing, just nothing they could do. They didn't know how they could possibly make up to us for their not being able to go, and they knew we wouldn't believe them and would think they were standing us up, but they weren't; they swore they weren't. They had to go back to the office (they were models) and work all evening on some mink coats.

Ralph was very gallant. He knew they couldn't help it. He knew about offices. He knew what a poor single girl in New York had to put up with. He knew everything; he understood; and he smiled and patted his girl, Helen, on the shoulder and arranged for us to pick them up the next morning, Saturday, as if nothing had happened because, as he said, nothing *had* happened and everything was wonderful. And they beamed and giggled and were grateful, and Effie—*my girl*—said to me, "Alec, you just mustn't think this happens all the time because it doesn't and I hate to make a bad impression the first time I meet somebody and I hope you'll tell me that I haven't. Have I?" What could I do but smile? We met them again at ten o'clock next morning.

At that time Helen said she was terribly sorry but she couldn't come until later in the day because there were still some minks to be photographed down at the office. She thought it was perfectly terrible to stand us up twice in less than twenty-four hours and she hoped we'd understand that she had to go down there or be fired.

So Ralph was gallant again. He knew about these things; he realized perfectly that there was nothing Helen could do. And he arranged for us to leave with Effie right away and for Helen, who wasn't to be finished with her minks until five-thirty, to hop a six-thirty train and meet us down there at eight. That would be wonderful, Helen thought, just wonderful and Ralph was so bright to think of it; but Effie looked worried and said she didn't know that it was right for her, an honest girl, to go off with two men alone even in broad daylight. Was it right? Certainly, Ralph told her, certainly it was right. She would be as safe with us as in her mother's arms. Certainly, I said. Certainly, Helen said. So away we went, with Effie sitting between us.

One of the listeners stretched out in front of the fire said that he didn't want to complain, but before they went too far would Alec mind so very much telling them where they were all going.

Alec said that nobody was supposed to know yet; everything would be revealed at the proper time.

The listener said that was all right, but for Alec's information he wanted to point out that he figured Alec and Ralph for college boys just out of short pants who had fixed up a mousetrap for themselves where a couple of mice could take them for their shirts, socks and everything.

Alec admitted that wasn't far wrong.

So the listener took off his shoes and wiggled his toes comfortably in front of the fire.

The cottage (Alec continued) had been closed all winter; it was like a tomb inside. We had to take the shutters off the main windows downstairs, find half-a-dozen switches, scattered everywhere, for the water pump, water heater, furnace and lights, take covers off the furniture, unstick doors and drawers, and clear out a bevy of sparrows on the front porch. After we had done all this we got the liquor, eggs, bacon and coffee out of the car and cooked ourselves what we called, variously, whiskey eggs, scrambled Manhattans, pullet-proof brunch, distilled oofs and oofs à la Seagramme. Effie had much less of this than we had, but enough so she stopped talking about the latest Book-of-the-Month selections, the shows she had paid six-sixty at Shubert's to see, and the difficulties a poor girl in New York had keeping up with the arts. After Ralph had built a fire in the big fireplace in the living room, and we had settled down on the couch, she decided that she was terribly glad she had come after all. For a while, she said, she had been just too scared to have fun, but now she thought everything was wonderful. The fire especially was wonderful, so homey, so romantic, so . . . homey. She thought the sea was grand (we were by the sea), and when she settled down she was going to have a cottage perched on the cliff right over the ocean where you could hear the waves pounding the rocks day and night and you could walk out on the beach—there would be a beach too—and pick up beautiful shells and walk barefoot in the soft sand. In fact she wanted nothing in life so much as a little place by the water, and maybe this was the place she had always seen in her dreams.

97

I pointed out that the cottage didn't meet her specifications: no cliff. But she said she'd be willing to forget about the cliff anyway, that was just an idle fancy, and as a matter of fact what she wanted, she guessed, was the very cottage we were in, especially if the dream house could come equipped with Ralph and me too.

I went out in the kitchen with Ralph and told him this was pretty thick at two in the afternoon even after whiskey eggs. But he said it was a lot better than before and Effie was my girl and where was my chivalry. So I went back and sat down close to her and told her that after all she was the first ingredient of anybody's dream house. Pretty soon her head was on my shoulder and she was purring like a cat.

Ralph took plenty of time in the kitchen. Then he came back in, gave me a big wink from behind her and said there was nothing in the world he liked so much to see as young love sprouting in the spring, but that he felt like an outsider, out of place, just an old grandmother, and so he was going out for a while if we didn't mind. He excused himself to gather, as he said, driftwood washed up on the shores of time for the fires of love. His exit would have been better if he hadn't had trouble getting the front door open.

So he left Effie and me with a kind of mission, but we had eaten too much and drunk too much to carry it out. When he came back an hour later, pounding and stamping and dropping great logs all over the front porch to show us, he said, what a gentleman he was in the presence of *l'amour*, we were asleep at opposite ends of the living room. He said we should have brought a chess set along; asked us if we thought we had come down here to take the cure; and wanted to know if there was anything he could do to make us more comfortable: tea perhaps? a couple of good books? some cards for double solitaire? I told him to go row a boat, and we started all over again on the whiskey.

"Do you know what agoraphobia is?" asked Ralph, after a

bit. Effie allowed as how she did not, such a big word. Ralph said he had it in reverse, and explained. Effie thought Ralph was very clever to be so clever, and she wished *she* had gone to Princeton and could say things like that. Ralph reddened a bit and said he wasn't being clever, he was merely suggesting that we go outside and enjoy the spring. That would be perfectly wonderful, Effie said, she would love to go out and was it cold? So we went out.

All the cottages were lined up in a neat row along the shore, shuttered, boarded up. The sand was smooth as a table right up to the tall grass and stretched in both directions— north toward Asbury Park, south toward Atlantic City—for as far as we could see, without a beach umbrella, a child's castle, a portable radio or even a Coca-Cola bottle showing. Effie said it certainly was desolate; she felt as if she were on a desert island. Ralph agreed and hoped it would stay that way. He said he didn't think he would hear the end of it from his parents if the neighbors took it into their heads, because it was such a nice spring weekend, to come down and open their houses too. What do you mean? asked Effie. She didn't see that we were doing anything wrong and she wanted us to know that she was a good girl and she wouldn't have left New York if she thought we were doing anything *bad*. I protested that she certainly was a very good girl and nobody was casting aspersions at anybody, and I went to the house and got the bottle and we all had another drink.

First, then, we considered wading. We took off our shoes and socks and tried it, and the water was so cold that we had to have a drink. Then we tried wading and drinking together and that worked very well: the water was warmer that way, though not very warm. Then we ran up and down the edge of the water until we were all breathing hard; and it occurred to me, because Effie was a very small girl, that I should run up and down carrying Effie. Effie kicked her feet and screamed when I waded in up to my knees with her and threatened to drop her, and when I put her down safe again on the beach she told me how strong I was and how wonderful it was to be with a man for a change after all those bleak weeks in that boardinghouse full of girls. Ralph said he supposed we wanted to be alone, and he went off down the beach about a hundred yards, balancing the bottle on his nose and skipping stones over the water. But he watched us all the time, and when he came back he said he thought it was a shame we weren't making use of all the facilities: why didn't we go swimming?

"No, no, no," Effie cried; "it's too cold!"

"No, no, no, it isn't," Ralph said. "It's healthy. It stirs up the metabolism. Its strengthens the red blood corpuscles. It's the best thing in the world for you if you go in just for a minute."

Effie wanted to know what the metabolism was.

"I'll show you," Ralph said. And he stripped down to his underwear shorts and said, "Look, it won't take a minute."

The listener in front of the fire said that he saw it all in his mind's eye, the three of them cavorting on the white sands, God being with them when they knew it not. But he was having trouble with the extra party, so would Alec please get that other girl the hell down from New York?

Alec said he was coming to that, but it was only about five o'clock and the other girl wasn't scheduled to arrive until eight. Furthermore he would tell his story in his own way, if the listener didn't mind.

No, the listener said, he didn't mind; but personally he couldn't stay more than three more days.

Ralph and I agreed (Alec continued) that Effie was being overscrupulous when she screamed and ran into the house at the sight of Ralph in his shorts. Ralph thought that must be the signal for us to rush in and drag her, happily protesting, back; but I suggested that we, or rather Ralph, had genuinely offended all her finest sensibilities. What sensibilities, asked Ralph. Effie? He had never heard of such a thing. But when she didn't come out again he redressed and we went in after her.

Effie was pouting inside. She didn't think it was nice for two men to take advantage of a poor girl this way, and she wanted us to know that unless we mended our ways she was taking the next train back to New York. I told her there was nothing wrong with people taking off their clothes—it was natural—and I mixed her a good strong drink to show her I was on her side. This restored her spirits. She was glad to know that I at least hadn't meant any harm, and she thought it was very chivalrous of me to be so understanding, and she wanted me to know that nothing she had said was meant to apply to me. But she continued to pout at Ralph, so Ralph began to give me dark looks over her head, and when we were alone to-gether out in the kitchen he said he thought it was a pretty cheap trick on my part to make up to her by putting him in the wrong. I told him I wasn't doing any such thing; after all it was he who had taken off his clothes.

"Well, for Christ's sake," Ralph said, and he went upstairs in a huff with a portable radio under his arm, leaving Effie and me on the couch in front of the fire.

Effie became unhappy. As the music began to drift down from upstairs she said that she felt terrible, just terrible, for making us fight; and she wanted me to go up and tell Ralph she hadn't meant anything.

"Who's fighting?" I said. "We're not fighting. Nobody's mad. Ralph just wants to be alone with his thoughts. He's a thinker. He does this every evening at six o'clock."

Effie wasn't so sure. She thought I was kidding her, and one thing she hated was not knowing whether or not somebody was kidding her.

So I told her that, yes, I was kidding her and Ralph *was*

mad, but that I was sorry and wouldn't do it any more. Besides, it wouldn't do any good to go upstairs and apologize; he would cool off and come down. Anyway it was too nice on the couch to go upstairs. "You're such a nice man," Effie said as she curled up next to me and stroked my head.

She did it very well. My head and the back of my neck tingled. I was so warm and comfortable from the whiskey and the exercise and Effie's stroking that I didn't ever want to move, and I didn't even hear Ralph come downstairs when he set out to get Helen. He banged the radio on a table and said he was frightfully sorry to have intruded upon us; he promised he wouldn't do it again; he would make enough noise to wake the dead when he came back. He went out, slamming the door.

Effie told me she didn't think Ralph was very well-bred. Nobody who was well-bred would have slammed the door.

"No," I said, "he's not well-bred. Are you well-bred?"

"Alec, that isn't nice!"

So it wasn't nice. So she stroked my head and the fire got warmer and warmer and the house was quiet as a tomb and she whispered to me that she thought I was just the nicest man she had ever met. I wasn't like the others. I was genteel. I knew how a poor girl felt. So I had another drink on this, and time passed, and we got to a certain point and she said no, Alec, really, Alec. I told her she was silly, but she said she couldn't. I told her it was natural, but she said she couldn't; it wasn't that it wasn't natural, and it wasn't that she didn't think I had the best intentions in the world; it was just that she couldn't.

"All right, all right," I said.

She thought it was wrong of me to get mad, and if I knew why she was acting the way she was, I wouldn't.

"I'm not mad," I said. "You don't need to explain anything."

Yes, she said, she thought she should explain. She owed it to me because I had been so good to her.

"But you don't owe me anything."

Yes, she thought she did, and she wanted me to know it wasn't because she didn't want to, but because her doctor had said she couldn't.

"Your doctor?"

Oh, yes, it was terrible; it had come to her as a terrible shock.

"What?"

Well, it was very hard for her to describe, and she wouldn't try to describe it, but she wanted me to know that her doctor had said that she couldn't because she had what he called an inverted womb.

"An inverted womb?"

By now we were sitting up pretty straight on the couch, looking at the fire; she was at one end of the couch and I was at the other. I told her that I didn't understand what the trouble was because I didn't know what an inverted womb was, or what it meant, but of course I was very sorry and why didn't we change the subject?

She wasn't sure what it was either, and she didn't think she could describe all the details right, but the doctor had said. . . .

I told her that really it was none of my business and I didn't see why she had to tell me the details. I would believe her, I wouldn't doubt her word for a minute, though admittedly I didn't see what an inverted womb, whatever it was, had to do with it.

"What *do* you mean, Alec?"

I said I didn't mean anything; why didn't we drop the subject?

So she said she couldn't possibly describe her condition properly, but that at any rate her doctor had said she couldn't have children.

For a minute I didn't say anything. Then I told her I still didn't see what that had to do with it; as a matter of fact I thought her inversion might be a very good thing, taking everything into consideration.

She burst into tears and called me the cruelest man she ever met.

Well, that was that. I sat at a distance on the couch for a few minutes, staring into the fire while she told me how cruel I was. Then I left her and went out in the kitchen to make some more drinks. Just then Ralph, from a block away, began blowing the horn. He blew the horn steadily all the way down the block, and when he turned in the driveway he screeched the tires, roared up to the house with the horn still blowing, jammed on the brakes and skidded on the gravel. He got out, opened all four doors of the car one by one and slammed them shut, and walked around the house shouting, Ahoy, ahoy, is anybody home?

It seems that Helen hadn't been on the train. He came in alone, and Effie ran to him sobbing and said that she never wanted to see me again and would Ralph take her to the railroad station immediately?

"There, there, there," Ralph said. "Has Alec hurt Effie?"

Effie clung to him and told him I had as much as told her she wasn't a nice girl, and she wasn't going to stay another minute in New Jersey being insulted and defamed and made a laughingstock. There, there, there, Ralph said. He was sure I hadn't meant any harm, but if I had meant any harm he would see to it that nothing would happen to Effie, not while he was around.

"For Christ's sake," I said. I picked up the radio and went upstairs.

The listener by the fire said he thought Alec had acted like a cad, a perfect cad; and if Alec weren't a big boy now he'd take him right over his knees and spank him.

Another listener wanted to know if that was the end of the story.

Alec admitted that it was, except for one thing.

Effie was Chinese?

Effie stole Alec's wallet?

Ralph told her an inverted womb was nothing to worry about?

Alec discovered another girl upstairs?

Effie came upstairs later and . . . apologized?

Ralph stole Effie's wallet?

Ralph came upstairs later . . . with Effie?

And apologized?

Alec said no, it was none of these things; at least, so far as he knew it was none of these things, but the point was. . . .

Aha, the point, said the listener by the fire.

The point was, Alec said, that he didn't know.

He didn't know what?

Alec explained that he had stayed upstairs all evening with the radio playing full blast, and that at midnight Ralph had taken Effie to the station for a train, but. . . .

But what?

What, Alec wanted to know, happened downstairs between nine o'clock and midnight?

Didn't Ralph say?

Ralph, Alec said, wouldn't say.

Well, for Christ's sake, said the listener in front of the fire. He put on his shoes.

Modern Science (*at 1930 Prices*)

It was surprising, really surprising, how few people in the world lived on any sort of schedule. They just went along looking at their old watches and the clock on the green and some grandfather clock in the hall that had been built before anybody knew anything about the needs of the modern world. They just went along living five minutes, ten minutes, maybe fifteen minutes behind time or ahead of time their whole lives without even realizing that for a very small expense and a little effort they could be right on the dot forever, or at least until the current went off. How could they do it? With electric clocks.

Efficient, accurate and cheap. Alec had two of them and he knew. He'd had one of them six months and the other a week and he hadn't had a bit of trouble. They'd been right on the nose every time he turned on the radio and the bong rang. It was remarkable. The clockmakers at Liggett's knew what was needed all right, and their prices were aimed right at the average man: ninety-nine cents. What an investment.

But he had to get that other one, the square green one, to make the set-up complete. Then he could have one on the bureau and one on the bookcase and one smack by the bed so that no matter where he was in the room he had one of them right in sight. Furthermore he couldn't be sure they'd have that green model on sale forever for that ridiculous price and he had the money right in his pocket, so there was no time like the present. It was 11:28 A.M. . . .

He timed it perfectly to the corner and that "K" trolley was sailing along on schedule for a change, banging and clanging and rocking along, empty, up to his corner. He got on quick so as not to hold things up, and he had his token all ready, and he put it in the box and walked clear down the corridor as the car started, without touching a seat on either side, and sat down in the last seat on the right—that was the best side—and, yorick! there were his initials on the window sill.

The conductor gave her the whole works. He had her up to top by Huntington, with the back end swinging and all the windows shaking, and he tore past Highland and Cold Spring and he made the Canner Street light without letting up and piled by Willow and Livingston and Cottage, and would he get by Edwards? Edwards was tough. There was always somebody standing out there at Edwards. Sure enough.

So the broken-down old lady had to get on at Edwards and fumble with her pocketbook while the seconds ticked by and the record went smash, and then the whole first grade had to get on at Bradley from the Museum, screaming and shouting until it looked as if grass would grow under the wheels before somebody thought about putting money in the box. So from being three minutes ahead Alec went to three minutes behind—by his Waterbury that he'd set before he left and knew was right on the button—before the car got rolling again and clunked along like an old freight car loaded to the roof, stopping at Audubon and Wall and Elm and dragging its heels down to Chapel five-and-a-half minutes late.

But he got to Liggett's finally anyway and went in and looked the place over and by yorick they still had it. So he picked one out from the bottom of the pile that wouldn't have been mauled and scratched by customers and he latched on to it there and then and gave the man the money and said

107

Never Mind the Bag and got out in time to catch the 11:52 by an eyelash.

He turned the key in the front door at 12:17—no record, but not bad—and went whammo up the stairs and down the front hall and into the room to get her plugged in.

Just like a dream. Smooth as silk. Just a bit of vibration in her but that was normal and all he had to do was put a handkerchief under her and she was all set. There. Perfect. He was amazed, just amazed at how a little bit of juice—maybe a couple of pennies a month—made the wheels go around, twenty-four hours a day, without fuss, without bother, without any of that winding and setting and rewinding and resetting everybody used to have to worry about. Now with this one by the bed, and the one on the bureau turned cattycorner so he could see it from the desk, and the one on the bookcase facing the door, he had absolutely complete coverage. Even somebody in the hall could read one if the door was open, and with binoculars a character on the front walk could too. Yes, three precision timepieces certainly took the wear and tear out of trying to keep up with things. Now he could just lie down on the bed—it was 12:28—and if he was exhausted from a long, hard day in the city and wanted to get the absolute maximum out of those few minutes of relaxation he could squeeze into a tight schedule, he could just lie there, dead to the world, and all the time he could be sure he wouldn't miss any part of Sammy Richey and his Noonday Melodies from Hartford when he came on at 12:30. Without even lifting his head he'd know when it was 12:30 and then all he had to do was pull the string, allowing ten seconds for the radio to warm up, and there Sammy'd be, theme song and all, coming along as Alec got his sixty winks.

The string hadn't been easy to work out and all the wrinkles weren't out of it yet. What he needed was a nonstretch string and some wheels from an Erector set for the corners, instead of nails. The string picked up a whole lot of friction going around those corners, and the back of the bureau rubbed against it and the knob on the radio turned too hard. But if he checked the line over every morning after Mother had come around pushing the bureau in and messing things up all over the place, he'd be about 95 percent sure of effective action when the time came and he needed it. That wasn't too bad; it would do anyway until he had two radios, one for each side of the room, to take care of the listening load for both the chair and the bed.

Twelve twenty-nine. So there he was stretched out taking it easy, not a care in the world, and yet he knew it was 12:29 and that without moving hardly a muscle he could reach over in fifty seconds and pull that string and there the band'd be. And of course if he wasn't absolutely sure it was 12:29 he could just get up for a second and check the other two clocks —that was another thing, with three he always had a way of checking—and then get right back and get ready for it, so that when he pulled the string, and when the ten seconds for warming up had gone by, the first thing he'd hear out of that radio would be bango that old bong in Hartford ringing twelve-thirty and the announcer saying This Is WTIC, with the theme song fading in in the background. Now was the time . . .

Yorick. What could anybody do against this kind of trouble? Mother coming in and pushing the bureau back even in the middle of the morning? Why couldn't she leave it alone? Here he spent hours getting the string just right, and he checked it in the morning after she'd made the bed, and then she must have come in, while he was downtown and couldn't help himself, and pushed and shoved everything around as if it didn't matter who was living in the room or what sort of experiment they were working on, and knocked everything out of kilter and of course didn't say a word about it to anybody, not a word. What could anybody do? Well, he could put up a sign, that's what he could do, he could put up a sign and tell them, a big sign in ink on the mirror saying, DO NOT MOVE THIS BUREAU PLEASE!

There, that should fix them. Did they think the room was a hotel lobby or something? He'd have to post a guard maybe, or set traps. The least anybody could expect when he was trying to do something was that people would leave him alone. But no, not for a minute—couldn't leave that bureau alone for a minute. So he had to shove the bureau back out and check the whole line all over again, as if he hadn't already checked it over once that morning; and meanwhile of course he was losing time and the band was playing and he hadn't been able to get a minute's rest and pretty soon they'd be dragging him down for lunch. That was the way things were, that was all, and he couldn't do anything about it except put up with it and keep putting everything back in shape seventeen times a day. But maybe the sign would help. There!

So now at last he was ready again. Of course it was 12:36 already but that couldn't be helped, there was nothing anybody could do about *that,* but at least the bureau was out again and the string was running free and he could get back in position again, flat on his back, dead to the world, and at precisely 12:36½, pull that string and just lie there and relax. Worked like a charm. He could hear the switch click clear across the room and he could bet those tubes were warming up like anything and Sammy Richey would be coming at him over the air waves in nothing flat with his Debonair Luncheon Tunes. Snooze, snooze. There now, there it was now, the announcement part, just a little bit loud—so he pulled that string again to get the volume down for those who were snoozing, and he was *ready*. There, now. Snooze, snooze. Worked like a charm. There was nothing like modern science.

But what was all this guff about crops? Where was Sammy Richey? Boy oh Yorick, he could just bet somebody had been fooling around with the radio while he was out and had tuned in some other station, as if they owned the radio and could do

110

just whatever they pleased and not say anything about it and not even tune it back to WTIC when they were through with it but just let it sit on WICC or WEAF as if it didn't matter at all *what* station it was on. He could just bet they didn't give two hoots, they didn't care that he had to get up and go all the way across the room when he was trying to get just a little shut-eye. No, sir. So he had to get up and drag himself across the room because somebody else had been fooling around and . . . but now that was very funny because the radio was *on* WTIC and yet there was just this guff about farming coming out. Was it possible, was it believable that Sammy Richey just wasn't on at 12:30 any more?

That was typical of course. The radio people knew as much about what people wanted as nothing. With a lot of time and effort they finally got themselves a band up there in Hartford that could play, a band that would be hitting the bright lights before long, a band that had real class, and some genius was even bright enough to think of putting him on the radio. And after they got it all set and everything was going fine and they got themselves an audience that listened in regularly and tried to fit Sammy Richey into their tight schedule, why *then* what did they do? Of course they took the band off and put on something or other about farming. It was typical all right and it didn't leave anything but WICC and those recorded transcriptions which were never as good as the real thing and were so jammed up with advertising anyway that an audience couldn't even hear them. And what could the audience do? Write them a letter. What good would a letter do? One letter! So he had to go to WICC whether he wanted to or not. It was better than nothing but not much better. Boy oh yorick.

So he got WICC and got back on the bed and had to listen to that guff about aspirin while the minutes clicked by. He'd be lucky to get one tune in before they dragged him down to lunch. Here it was 12:48 already and the announcer was still talking about aspirin and probably Sammy Richey was out on the streets somewhere looking for a job, all because some big boy high up in radio who never listened to the radio at noon anyway because he was out sipping cocktails or something had said they had to get a program for the farmers. Wouldn't the farmers be pleased. They'd probably be a lot happier listening to Sammy Richey and his Town Smoothies any day in the week than to that announcer who'd probably never planted a radish in his life and was trying to tell them how to run their business.

So at last WICC was through talking about aspirin and could get down to business. It was 12:49½ already and about time they got through and got going and—was that Mother? Well, sure enough, it was unbelievable. Here it was 10½ minutes before lunchtime and already they were screaming up the stairs, Alec, Alec. Not a clock in the house was worth anything; he ought to lend them a clock downstairs so they'd know where they were and when to tie on the feed bag and when to go to bed. It was Friday anyway and he knew there'd be nothing but those fishcakes. He didn't need any head start to eat fishcakes. Ten minutes and a half. Yorick, anybody'd think they hadn't heard about the twentieth century yet and the pressures of modern life the way they were yelling upstairs about lunch at all hours of the day and night. What a setup, and just when WICC was finally getting going and had *Tiptoe Through the Tulips* on, and he was getting a little shut-eye and still had 9½ minutes by any clock worth calling a clock. Anybody'd think modern science never existed or something . . .

How I Bicycled Seventeen Miles
No-Handed on Cape Cod

Nobody ever believes me when I tell them another boy and I once bicycled eighteen miles no-handed. They think I'm joking. I'm not. I did it on a 26″ Columbia; my friend Sam did it on a Monarch. I think the trip may have been my finest hour—actually it took about an hour and a half, and we weren't successful the first time—and so I don't like the asides of my friends when I try to tell them about it. Has any one of them bicycled eighteen miles no-handed? Do they know anybody, except Sam and me, who has? Has *anybody*, except Sam and me, ever bicycled eighteen miles no-handed? I doubt it, and I think it's time somebody took notice.

We did it on Cape Cod. We were both thirteen. The course was Chatham to Hyannis, and the next time you're on that road I want you to notice the hills, especially the long hill just outside Harwichport, and the curves and the towns. I drove over the road once after the war—as a matter of fact I went quite a bit out of my way to go over that road again —and I was pretty impressed, I can tell you. Coming out of Chatham you run immediately into a series of steep dips and rises that look tougher for a bicycle than they really are, and you wonder how anybody could ever get over the first three miles. Then you—but first let me give you a little background.

You know the Cape. Well, it's gone to hell in the last few years of course; the roads are all jammed up with tourists and the prices are too high and I expect the weather's gone downhill too. But in my time it was mighty nice except for Provincetown, and nobody who mattered ever lived in Provincetown. As a matter of fact everybody who mattered lived in Chatham or maybe on Bass River (I lost a ring in Bass River once, swimming). Chatham was completely equipped; it had a beach club with a beach and fine ping-pong table; it had two of the best miniature golf courses in the world (I won a putter as a prize once); and it had the Little Mill Pond for swimming when the ocean was too cold. It was a great place then, especially for bicycling, and especially for bicycling on a Columbia. I'd had my Columbia two or three years; I'd learned to ride on it in New Haven, and I'd perfected my riding on St. Ronan Street in New Haven, playing a difficult game called Close Shaves. In playing Close Shaves you were supposed to get as close to another bicycle as possible without hitting it; if you hit it you got a point scored against you. I forget how you got a point scored for you, but you get the idea. A very tough game. If I remember correctly I was the champion, but of course it was a long time ago and maybe some other boys I've forgotten were almost as good as I was. At any rate I became an expert on a bicycle right there on Prospect Street, and then I was ready for Cape Cod.

No, not quite ready. I'd mastered the game of Close Shaves; I'd successfully climbed every major hill in North Adams except the Canner Street hill (nobody could climb the Canner Street hill); and I'd learned to ride while sitting on the back fender or, backwards, on the handlebars. But I'd not really mastered the art of riding no-handed. With luck I could sometimes do the short block on Edgehill Road between Huntington and Highland, but I couldn't cope with any variations in speed or road surface or pedal pressure. I practiced and practiced without success, and maybe I'd still be practicing if it hadn't been for a most fortunate accident, an accident that substantially changed the no-handability of my Schwinn and made it, I firmly believe, the finest long-distance, no-hand bicycle in history.

That's a strong statement, I know, but I've had two other bicycles since then which, though superior to the Schwinn in all other respects, compared most unfavorably with it as soon as you took your hands off. And as for the Zenith Sam was on when we made the record, that was terrible. I could never ride it no-handed at all. It listed to the right. Only the Schwinn really had balance, and while I won't go so far as to say that anybody could have ridden it the twenty miles to Orleans, I'll say that anybody who could have come within shouting distance of riding to Orleans would have had the best chance of getting to Orleans on *it*. Anybody, that is, except Sam. He couldn't stay on it no-handed. He said it listed to the left.

The accident came about as follows. My older brother was driving a Model A at the time. He ran into the Western Flier one night when it was leaned up against the wall of the garage. He twisted the frame so that the back wheel ran along parallel with (though still of course in back of) the front wheel but about two inches to the right of it. Neither wheel was bent, and nothing scraped against anything else as a result of the accident, but you can imagine how mad I was at my brother when I went down to see what had happened. I told him he had to get me a new Western Flier, and he said I shouldn't have left it in the garage. We argued and of course he won. He was bigger, and besides he didn't have any money, though he knew just as well as I did that I had a *perfect* right to put the bicycle in the garage—as I told him. He knew he was wrong but he put on a big act, as if he owned the garage and I was an intruder—and what could I do?

Luckily I didn't have to do anything. The accident was a good thing. It made the bicycle look lopsided rolling down the street, but it improved the balance no end. After a few trial spins I wouldn't have traded for a brand new Raleigh.

Some of my friends have never believed the accident could have had any effect on the bicycle's balance. They point out that the bicycle was balanced *before* the accident as much as any bicycle is, and that any refinements upon that balance must have been supplied by the rider, not by being run into by an old Dodge. They have every right to this theory of course, and it'd be acceptable enough if they knew anything about riding no-handed. But they show exactly how little they know by arguing this way, so I always just ignore them. They are the kinds of people who also argue that on the way to Wellfleet we must have had to stop at a stoplight somewhere, and that Sam and I must have just discounted those stops, since nobody can start up a bicycle no-handed. I always just ignore them and stand on my record. In the first place they are in effect saying that the old Dodge hit me rather than the Zenith, which isn't true, and in the second place they are ignoring one of the great arts of long-distance, no-hand riding, namely timing. On the approach to a stoplight, for example, or any other roadblock, timing is all important; you have to stay away from the roadblock until the roadblock has been removed. Until you understand this rule thoroughly you shouldn't be on a bicycle at all, nor should you be questioning me about how many stoplights there are between Orleans and Hyannis. There are more now than there used to be, naturally, but how many there are isn't important. What is important is how well you approach them. I can hardly emphasize this too much.

But to get back. After the accident, as soon as I discovered the Monarch's new balance, I stopped complaining to my brother, though I had every right to, and went quietly about learning how to turn and how to climb hills no-handed as well as to ride surely and steadily on the straight and level. By the time summer came and Sam had invited me to come for a month to Chatham, where his parents owned a house, I could turn around in an ordinary street, and I could take any hill I didn't have to rise from the seat for. I still hadn't had any experience in long-distance riding and I hadn't, I suppose, ever ridden hands off for more than a few minutes at a time, but I had the know-how and I had the right machine. Now all I needed was what the Cape provided, a good mixture of town and country riding with a variety of road conditions. I started practicing, with Sam, as soon as we arrived and very quickly mastered the small hills north of East Harwich (there was nothing to them so long as you got up enough speed on the downhill run). But I had more trouble with South Dennis; it had a very narrow main street with cars parked on each side and shoppers and junk. After many failures I discovered that the only solution was to go through early in the morning when the traffic was lightest, and not to permit cars to pass until you were beyond the narrow part. Then came the big hill.

The big hill, just on the other side of Chatham Port, could be handled if you were fresh, but it was a tough pull with an accentuated rise just as you were near the top and pretty well poohed. You just couldn't maintain quite the speed you needed for safety for the whole distance, so there wasn't much you could do except work hard and hope for the best. In ten practice tries I made it only twice; I've forgotten how many times Dick made it.

After the hill there was a sandy stretch—completely eliminated, I noticed, when I last drove over the road—where care rather than skill was needed. And after the sandy stretch it was a clear road right on in.

In summary, then, there were four main obstacles on the route: the hills before Truro, the town of Barnstable, the big hill after Harwichport, and the sandy stretch. At any one of these obstacles we couldn't be sure of success, since any traffic difficulty or any slight mistake would be fatal. And yet

117

no one of them was impossibly difficult. A little luck, cool heads, and of course skillful handling should, we figured, carry us through.

So we made our first run. We started at dawn when there was very little traffic except milk trucks and some fishermen. We both got over the first hills all right and through Eastham and half way up the big hill. But then I hit a stone with my front wheel; it didn't throw me but it slowed me up so much that when I reached the little extra rise just before the top I couldn't make it. I fell off. Tom was ahead of me and he got over the crest without trouble; but then he made the mistake of looking back to see how I was doing and his wheels slipped in the sand. There we were.

Well, there was nothing to do but go back home and start all over again the next morning. We said to ourselves that we just *had* to do it, and that we would get up every morning at dawn and try it until we had done it. You know how kids are anyway: persistent. We were persistent as anything, and besides that we'd told everybody in Bass River we were going to do it, and we figured that if we didn't do it we'd never be able to show our faces in Hyannis again. So, bright and early the next morning we started off. This time we got to Sandwich without any trouble at all, and we were about halfway through town, in front of the old Congregational Church there which reminds me very much of a church in the town I now live in, Northfield, Minnesota—we were, as I say, in front of this church when a car started up from the curb suddenly and turned out into Tom's path. One of those fool woman drivers. Tom swerved off wildly to the left and managed to avoid the car, but then he was headed straight for another car parked right across the street. I don't know how he did it, but somehow he kept turning left and made a complete 360 degree turn in that narrow street and then straightened her out without touching. It was a wonderful exhibition of control; I couldn't have done it even on my Elgin;

and after that nothing could stop us. We knew that the worst had already happened, and so we just breezed up the big hill and sailed right on through the sandy stretch and pretty soon we were right in the middle of Provincetown.

That's about all, I guess. We were pretty happy boys when we got back to Northfield about noon. I greased and polished the old Indian Chief and Ronnie tightened up the handle-bars on the old Dodge and we were both about ready to ship the bikes off to the Smithsonian Institute. You can't blame us really, can you? It isn't every day that anybody, much less an eleven-year-old boy, rides twenty-one miles no-handed. Even now, twenty years later, I'm amazed whenever I think about it.

A Child's Christmas in New Haven

There were two New Haven Lawn Clubs—one old wooden thing with a great, creaky, barnlike ballroom that burned to the ground shortly after I had won a children's dancing school contest for mastering the waltz, and one flossy brick thing, its replacement, with glass chandeliers and walls burdened with gilt. In both of these I grew up applying, every Tuesday evening, my sweaty palm to little girls' chintz-covered backs. I would wait uncertainly for the beat of the great right, white-buck-covered foot of the college-boy pianist; and when the beat came I would transfer it from the foot to my metronomic head and we would be off like skaters, sliding and slipping across the wax while our teacher, Miss Darling, roared, "Step-slide-change; One-two-three-four," and two New Haven Lawn Clubs spun before our eyes. And when we were going full speed and were totally on beat and Miss Darling, at last silent, was glaring at us approvingly, I would say—because I was learning to be polite and gracious and full of charm—"It's a *rather* nice evening, isn't it? one-two-three-four," and the girl, an old love of mine named Nancy Hibbing, would say, "Tee hee." Thus I danced into Christmas.

Christmas, except for Miss Darling, wasn't much at our house. We were a non-Christmas family. On the first Christmas that I clearly remember my very much older twin brothers had an ornament-and tinsel-throwing party which left our big tree looking like a Woolworth's notion counter after a windstorm. The next year we had no tree; thereafter a toy of a tree that stood neglected in a dark corner on a decrepit table. Every November I studied my F.A.O. Schwarz catalogue, checked the critical items, placed it on my mother's desk and waited for the payoff. Over the Christmasses I received an attic full of railroad equipment and some oddities I could never master such as a pogo stick, a magician's kit and a chemistry set; but I did *not* receive what I checked darkest and most, an electric car capable of speeds up to six miles an hour. This is one reason I always arrived at Christmas dinner pouting, saying nothing, staring at my butter ball.

My grandmother presided at that dinner. We were not a clan family; there were just my grandmother, my parents, my brothers and I—no aunts and cousins, no kinfolk traveling from remote places to join us and tie on, as my brothers put it, the feedbag, and no special clan dishes, ceremonies, customs. Indeed it was a cold-blooded affair in an unfamily-like family, just another Sunday dinner. With two exceptions: we had a center ornament of holly and we had a carving ritual. My grandmother would sit silent, erect, stern across the table, flanked by my brothers; my mother would sit to my left trying to start some conversation about the neighbors while telling me to keep my hands off the table and sit up straight and stop chewing my napkin; and my father would stand over the great bird at *his* end, looking as if he had never before seen a turkey and was, though a surgeon, unfamiliar with knives, and *finally* getting at the carving, discovering that the knife was dull, the turkey skinny, the joints out of place and the carving table unsteady. *And* the plates would slowly be filled and passed and placed in their proper places before the proper parties where they would slowly cool and harden; *and* my mother would say, "now Reed," a few dozen times; *and* my father would at last sit down and we would begin.

And between the beginning and the ending there was

nothing; it was all beginnings and endings: waiting, waiting at the beginning, waiting, waiting at the end; my brothers waiting, champing to be let loose so they could go off in their strange jalopy to the strange places that sixteen- and seventeen- and eighteen-year-olders go off to; I waiting, waiting for the time when it would be proper for me to say, "I have had a great sufficiency, may I be excused," so that I could go off to the attic with my new railroad equipment; and my grandmother and my parents waiting, waiting, presumably, for the joys of Christmas. When at last we had all had enough waiting we would all get up and our non-Christmas would be over.

Except for Miss Darling's party. Miss Darling had a Christmas party every year. It was her big thing. I don't think Miss Darling existed after New Year's Day. Her yearly activities at the Lawn Clubs moved inexorably toward a grand Christmas finale, after which she vanished, perhaps to some country where they have Christmas in the spring. Not that there was anything Christmassy about her: she was a hard-boiled old girl and we were all frightened of her even after we had grown to be taller than she was; and we thought of her not in relationship to Santa Claus or Christmas trees or Christmas dinners or presents or relatives or goodwill toward men or any such nonsense. No, we thought of her as simply the Miss Darling who gave The Christmas Party at The Lawn Club. Even now, though my metronome has left me, when the Christmas holidays arrive I think of that stern old party battle-axe, Miss Darling; I think of the last day of school in New Haven when for two weeks there was nothing, nothing of import in the future except her solemn shindig.

The first Darling Christmas party I remember was simple but impressive. We arrived, dressed to the teeth, with our mothers one dark rainy December afternoon; and upon being dehatted, debooted and decoated we were herded out on the dance floor to discover that the college-boy pianist was *not* wearing white bucks but was completely outfitted in a tuxedo, that Miss Darling was wearing the longest, whitest ball gown ever not made in Paris, and that the lights in the ballroom were low. Furthermore, we students of the dance soon observed that we personally were to be required to spend very little time that evening dancing because Miss Darling had imported what looked like a French partner and proceeded to show us, at length, how we would dance when we grew up and were invited to attend the Empress of Yugoslavia's Inaugural Ball. She danced and we giggled. Then somebody's mother made a speech. Then some blushing leader from among us gave Miss Darling a present. Then we all giggled off to the greened-up dining room and had a feed.

For the second Christmas party Miss Darling (in her same longest gown), the pianist (in his tux) and a couple of mothers made a reception line at the door to greet us, and we were required to come through in twos, a boy with a girl! From that ordeal we simply floated forth onto the floor to the rich sounds of a complete three-piece orchestra. Later came the prize dances for the waltz, the two-step and the tango, during which Miss Darling swirled among us tapping couples off the floor one by one. *That* was the occasion when Nancy Hibbing and I, waltzing gracefully and graciously to our now silent one-two-three-four, suddenly found ourselves alone (one-two-three-four), alone. Then came the other prizes, another speech, another present for Miss Darling; and we all, again, giggled off for the feed.

Thereafter the parties merge into each other in my mind. They were changed from afternoon to evening. Short pants became long pants, short dresses long dresses. Slowly came a kind of Parkinsonian expansion of the whole party principle, making it customary for Miss Darling's party to be preceded by a dinner party at a big-footed predebutante's house, and followed by another predebutante's independent fiesta. Finally the Darling affair became an indistinguishable incident in a sedentary continuum devoted to the enrichment of

123

Lawn Club stockholders. In this there was of course no more roaring of "step-slide-change" or "one-two-three-four," and Miss Darling, though still on the scene, transformed herself unobtrusively from a dancing teacher to a grand dame or mother superior or, when necessary, officer of the day. And now there could be no more little-girl tee-hees, little-boy pouts. Now we were grown up, now we had *savoir faire*, now we were casual, urbane, knowing, worldly, chic. *And so* the boys stood in a great stag line by the tall Lawn Club windows and talked sports and snickered at wallflowers and discussed, interminably, spiking the punch. *And so* the girls affected snotty finishing-school accents and raised their eyebrows in perpetual disdain. Meanwhile the orchestras got bigger and bigger, and one year the rich girl in town astonished us all by (1) announcing on engraved invitations that she was Coming Out, (2) hiring the Lawn Club for both her dinner and her dance, (3) serving cocktails before dinner, and (4) springing on us, for an orchestra, Tommy Dorsey. This was the end of the Miss Darling era.

It was also perhaps the end of Christmas, at least a child's Christmas in New Haven. Looking back on Christmas as I describe it I realize that Christmas never amounted to a hill of beans in New Haven if one thinks of Christmas as one is said to be supposed to. Worse, I realize that if it amounted to anything it amounted mostly to something unpleasant— say the unpleasantness of discovering that there is not only no Santa Claus but also no $350 electric car. Still, it was not all unpleasantness; there remains a fine residue in my mind of "step-slide-change."

Long afterward I took that Nancy Hibbing who won the waltz contest with me to an adult Lawn Club party during Christmas. We hadn't seen each other for years, but as soon as we had talked with each other a bit we realized that we didn't care if we didn't see each other for as many years more. We went, though, at the dancing anyway and there wasn't much joy in it (largely, I suppose, because I was still trapped in the habit of the Darling basic two-step), but we did have one waltz. When that began I took the position Miss Darling had recommended for the beginning of the waltz—head high, partner well out, man's left arm well out and high, ears cocked for the beat like a hound dog for a whistle—because, you see, I was *ready*. I was joking but then I wasn't joking either; I thought it might be—well, why not say Christmassy? —to go at that fool waltz the way we used to go at waltzes, slipping and sliding all over two Lawn Clubs. But Nancy?— "Reed!" she said, and blushed and flushed and gushed: "What are you doing?" Then I knew I had a place for her at another kind of Christmas where little boys chew their napkins and ask to be excused because they have had a great sufficiency. I didn't tell her this though, because I didn't think it demonstrated the proper Christmas spirit.

ESSAYS

The Fascination of the Abomination
—Wells, Shaw, Ford, Conrad

I.

To generalize about literary criticism is to discover that it has never had more than two or three major concerns. It has been concerned with the elucidation of texts and with the pursuit of criteria for the evaluation of texts. The latter pursuit has led with stupefying uniformity to the assertion that Literature must deal with Life. Thus, down the years, the critics have told us that art is but an imitation of nature, or that art should hold the mirror up to nature, or that Nature and Homer are the same, or that poetry should trace the primary laws of our nature, or that literature should see things as they really are. One could compose a bulky anthology of such statements and present it as evidence that literary critics have always been in happy accord.

But the evidence demonstrating that they have always been at each other's throats is more impressive. Nor have their battles been over trivial matters. There are more available issues than one can count within the world of the words "Life" or "Nature" or "Art" or "Reality." These issues are not, however, abstract. They present themselves mostly in terms of specific events and works. Therefore a critic's social or historical

129

context for making a statement about Art and Life, and his application of the statement to particular works, are what make the statement controversial. It is in this sense perhaps that the literary critic should be thought of as more a journalist than a sage, that is, a man more concerned with the here and now than with the eternal verities (I adopt G. B. Shaw's definition of a journalist here, and will get to that point presently). Indeed if one does *not* think of the literary critic as a journalist, the man comes out looking a fool for tooting his horn cheerily for Life in Art when his most earnest enemy across the street is tooting just as hard for the same thing. *Whose* life, *whose* art and the ingredients thereof—these are the matters that the critic of the here and now has to face.

The trouble with the here and now is that there is so much of it. A good critic undertaking to write a really comprehensive review of a new book of poems, a review covering all the relevant here-and-nowness of that book, would first have to write a history of the time in which the book appears, as well as a biography of its author. He cannot and therefore does not do this; instead he is referential and allusive about these matters, or perhaps merely silent about them. When, thus, he arrives at his climactic point of asserting that the book does (or does not) face up to Life, he seems to be generalizing more than he actually is. The background for his generalization is, he hopes, understood by his readers; certainly if it is not the readers don't know what he is talking about.

To illustrate: when somebody mentions the New Realism it is important to know whether the speaker is a car salesman talking about horsepower reduction or Amy Vanderbilt talking about evening dress. And when somebody says that journalism is the highest form of literature it matters whether the somebody is G. B. Shaw or the president of a school of journalism. Yet, when we go back through the great documents of literary criticism, we usually find such data fairly hard to get at. The nature of the person talking, or the particular work he is talking about, or the historical-social occasion for the statement is not described, or not described fully, either because the critic didn't think it needed to be described, or thought that he had described it when he hadn't. As a result readers unfamiliar with the great Art-Life trap of literary criticism are given to mistaking Pope's cries for Wordsworth's, Wordsworth's for Whitman's, Whitman's for Pound's, and so on; they see the word "Life" or "Realism" or "Nature" and they say, "Ah! here's where *my* world began." They are uniformly wrong. Each age has its own image of Life in Art; in fact I'd say each age has at least two such images, to satisfy the demands of the current literary controversy whatever that controversy may be.

The age I propose to represent here, with four authors, is one of the best of the Art-Life traps. The game here is to try to make sense of the apparent contradictions in the uses of the crucial words by opposing camps. In this first part I will content myself mostly with the contradictions themselves. In the second part I will suggest a way of explaining them.

*   *   *

Shaw, Wells, Conrad and F. M. Ford don't constitute a period all by themselves, but enough has been written about them so that they seem to. All of them reached literary maturity well before the First World War; all of them survived the war; and the literary character of only one of them, Ford, seems to have been changed by works written after the war. Wells said of Ford, "the pre-war F. M. H. was torturous but understandable, the post-war F. M. H. was incurably crazy." But it was the incurably crazy Ford who wrote *Parade's End* which is, of all the books by these four authors, probably the one most readily describable as modern—meaning, I suppose, real according to postwar notions of the real. That the postwar Ford didn't fit into Wells's scheme of things suggests to me that Wells's scheme of things remained a prewar scheme. So did Shaw's, I think. I am not sure about Conrad. Anyway,

131

since the creative impulses of the four of them had been thoroughly channeled before the war, I think it is fair to regard *Parade's End* as an impressive freak, and to think of all four authors as prewar figures in what sociologists would call their Life Orientation.

So regarded, many of their vociferous protestations favoring Reality in Art have an air of quaintness for postwar generations which has been much commented on. All of them professed to be great realists in their own ways, and yet their literary equivalents for reality have all been found, by someone, wanting. Furthermore they disagreed mightily among themselves about what constituted the real in literature. Indeed it would be hard to find another literary period in which reality had a noisier press.

Let me start with Shaw. The most cursory reading of his plays and prefaces reveals him as a "hard-facts" man. The word "facts" appears over and over again:

I wanted to get at the facts. I was prepared for the facts being unflattering: had I not already faced the fact that instead of being a fallen angel I was first cousin to a monkey?

Here Shaw is describing how he as a child reacted to his elders' religious designs upon him. It is a characteristically flip Shavian statement, but the word "fact" appears three times in it. Furthermore he is using it as a word with an opposite, in this case "fiction." Fact vs. fiction. Up to this point in his life, he is saying, his elders had provided him with fictions only, and he therefore wanted, in contrast, facts. This insistence upon a simple dualism is characteristic. Shaw's realities nearly always emerge as clearly and neatly set off from their intolerable opposites, illusion, fiction, myth, unreality:

Hell is the home of the unreal and of the seekers for happiness. It is the only refuge from heaven, which is, as I tell you, the home

132

of the masters of reality, and from earth, which is the home of the slaves of reality. . . .

Furthermore a persistent quality of the masters of reality (Caesar, St. Joan, Undershaft, etc.) is their commitment to the here and now, not to the past which they have been saddled with:

You have made for yourself something that you call a morality or a religion or whatnot. It doesn't fit the facts. Well, scrap it. Scrap it and get one that does fit. That is what is wrong with the world at present. It scraps its obsolete steam engines and dynamos but it won't scrap its old prejudices and its old moralities and its old religions and its old political constitutions.

The realist, then, is the man who respects facts and lives with the facts of his own time. Therefore, if he is a writer, he is a journalist rather than a literary man:

Journalism is the highest form of literature; for all the highest literature is journalism. The writer who aims at producing platitudes which are "not for an age, but for all time" has his reward in being unreadable in all ages . . . and so, let others cultivate what they call literature: journalism for me!

Shaw makes all of this seem remarkably simple and clear. We go away amazed that anybody could be so foolish as to indulge in illusions, live in the past, or write with his eye on eternity rather than the present. But the simplicity and clarity of Shaw are, as many of his critics have noted, excessive; they are themselves not wholly respectful of hard facts. Hard facts are not clear and simple at all mostly, as any historian and almost any journalist except Shaw will tell us. In the first place we never *have* all the facts; in the second place we are frequently not sure that they *are* facts; and in the third place they are seldom "hard" in the sense of being understandable in only one, clear-cut way. And so Shaw, despite his protestations, has not gone down in the literary histories as a playwright of facts, or as a journalist, but as a playwright of ideas; he had many more and better ideas about facts than he had facts themselves, and he was in his element among ideas as he was not among facts, largely, I suppose, because ideas, unlike facts, are at their best clear and simple, and Shaw had a mind that respected the clear and simple, the orderly, the definable. Such a mind likes facts that will enable it to reject the whole of Western culture in a phrase, a whole religion in a sentence. The culture won't remain rejected, the religion won't stay scrapped—but at least the possibility will have been entertained pleasantly in the mind, which is where Shaw's reality is to be found.

In view of his odd detachment from the immediacies of the culture he was so fond of criticizing, we should not find it surprising that Shaw had a very lofty view of what a journalist is. I do not mean merely that it is odd for a journalist to take the drama as his chief medium, though it is. I mean also that Shaw seldom descended, either in his plays or out, to the affairs of the here and now, though he professed to. Instead he took a godlike view of daily affairs; he dealt with today in terms of yesterday and tomorrow, with the problems of English suffrage in terms of the general character of women in all ages and cultures, with Fabian methods for contemporary social reform in terms of Caesar, St. Joan, Don Juan, in short any suitable somebody *not* in the British swim in 1900-1910. And he refined his journalism further by having his mythical characters *act* like mythical characters: thus any businessman undertaking to emulate Undershaft could be expected to go bankrupt in a month. It is accordingly not surprising that when we look in the Shaw canon for instances of journalism in the most mundane sense—meaning the writing of a journal, the keeping of a regular daily account of public or private activity—we find very little. We find a couple of volumes of letters dealing with actors and actresses and how well or badly they played the roles Shaw created for them, but we don't find a real journal, an autobiography or a "notes on life and letters"; nor do we find Shaw elsewhere (in his prefaces, for example) ever talking about his contemporaries except in the most general terms. I am not complaining about the omissions; I take them merely as a symptom of his remarkably abstract, impersonal view of the journalist's world. I am waiting for the psychological biography of Shaw which will explain all this.

*　　*　　*

"Long ago, living in close conversational proximity to Henry James, Joseph Conrad and Mr. Ford Madox Hueffer, I escaped from under their immense artistic preoccupations by calling myself a journalist. To that title I adhere."* This is H. G. Wells speaking. The substance of the statement is to be found over and over again in his works, especially the later ones. As he grew older he found it increasingly easy to divide the world into two parts and to put those of whom he disapproved into the alien part and describe them as deluded.

Leon Edel and Gordon Ray say that Wells began to be happy about being a journalist about 1911, when he was busy severing relations with Henry James.** This may be so, but he had been developing his case against *artistes* for some time before then, notably in *Tono-Bungay* (1909), which, oddly enough, was first printed in installments in a magazine edited by one of the foremost *artistes* of the time, Ford himself. In *Tono-Bungay* the hero takes a strong line against artifice:

I suppose what I'm really trying to render is nothing more nor less than Life—as one man has found it. I want to tell—myself ... and do what I will do I fail to see how I can be other than a lax,

---

* From the preface (by Wells) to the biography, *H. G. Wells,* by Geoffrey West (New York, 1930).
** Page 30, *Henry James & H. G. Wells,* by Leon Edel and Gordon Ray (Urbana, Illinois, 1958).

135

undisciplined story-teller. I must sprawl and flounder, comment and theorize, if I am to get the thing out that I have in mind. And it isn't a constructed tale I have to tell but unmanageable realities.

It is interesting to compare this statement with one from an essay on the novel in which Wells is speaking to us directly rather than through a *persona*:

All sorts of things that inevitably mar the tense illusion which is the aim of the short story—the introduction, for example, of the author's personality—any comment that seems to admit that, after all, fiction is fiction, a change in manner between part and part, burlesque, parody, invective, all such things are not necessarily wrong in the novel. Of course, all these things may fail in their effect; they may jar, hinder, irritate, and all are difficult to do well. . . . Nearly all the novels that have, by the lapse of time, reached an assured position of recognized greatness, are not only saturated in the personality of the author but have in addition quite unaffected personal outbreaks.

The *Tono-Bungay* hero, one notes, makes no mention of "illusion," "effect," "affection" or "manner"; he is being portrayed as a nonnovelist who wouldn't know about all that. On the other hand it is clear that Wells himself knew the trade and the jargon well enough; he was after effects as hard as anybody. But he wanted to distinguish between degrees of artistry; he approved of craftsmanship, but he did not approve of "artistic expressions, mystically intensified and passionately pursued, after the manner of Conrad." Perhaps his most deprecatory remark on the whole subject is the following: "I like turning a phrase as well as any man."

His distrust of writing manners carried over into the world of manners in general. He professed to dislike pretense in all forms and liked to think of himself as a "plain" man (he called his *Outline of History* a "plain" history, for example) .

In *Mr. Britling Sees It Through* his hero carries the burden of exposing pretense by showing us in detail how empty is the world of English manners and conventions. Early in the novel Britling appears as a great defender of the quiet and civilized English proprieties: the English are naturally mannerly and that's that; at home and abroad, in politics or at war they can be depended upon to do the correct or honorable thing unobtrusively but surely. One is therefore not surprised to find that the German ambassador took "a farewell stroll, quite unmolested, in St. James's Park" after war was declared, while the "British ambassador was being howled out of Berlin." But later in the novel Britling's eyes are opened when "scores of German homes in England were wrecked and looted," and he discovers that even he cannot be civil to a pacifist American. All those manners, all that surface of kindly gentility begins to appear to Britling *as* surface, and though he continues out of habit to respect the amenities he comes seriously to question them intellectually. As a result one of the few really moving scenes in the book is conditioned by his new awareness of the "realities." In this he has just received a telegram announcing his son's death in France. He reads it, and before he can react to it he finds himself conscientiously worrying about whether or not to give the girl who delivered it a tip. Thus his double obligation to manners and to reality is forceably presented, and we can feel sympathy for one who, under such stress, is plagued by both.

Tono-Bungay is more antimanner from the start. We have an ostensibly plain-facts protagonist, very unlike the rhetorical Britling; and we have a setting among chambermaids and middle-class tradesmen rather than among the mannered gentry. Wells was himself the son of a chambermaid and a shopkeeper, and in his youth he was apprenticed to a draper and a druggist. I don't want to make much of these "plain" biographical facts, but the validity of the scenery and detail in *Tono-Bungay* is, compared with *Mr. Britling*, striking, and it is matched by a genuineness of feeling against the gentry that one doesn't find in the latter. In *Tono-Bungay*, furthermore, there is no problem of *gradually* revealing the vacuousness of the gentlefolk: they are all idiots as early as page 14:

I began to question the final rightness of gentlefolks, their primary necessity in the scheme of things.

The questioning goes on through the novel, but it is more than questioning. It is assertion, plain and simple, of the final unrightness of all the established forms of England:

One frost and the whole face of things will be bare, links snap, patience end, our fine foliage of pretenses lie glowing in the sun.

The foliage of pretenses includes the gentry, the aristocracy, and the Established Church as well as the new merchant class in England which aspires to the foliage:

. . . the kindly, empty faces of the Royal Family appeared and reappeared, visiting this, opening that, getting married, getting offspring, lying in state, doing everything but anything, a wonderful, good-meaning, impenetrable race apart.

I avowed outright my entire disbelief in the whole scheme of revealed religion.

I hadn't fought ten seconds before I felt this softness in him, realized all that quality of modern upper-class England that never goes to the quick, that hedges about rules and those petty points of honor that are the ultimate comminution of honor, that claims credit for things demonstrably half done.

These instances from the early novel may be matched from many of the later, but one should be sufficient. *Brynhild, or The Show of Things* takes us thirty years onward in Wells's career, but in it his distrust of mannered styles and persons is still sizzling. And in it, as in *Mr. Britling,* this distrust manifests itself primarily when the subject of rhetoric comes up. The villain of the piece, Rowland Palace, is a kind of no-good Britling. Vain, wholly concerned with "show" at the expense of the realities, he is a man of polish, of finish, who has apparently never *said* anything with any meat on it. His opposite, another writer, doesn't "believe in the surface" as Palace does, and so his style is "rough," "patchy," "a splutter," being the product of one "trying desperately to say something more than can be said." Naturally enough we are expected to admire these splutters because they are not fake. The fact that Wells's own style is far from a splutter is admittedly disconcerting, but Wells doesn't expect this to undermine his thesis in favor of no-nonsense incoherence. He even backs up his hero's incoherence with the incoherence of the heroine, who is a "quiet lovely." *She* is not given to pomp and ceremony; *she* is not fooled by façades; *she* is even rather proud of the fact that she is "incapable of conversation." So when she and the hero get together it is a real love match; they can sit around talking about the inadequacies of talk:

"Speech was a great invention," he philosophized. "I am sure the wicked gods were afraid when men got hold of it. They thought human beings would get together and it would be all up with Olympus. Needlessly! What use do we make of speech? What use do we make of anything? Triviality or mischief. . . ."

From such evidence I think it is clear that Wells, if he had had his way, would have swept rhetoricians and *artistes* off the face of the earth. The evidence is even stronger in his nonfictional work. In *Experiment in Autobiography* he knocks about at most of his literary colleagues for their artifices. James was a lost cause, he felt, and Conrad was worse; Conrad "had gone literary with a singleness and intensity of purpose that made the kindred concentration of Henry James seem lax and large and pale." Ford was perhaps not quite so bad—and indeed the personal relationship between Wells and Ford seems to have remained a friendly one—but he "talked criticism and style and words interminably" and he was a terrible *poseur:*

What he is really or if he is really, nobody knows now, he least of all; he has become a great system of assumed personas and dramatized selves.

Even hard-facts Shaw did not escape Wells who found in him deficiencies as a journalist such as those I have suggested:

. . . early circumstances . . . had inclined him to rebellion and social protest; but otherwise he was as distinctly over against me and on the aesthetic side of life as H. James. To him, I guess, I have always appeared heavily and sometimes formidably facty and close-set; to me his judgements, arrived at by feeling and expression, have always had a flimsiness. I want to get hold of Fact, strip off her unessentials, and, if she behaves badly put her in stays and irons; but Shaw dances around her . . . he thinks one can "put things over" on Fact and I do not.

Set up against all of these gentlemen, in Wells's mind, was of course Wells himself. He had, if he did say so, managed to avoid dramatizing himself, building up a world of paper dolls as the others had. They had "lapsed into arbitrary, inconsistent and dramatized ways of thinking and living" and were, as a result, essentially uneducated:

These vivid writers . . . remained . . . abundant but uneducated brains. Instead of being based on a central philosophy, they started off at a dozen points; they were impulsive, uncoordinated, wilful. Conrad, you see, I count uneducated, Stephen Crane, Henry James, the larger part of the world of literary activity. . . .

On the other hand Wells himself, having been brought up and educated amid "non-dramatizing, systematic-minded people," kept his "*persona* under constant scrutiny" and tried to see himself "as far as possible without pretenses."

These are the words of Wells late in life, but one of his most celebrated outbursts against pretenses took place in 1906 when he read before the Fabian Society a paper entitled "Faults of the Fabian." This is well described in Hesketh Pearson's biography of Shaw.* Wells said that Fabian "socialism was in the air and should be brought down to earth"; he offended some of the members thereby, and so a post-mortem debate occurred during which Wells lost his temper and called the Fabians "liars, tricksters, intriguers." Shaw cheerfully agreed to his own lying; the others were less pleased. Shaw pacified Wells and the others, but a year or two later Wells resigned from the Fabians, persuaded that the society was not his dish. Hesketh Pearson agrees, saying that Wells was simply not to the manner born. Not only was he not well-bred (that curious feature of the early Fabians), but he couldn't contend, dramatically or rhetorically, with the others on a public platform. Nor was he the theorist or delighter in theory that Shaw and most of the others were. So, for Wells the Fabians, though professing to be realists, were in a sense comparable to the literary artificers already mentioned. They also failed to face up to "unmanageable reality," being instead always busy trying to manage it.

Wells later described his Fabian paper as one of his great mistakes, but this is presumably because he thought he handled the affair badly, not because he thought he was wrong. His convictions against his literary and political colleagues remained steady, and he became surer and surer that although his brain was not fundamentally "a particularly good one," it had happened upon a Great Truth. Eventually his enthusiasm about his own vision of reality quite mastered such humility as he began with:

> . . . it is by mere chance and opportunity that I have been among the first to give expression to this realization of a guiding framework for life. But I have been among the first. Essentially, then, a

---

* Pages 220-230, *G.B.S., A Full-Length Portrait,* by Hesketh Pearson (N.Y., 1942).

main thread in weaving my autobiography must be the story of how I came upon, and amidst what actions I doubted, questioned and rebelled against accepted interpretations of life; and so went on to find the pattern of the key to master our world and release its imprisoned promise.

Strong words! But as I read them and try to apply them to the particular delusions I am concerned with here—the delusions, that is, that everybody except Wells was reported to be imprisoned by—I keep coming back to the simple hard fact that Wells throughout his life kept writing novels. I can't explain away this fact simply by saying that the novel form was a convenience for him, or by saying that he also wrote things other than novels, or even by saying that the novels he wrote were, as he himself said, discursive. Granting that there are novels and novels, and that a Wells novel is probably closer to a Dickens novel than a Conrad novel, I cannot grant that Wells was the plain journalist he described himself as being. To the Shaw sense of that word he conformed perhaps better than Shaw himself: he *did* write about the here and now constantly; he *did* write about himself and what he saw happening around him. But his essential artfulness in doing so is hard to deny despite his own constant denials. There is no Wells novel without art; there is indeed no Wells novel with as little art as we normally attribute to the shapeless realist novels of a later time. Wells was simply not a realist in the Dreiser, Farrell sense. Some of his novels are more blatantly fictional, artificial, contrived than others, but any of them is closer to a Shaw play than to any novel I can think of to which we might now, even loosely, apply the word "realistic." Like a Shaw play a Wells novel is heavily dialectical—or, if that's too technical a word, disputatious. Much of the art of it is the art of argument, an art that the modern realists omit almost completely, perhaps because they think their characters can't be real and still talk that much. For Wells, as with Shaw, the height of realism or naturalness was apparently to be achieved by putting a couple of idea men in a room together and having them talk about art, life, conventions and social reform—and I submit that nothing is more foreign to the modern image of realism than this. Furthermore, Wells, despite his complaints against Ford and Conrad, did believe in and did indulge in the mysteries of literary artifice. If he had been granted a tape recorder he wouldn't have known what in the world to do with it. Testifying to his artfulness was artificer Conrad himself, who praised him up and down in at least a few letters for his "imagination," his "power of realization," his "absolutely convincing effects," in short all the qualities that Wells's men of pretense and quackery possessed. Also testifying to the art are the unartful heroes whom Wells created. Britling should suffice as an example of this, being the kind of "honest" man Wells frequently adopted as a central figure. Near the end of this novel Britling, having always been too glib, too ready with easy answers to the world's problems, subsides painfully into the silence of awareness of the insufficiency of rhetoric. But is this *Wells* subsiding? Heavens no, Wells subsided less than perhaps any writer in history.

*   *   *

Complaints against Shaw as a hard-facts man have already been voiced above. Ford Madox Ford's complaints were, however, far more shrill than any of these; he devoted a whole book to Shaw's "facts."

The book was called *Between St. Dennis and St. George* and purported to be a "sketch of three civilizations." It stands up better, though, as simply an attack on Shaw. Shaw is the representative villain in the book, the horror most commonly referred to; and Shaw's wartime essay, "Common Sense About War," is exploded line by line and fact by fact in a dense and lengthy appendix. All the heat that a year of war had engendered went into the book, which was written *for* the British government and which Ford acknowledged to be an elongated polemic. In aim and tone it is perhaps comparable to the MacLeish-Van Wyck Brooks attacks upon the "irresponsibles" before and during World War II.

Ford was most anxious to acknowledge Shaw's artfulness, and indeed used it as a weapon against him. Briefly, his case was as follows:

My quarrel with Shaw . . . is not that he has written brilliantly about facts, but that he has invented facts and has then written brilliantly about them. Without giving us any *Quellen* at all— any documents by which we may check his utterances—he has written many brilliant sentences with the object of inducing the reader to believe that the German national psychology is exactly the same as the British national psychology.

I note that the word "brilliant" is used three times. I think it is fair to say the premises here are premises Shaw himself might have used, though hardly against Shaw: Shaw's brilliance produces a fine illusion that is simply not backed up by fact. No *Quellen*. As simple as that. It was Ford's thesis that the time (1915) was "at hand when the historian and the historian's methods" should "come into their own again." Nobody respected facts any more; people lived "in an immense cavern, in an immense Hall of the Winds, in a vast Whispering Gallery—of rumour." And though there were as many rumorists as there were journalists and old wives, one rumorist was preeminent among them: Shaw. Shaw had taken the position that the English and French were as responsible as the Germans for the war, and though his position was of course not a popular one his way of arriving at it seemed, to Ford, characteristic of the age. Ford couldn't keep his temper about it at all. He so disliked, he said, to call it imbecility, that he had to "style it sheer intellectual dishonesty." He went on:

Mr. Shaw, Mr. Brailsford, Br. Bertrand Russell and their confreres employ, in short, in dealing with matters of real history,

144

precisely the methods of "intellectual fictionists." They invent and clothe dummy figures with attributes which have some faint resemblance to the attributes of the persons or the ideals that they pretend to portray, and then, getting these characters into circumstances of their own devising, they proceed to foil, confuse and hopelessly confuse their puppets according to the traditions of Adelphic melodrama.

So Shaw was described as a fictionist, *not* dealing with "real history" but concocting fantastic illusions for his own presumably dark ends. Ford then proceeded to try to counter the Shavian melodrama with as much "real history" as he could grub up on the spur of the moment, thus, it is to be noted, setting himself up as the real hard-facts man in the case. He denied, for example, the premises of those "lazy and loose-thinking analogists" (of course, Shaw) who asserted that

British, German and French are alike governed by flagitious and hereditary ruling classes—are alike inspired by insidious and concealed sentiments of militarism—are alike, in reality, bulldogs while desiring to present the aspect of gazelles.

And for his own *Quellen* to defend his denial he referred at tremendous length to all his own readings of and meetings with representatives of the three nationalities, coming up at last with the statement that he had

no doubt whatever in saying that the English were unmartial to a degree that rendered them a danger to peace, while the Germans were martial to a degree that rendered them absolutely ridiculous.

At this distance the argument is perhaps of little consequence, but I find it interesting that Ford should be trying to beat Shaw at his own game. One may very readily question Ford's facts as well as Shaw's (especially since Ford has been reported to have been a colossal liar), but the fact that he found it important to *be* a hard-facts man, not a master of illusion, not just one of those arty chaps, is instructive. Furthermore, I think it can be shown that Ford liked to think of himself as a hard-facts man in his novels as well as his propaganda pieces for the government. The trouble is that he, like the others, had his own view of what a hard fact is. Just as Shaw's and Wells's hard facts got mixed in with ideas and art, so did Ford's get mixed in with art, "rendering," form.

Robie Macauley has described Ford's book on the English novel as "crotchety," and this is an understatement.* It is dense, contradictory and immensely annoying. It plumps for art and reality with equal vigor, and just when it should be working up a fine alliance it abandons the project. This is well illustrated by Ford's discussion of the difference between a nuvvle and a novel. An artist, he said, had to manage the realities; otherwise he was an escapist who wrote a nuvvle. A nuvvle was a "commercial product that Mama selected for your reading" and that avoided the "problems of the day" and that set up a "Manor House, inhabited by the Best People." A novel on the other hand, well, that was not so easy. It faced up to things all right, as Wells or Shaw would have approved its doing; and it was the sort of thing one couldn't help writing. But its emergence as a novel rather than a nuvvle didn't, oddly, seem to depend upon these urgencies. Instead a novel depended, for its novelness, upon three admirable formal properties: it was rendered rather than told; its characters were treated with aloofness; and its author kept his comments and prejudices out of it.

Such a switch—from the novel's materials to its procedures for rendering the material—suggests something of the same sort of dialectical confusion to me as that propounded by Wells whenever with eloquence he decried eloquence, or by Shaw whenever he brought forth an idea and called it a fact.

---

* Introduction by Robie Macauley to *Parade's End* (New York, 1950).

146

It is perhaps a more modern confusion, however, since Ford prefers to talk about the reality of a novel in the novel's own terms rather than pretending, as Shaw and Wells did, that raw life would establish the terms. This made it possible for Ford to insist on the realities and at the same time to say, "the story is the thing, and the story and then the story, and . . . there is nothing else that matters in the world," a statement wholly alien to Wells, who professed to think of story as ornamental. The modern word for the Ford position is, I believe, "auto-telic," but while there is a good bit of fuss in our classrooms about treating poems and stories on their own terms (letting *them* establish the reality), I don't think Ford or James or Conrad or any of the later apostles of rendering were either capable or desirous of positively divorcing an artistic reality from its worldly counterpart. What writer, after all, is? To put it differently, they were as conscious of their obligations to something outside their art as Shaw and Wells were to something outside the unmanageable realities, but the focus in each case was different: Wells and Shaw didn't like to admit to artifice; Ford talked of reality in terms of artifice. Further-more Ford was committed to a quite different kind of artifice from those of Shaw or Wells. I suppose that we now call it impressionism. This was a novelty, at least to Wells, and so he was struck by its artificiality. Such matters are hard to gen-eralize about but, to put it crudely, the argument between the two camps seems to resolve itself at least partly into a disagree-ment about the validity of different artistic techniques— though there is a deeper disagreement that I will get to presently.

The case of Tietjens is appropriate to illustrate the techni-cal difference, but it also carries on Ford's contempt for Shaw's kind of realism. Tietjens is Ford's version of a realist; he is a kind of antidote to the Shaw realists who have no *Quellen.* He knows everything he has ever read by heart; he can tell a genuine Chippendale from a fake at fifty paces; he knows horses and birds better than any man in England. Furthermore he is anti-Shavian politically. He does not move ahead in a Machiavellian manner, but over and over again rejects that kind of leadership, turning down high posts, insulting those who might help him on, hating "any occupation of a competitive nature." Nor is he, like Shaw's heroes, contemptuous of the past, of tradition, of conventions: he refuses to get a divorce because one does not *do* that; he is the first to ask for the removal of two city slickers from a highbrow golf course because they are unmannerly; he is "so formal he can't do without all the conventions there are and so truthful he can't use them." Nor is he, like Shaw's heroes, a man of common sense: he is always getting into "obscure rows" about principle that only do him harm, and he goes off into the thick of the war though any man in his position, as several examples in the book indicate, could readily have stayed at home in a bank. So his realism, which is insisted upon, makes him a figure wholly unlike Shaw's Caesar, St. Joan or Undershaft. Equally alien to Shaw (or Wells) is the manner by which his actions are presented:

An immense tea-tray, august, its voice filling the black circle of the horizon, thundered to the ground. Numerous pieces of sheet-iron said, "Pack. Pack. Pack." In a minute the clay floor of the hut shook, the drums of ears were pressed inwards, solid noise showered about the universe, enormous echoes pushed these men. . . .

This, if you will, is rendering. The sights, sounds, sensations received by Tietjens and others in the hut are "recorded" (the word is deceptive) rather more directly than would be the case in a conventional narrative, where it first would be announced that a bombing *was* taking place, that the scene was a battlefield, and so on. Ford, as any reader of *Parade's End* knows, worried incessantly about the pace of his novel; he didn't want the action to stop while the exposition went on, and so he, like so many of his successors, devoted a good deal of his artifice to the tricky problem of getting in the exposition and the action simultaneously. This left him, like Conrad, to numberless struggles with Point of View; he shifts us, sometimes with almost no transition, from the events as received by one mind to the events as received by another; but almost always the minds are the minds of the people there, on the scene, in the action, rather than the mind of the author—hence Ford's comment that an author should keep his comments and prejudices out of his novel, a comment with which Wells could not agree. Wells kept insisting that the artist should talk *about* his experience through his novel. Now when one talks about something one has the primary obligation to set everybody straight, to organize the material, provide background for it, and so on. When on the other hand one renders, in the Ford sense, experience, one has an obligation to the experienc*er* which takes precedence over the obligations to exposition, clarity, order. Accordingly Wells and Shaw, with their clarities, could protest about the mysteries of Ford and Conrad; but Ford and Conrad could turn around and complain that Wells and Shaw did not deal with the immediacies. All in the name of reality.

*   *   *

Wells had a character in one of his novels say of Conrad,

   "Pink caviar. Special taste, I mean. Such richness. Turns the simplest ideas into mysteries. Adds a complication to life on every page. Says nothing in a kind of literary agony."

Wells wasn't always so ungenerous. The two were friends for a bit, and exchanged compliments. Still, as I have indicated, Wells had a good many harsh criticisms of Conrad to offer up in his later years, and the two apparently didn't correspond after 1905. Furthermore, even during the period of good feeling, Conrad's praise of Wells was apparently mostly for

Wells's ears. Thus in July, 1905, Conrad wrote to Wells to say, using the third person, that Wells was "unique in the way he approaches his facts and absolutely distinctive in the way he leaves them," yet in February of that year he had written to someone else to say, "the grave of individual temperaments is being dug by H. G. W. and G. B. S. with hopeful industry." Assuming that individuality and uniqueness amount to the same, I can only find the statements contradictory; they suggest that Conrad, although polite and ready to look for the virtues he wanted to find in Wells, had trouble finding them. As for G. B. S., Conrad is reported to have once wanted to bite him.

Despite his detachment from these hard-facts gentlemen, Conrad of course, like all the others, had hard facts on his mind too. The hero of *Victory*, Heyst, is probably the strangest hard-facts figure in my portfolio:

"Are you interested in . . .?"
"Facts," broke in Heyst in his courtly voice. "There's nothing worth knowing but facts. Hard facts. Facts alone, Mr. Tesman."

As a result of this conversation, Conrad related, Heyst became known for a while as "hard-facts" Heyst. The label is surely ironic, however, for Heyst also became known as a utopist, a perfect gentleman, a spider, a wanderer, a devil and a spy; furthermore the above description of him as a hard-facts man is immediately canceled out by a description of him "mooning" about the Java Sea. I don't know that it is wise to look for a model for Heyst, yet Wells and Shaw, as well as Conrad himself, qualify for the job in some respects (so, unfortunately, does all England or perhaps the Allied Powers; for the tale may be taken as a murky parable of World War I) . Wells and Shaw certainly had an excessively clear view of what a fact is, and Conrad had an artist's view. For Wells and Shaw a fact was an idea or an ideal; for Conrad it was something which could be made to stand for something, and so a Conrad fact partook of the slipperiness of a Wells-Shaw fact. All of these men could be said to have dreamed up their ideological or emblematical clarities; they all could be said to have "mooned about" their intellectual or artistic Java Seas. Furthermore, the fate of Heyst might reasonably be taken as Conrad's comment upon the capacity of someone like himself, or Wells or Shaw, finally to cope with Life. Heyst in the mundane world was totally helpless: in the first place he withdrew from it, was not up on the here and now (Wells's complaint about Conrad); and in the second place he couldn't handle it when it came to him—he merely talked or thought about it, à la Wells or Shaw. I will return to this novel, but I think it is clear that Heyst's inability to "get to the quick," mixed with his inheritance from his father of an abstract materialism and his indisposition actually to act—all these are qualities my four gentlemen have been accusing each other of. Conrad obviously thought it was academic and undramatic, as well as unrealistic, for a Heyst or a Shaw to go around *discussing* reality when he was being flooded by it through his five country senses. And yet if Shaw was the biggest talker on his side of the fence, Conrad was surely the biggest talker on the other. If Shaw was weak on the here-and-now of "experienced" reality, Conrad was equally weak in the world of ideas. In the first place Conrad was a perfectly terrible literary critic; he couldn't talk about literature except in the murkiest terms:

Crane was concerned with elemental truth only; and in any case I think that as an artist he is non-comparable. He dealt with what is enduring, and was the most detached of men.

This war book *The Red Badge of Courage,* so virile and full of gentle sympathy, in which not a single declamatory sentiment defaces a genuine verbal felicity, welding analysis and description in a continuous fascination of individual style, had been hailed by critics as the herald of a brilliant career.

151

And in the second place, despite his enthusiasm for detachment, he was incapable of getting out of himself. As a result he could never allow any of his characters the privilege of carrying the burden of talk—that had to be done by himself or by his own shadow, his narrator. As with Ford everything about Conrad's characters is interesting to him except what they say, and so they say very little, and when they say it they are interrupted constantly by the narrator's lush sensory monologue. This playing down of conversation, which we later see in Hemingway, Faulkner and others, is, I suspect, what annoyed Wells most; he could no more have engaged himself to write a hundred-page story in which the hero speaks five significant words—"exterminate the brutes" and "the horror"—than Conrad could have engaged himself to write a novel with a lippy journalist at its center. In view of their different feelings about where reality lay this is hardly surprising; what is surprising is that Conrad never seemed to realize that the technique to which he was committed made meaningful dialogue practically impossible. He kept trying to write plays. One wonders where he thought the actors' speeches were going to come from, and after reading his unrecognizable dramatic version of *The Secret Agent* one still wonders. A true Conrad play would be a kind of pantomime with everyone looking deep, gesturing madly, and brushing aside mosquitoes and palm fronds, to perfectly tremendous background music.

This is not to say that the pantomime would be devoid of hard facts. It is only to say that the actors involved would not be expected to vocalize about them; indeed they would be speaking out of character if they did so, for their awareness of hard facts was conceived by Conrad to be an emotional rather than conceptual awareness; their response to the hard facts had, accordingly, to be somehow more or less than verbal, a response that they themselves could not be expected to describe any more than Benjy could have been expected to write the first chapter of *The Sound and the Fury*. And so, dramatically, such characters were the weakest of reeds; they needed their author to be on stage constantly, mouthing for them, telling the audience what their thoughts and feelings were. This is one reason why Conrad *was* on stage all the time, why his novels took the form they did, and why they were completely unsuited to the theater.

I think this is also why Conrad's art seems arty to those who, like Wells, have a nagging suspicion that artists are, like Heyst, not responsible about Life. When a character speaks to us directly he may be judged directly for what he has said; but when a character is not permitted to speak he may be known to his audience only at secondhand; the audience's opinion of him is thereby diverted by its interest in the intermediary, the author who created him. Thus we arrive at a kind of paradox that the artist like Conrad, who is concerned with the immediacies of Life, with the here and now in the most obvious and defensible meaning of the here and now, the here and now of an individual's sensations and feelings—we come to the paradox that this kind of artist is apt to be more of a contriver, more of a pink-tea man than the Wells kind. One has to get over the hump of the method before the hard facts, if there are any, emerge.

Obviously Conrad's admirers have gotten over that hump. His rather conspicuous artistry, his verbal mystification, his concern with transitions and point of view, all the matters that Wells professed to be scornful of, have not prevented them from discovering the realist in him. To conclude, then, this part on a note of confusion, let me quote from a modern English Marxist critic, Arnold Kettle.* Conrad, he says, is one of only two "considerable writers in English"—the other is Rudyard Kipling—who have looked the phenomenon of imperialism "in the face." And only Conrad looked at it "honestly enough to become a great artist." Kettle goes on to say that *The Heart of Darkness* is "perhaps the most horrifying

---

* Page 69, Vol. II, *An Introduction to the English Novel,* by Arnold Kettle (London, 1953).

description of the effects of imperialism ever written," and he praises "the scorn bestowed on the Tropical Belt Coal Company in *Victory*," as well as the sympathy displayed for the natives in *Lord Jim*. Admittedly this may be taken as praise for Conrad's political *line* rather than for the kind of fact-facing I have been discussing—but reading Wells one doesn't get the impression that Conrad had any line at all; Wells described him as a writer about the "incalculable sea" who had no time at all for political or social issues. The disagreement about both the merits of Conrad and the direction of his work is fundamental, and Kettle confirms it by turning around and describing Wells as "hamstrung by his petty-bourgeois outlook . . . he cannot bring himself or his main characters to participate fully or sympathetically in life as it actually is." In other words Wells didn't deal with the hard facts; he was not, like Conrad, "concerned essentially with the real, material world." Thus the argument goes on. And on.

II.

I think it should be clear by now that both parties in this argument in their moments of pride thought of themselves as doing what every student of American Literature is taught is a fine thing: striking behind the mask. In their weak moments on the other hand (as in *Mr. Britling* and *Victory*) what upset them (and what delights their opponents) is their inability to do so. Ultimately, then, no discussion like this one can be expected to end until the problem of what *is* behind the mask anyway is broached, loathsome though such discussions usually are. Mine will be fairly brief. It takes its cue from some remarks by Howard Nemerov in an essay on Thomas Mann, for which I am most grateful.* I will start

---

* "Themes and Methods: The Early Stories of Thomas Mann," by Howard Nemerov (*The Carleton Miscellany*, Winter, 1961).

with *The Heart of Darkness* and *Major Barbara;* their details are excessively familiar, but for my purpose this is an advantage.

The affinity between the two works is slight. In both there is the usual concern for stripping away Pretense and getting at Truth. Major Barbara is the deluded one in Shaw's piece, Kurtz in Conrad's; Major Barbara is set straight by Undershaft, Kurtz is set straight by—what? the jungle? The nature of their error is also vaguely comparable; Major Barbara has an "obsolete" morality or religion that she has to scrap; Kurtz has a number of things—science, progress, light, eloquence, love, poetry, "great things." But even at this point an important difference between them begins to emerge: Kurtz's error radiates outward from the hard center of a false imperialistic idealism to a deliberately murky aura or emanation surrounding this center (thus we get the mystery Wells so disliked), while Major Barbara's error remains pretty static, dependable, clearly defined. Furthermore, the correction of the error is, in Major Barbara's case, clear and indisputable: she marries happily into the munitions plant. But for Kurtz the correction is not clear at all: true, he dies (that's clear enough), but his legacy to Marlow is at best an ambiguous one alternately repelling and attracting Marlow and leaving the reader with the confused impression (which I think is the correct one) that Kurtz's error has been simultaneously expunged and perpetuated, damned and whitewashed. In other words the conclusion of *The Heart of Darkness* leaves the stage still dark, while all Shaw's lights go on at the end and everybody (including the audience) leaves with a firm resolve to face up to things.

I have already mentioned that Conrad was incapable of writing a play because he had to be onstage himself all the time. I blamed the deficiency on his rendering principle. Let me suggest that another and related reason is that he felt involved in, committed to his characters as Shaw never was and

155

I suppose no writer of comedy ever has been. This personal involvement, which is like Ford's with Tietjens, was apparently indispensable to him; without it his characterizations lose all their power; with it they have a quality which cannot be discussed mechanically, abstractly, lightly as Shaw discusses his characters in his prefaces. I suppose that what this means is, crudely, that Shaw looked out, Conrad looked in for the image behind the mask; that Shaw had either no delusions to scrap or preferred not to reveal them, while Conrad could do nothing *but* reveal them. At any rate the results are what we have: an ebullient comedian of dialectic; a morose, self-centered hypochondriac of "art."

There is no way of getting at Shaw. He is either the most masked or the simplest of all our great playwrights; but we can get at Conrad on every page, though obscurely, sharing Wells's frustration. *The Heart of Darkness* may, for example, be read as a kind of spiritual biography of Conrad in which the key figure is not Kurtz but Marlow. Marlow is a thin cover at best; his function seems to be to keep up the appearance of objectivity and detachment (an ideal for both Conrad and Ford) while Conrad simmers relevantly in the wings. Marlow has an important technical contribution to make to the story—which would be a blunter, more political, more journalistic affair without him—but he remains for all that the voice of Conrad, the voice of the artist; and as such he is far from a passive figure, a simple narrator, a device. He is actually one of the characters in the drama, and he is acted upon by Kurtz, the jungle, the ladies with knitting at home, even the Intended. Indeed, in this story as in *The Secret Sharer* and others, the narrator comes to share the problems of the protagonist and therefore to identify himself with him. The progression in *The Heart of Darkness* is not merely from delusion to truth; it is also from detachment to commitment. As Kurtz is revealed to us, Marlow is involved with him, so that at the end the whole problem has been insensibly transferred from Kurtz ("he dead") to Marlow (he talking).

156

At the beginning Marlow is the man looking for a job, and he takes *any* job, and has nothing but the most common cynicisms to offer up about his actions; in the middle he has heard the name Kurtz, has been subjected to some of the legend surrounding him, and finds himself inexplicably attracted; at the moment before he actually meets Kurtz he realizes that he has eagerly been waiting to hear the man talk; and after the revelation of the horror of Kurtz he suffers the further realization that somehow he had been committed to Kurtz all along: "It was written that I should be loyal to the nightmare of my choice. I was anxious to deal with this shadow by myself alone."—I suggest that if the line were to read "this shadow *of* myself," the change would cause not a ripple in the text. For it is the subordinate theme of the story that Marlow absorb the trials, the revelations, the experience of Kurtz; that he in some manner cope with all this even though he is just a ship captain, not an ivory merchant, just a narrator, not an official successor; that he be Kurtz's executor; that he carry all Kurtz's papers, messages, sermons back to the world; and that he also keep the secret of "the horror" from the Intended. These are important missions. Marlow is playing the recording angel here, but he is doing more than that: he is playing the part, vicariously, of the man he is recording.

But what is it, in the case of Kurtz, that he is recording? Here too the difference with Shaw is evident. Kurtz is no Major Barbara; his delusion, which the author though undeceived paradoxically shares, is not to be corrected by a revelation scene at Salvation Army headquarters. And Marlow is a cynic from the beginning; he sees the attraction of the delusion:

Hunters for gold or pursuers of fame, they had all gone out on the stream, bearing the sword, and often the torch, messengers of the might within the land, bearers of a spark from the sacred fire.

What greatness had not floated on the ebb of that river into the mystery of an unknown earth!

but he also sees the repellent:

. . . it is like a running blaze on a plain, like a flash of lightning in the clouds. We live in the flicker. . . .

He sees in fact both sides and recognizes that they work together; the fascination persists not only in the face of the disgust but is in a way a result of it; thus the fine phrase, "the fascination of the abomination." Major Barbara on the other hand has no ambiguities in her; for her the discovery of the abomination is the turning point in her career, the revelation she and we have been waiting for. For Marlow it is not so much a revelation in store for him as a confirmation of what he had always known but not experienced at firsthand; and one of the difficulties of the story, technically, is to sustain his expectations in Kurtz when he knows better than to have expectations. This is done laboriously; Conrad distinguishes between those who go at it blind and the great ones, the ones who try to redeem the horror by conviction rather than neutral acceptance, by leading rather than following. When he comes at length to the discovery, which is Marlow's, that the greatest leader of all, the one most fully committed, the one truly in the service of an ideal, is even more completely enslaved by the horror than the others, he is really merely in possession of what he had already possessed. He had known that what was the case would be the case, but it took the trip up the river and confrontation of Kurtz to make him know it feelingly. This is what I mean by Conrad's involvement; this second step, by which the author's own representative is himself faced with the revelations to which he subjects his fictions, this step is what one can never find in Shaw. For Shaw to identify himself with Major Barbara—though she be pleasantly naïve and beguiling—would be absurd. She is simply not of the author's camp; she is one of the deluded of whom we say, as we leave the theater, "Well! I'm glad Shaw straightened *her* out."

Nor is it idle to think of Marlow quite specifically as the artist sitting at his desk scribbling all this. Conrad wants us to know from the beginning that his story has to do with more than ivory, white exploitation and so on:

The yarns of seamen have a direct simplicity, the whole meaning of which lies within the shell of a cracked nut. But Marlow was not typical (if his propensity to spin yarns be excepted), and to him the meaning of an episode was not inside like a kernel but outside, enveloping the tale. . . .

He also wants us to know that the darkness up the river has its affinities with a smaller river, the Thames:

"And this also," said Marlow suddenly, "has been one of the dark places of the earth."

Furthermore, when Marlow gets "out there" to the big river, he describes the scene in stage terms; he becomes a hard-facts playwright worrying, about the reality of the scene he is both witnessing and creating:

Every day the coast looked the same, as though we had not moved; but we passed various places—trading places—with names like Gran' Bassam, Little Popo; names that seemed to belong to some sordid farce acted in front of a sinister backdrop.

Sometimes the scene rings true:

For a time I would feel I belonged still to a world of straightforward facts. . . .

But then the old staginess sets in; everyone is merely playing a part, the action is weak and unconvincing melodrama:

Pop, would go one of the six-inch guns. . . . There was a touch of insanity in the proceeding, a sense of lugubrious drollery in the sight; and it was not dissipated by someone on board assuring me earnestly that there was a camp of natives—he called them enemies!—hidden out of sight somewhere.

Then, at a perplexed moment before the confrontation of Kurtz, Marlow has a good Shakespearean peroration ready for us on the ineffectiveness of the artist, the "conveyor" of all this, to get the hard facts into his wooden '0':

. . . No, it is impossible; it is impossible to *convey* the life-sensation of any given epoch of one's existence—that which makes its truth, its meaning—its subtle and penetrating essence. It is impossible. We live as we dream—alone.

He comes back to the same theme a bit later, describing the "conveyor" as a kind of minor conjurer with a trick deck of cards or a hat full of rabbits faced with trying, say, to get the sun up:

When you have to attend to things of that sort [minor details], to the mere incidents of the surface, the reality—the reality, I tell you—fades. The inner truth is hidden—luckily, luckily. But I felt it all the same; I felt often its mysterious stillness watching me at my monkey tricks, just as it watches you fellows performing on your respective tight ropes.

Then, upon his meeting with Kurtz, the man he is destined to be loyal to, what is it that first attracts him?—not his ivory, not his ideas, not his commanding presence, not his handling of the natives, but his voice:

The man presented himself as a voice. . . . The point was in his being a gifted creature, and that of all his gifts the one that stood out preeminently, that carried with it the sense of real presence, was his ability to talk, his words—the gift of expression, the bewildering, illuminating, the most exalted and the most contemptible, the pulsating stream of light, or the deceitful flow from the heart of an impenetrable darkness.

The last passage is instructive in many ways. Not only can we observe a curious switch by which Kurtz rather than Marlow suddenly emerges as the artist, the conveyor (Marlow says elsewhere that Kurtz "was very little more than a voice"), but his voice, aside from all his other credentials, is itself identified with his darkness. With his darkness *and* his light. Somehow here the problems of Conrad presenting the case of Kurtz and the problems of Kurtz himself merge. The merging is just the kind of thing that Wells objected to—but as it is prepared for and insisted on throughout the story it cannot be ignored. Kurtz is the imperialist perhaps, and Marlow is the artist; but the two participate equally in the ambiguous service of progress, culture, light or merely "all the dead cats of civilization." Also Kurtz and Marlow share the same ambiguous feelings *toward* the enterprise. Just as Kurtz is fatally drawn to actions which his "voice" never confesses to for an instant until the deathbed scene, so is Marlow first drawn into intimacy with the man he knows he should detest, and then driven to perpetuate Kurtz's own falsehood by lying for him at the end. Indeed I think it is difficult to carry the analogy here between artist and imperialist further than Conrad intended it to be carried. The two fare forward together; the horror for one in the ivory trade is the horror for the other in a study in Essex.

Victory is *The Heart of Darkness* inverted or reversed, the other side of the same coin; and as it is a war novel it may be compared with *Mr. Britling Sees It Through.* The abomination is certainly present for Heyst, but he doesn't go eight hundred miles upriver for it; he goes an unspecified number of miles out in the Java Sea to get *away* from it and then it comes to him. Britling's case is similar; Britling was con-

161

fronted with the abomination of the war though he certainly didn't want to be; he went out of his way to look at the war through rose-colored glasses until finally the hard facts made it impossible for him to do so any longer. Both were in other words passive figures for as long as they could be, and when the confrontation came it wasn't their doing as it was, certainly, for Kurtz. But here the similarity ends. Heyst's wrongness is solved by making the confrontation stick, by in other words making a tragedy of it—nothing is more hollow, as Heyst's total despair and suicide testify, than his victory over Jones and Ricardo. The abomination has won, and the only solace to be found is in the knowledge or awareness of the abomination that Heyst has been feelingly presented with.

But Britling? Britling does not confront the confrontation by despair, by suicide. No, his conclusion is much more sensational: he turns to God. He turns with a vengeance; he abandons his art, his journalism, his all; he sits up all night scribbling sentences which he then crosses out; and as the down comes he is suddenly struck all of a heap by religion:

He is the only King. . . . Of course I must write about Him. I must tell all my world of Him. And before the coming of the true King, the inevitable King, the King who is present whenever just men foregather, this blood-stained rubbish of the ancient world, these puny kings and tawdry emperors, these wily politicians and artful lawyers, these men who claim and grab and trick and compel, these war makers and oppressors, will presently shrivel and pass—like paper thrust into a flame. . . .

I do not wish to ridicule this conversion; Wells has already done so himself in his *Experiment in Autobiography*. There he amusingly describes the war years as a period of real funk for him; not only did he misunderstand the war and achieve immortality by coining the phrase "the war to end war," but he also, though a good healthy atheist, "confused and misled" his "more faithful readers" by the introduction of deity. He

162

partly defends himself by saying that at least his deity was not orthodox:

At his best my deity was far less like the Heavenly Father of a devout Catholic or a devout Moslem or Jew than he was like a personification of, let us say, the Five Year Plan.

But on the other hand he seems genuinely ashamed of himself. Here was an occasion when he had failed to face up to hard facts:

What we have here is really a falling back of the mind toward immaturity under the stress of dismay and anxiety. . . . It is a good thing to imagine the still companionship of an understanding Presence on a sleepless night. Then one can get to sleep again with something of the assurance of a child in its cot.

Maybe so, but the incident does not seem to me to be such a momentary relapse as Wells indicates. There is surely a connection between the elevated image of the truth which Wells retained throughout his life (both in his great plans for world federation and in his insistent fictional discoveries that when lies are exorcised all is well), and his managing to find God at a moment when the earthly counterpart of God was clearly an abomination. He, like Shaw, seems to have had an abomination for abominations.

It is at this point that my two camps seem finally to begin to move distinctly apart. The Wells conclusion for *Britling* is as far removed from Conrad as it could well be. Or from Ford either, for that matter. Ford's Tietjens follows the Kurtz-Marlow pattern in many respects; Tietjens is resigned to the horrors of the war and what it is doing to his civilization (as Britling could never have been). But he is far more than resigned; he is in other words more like Kurtz than Heyst. Far from letting the horrors filter in on him as they did slowly to Britling and Heyst, he has to take positive action

163

to subject himself to them; he has to go off to the war's heart of darkness; he has to be battered physically, spiritually, economically by it. And for him the solace, such as it is, is the solace that Marlow attributes to Kurtz, the solace of finding the horror and affirming it:

> Better his cry—much better. It was an affirmation, a moral victory paid for by innumerable defeats, by abominable terrors, by abominable satisfactions. But it was a victory! That is why I have remained loyal to Kurtz to the last. . . .

The Kurtz cry, it must be remembered, was not "God" but "the horror."

Now I don't know that one can go further with the split without going into the appropriate ids and egos. What is it that makes one man strike behind the mast *with the intention of* finding God or "the pattern of the key to master our world"—and another do so with the previously fixed opinion that what he will find there is dead cats. Both impulses have a grand tradition. The fascination of the abominable begins with Eve and the apple. One may invoke the shades of any number of literary and religious figures who shared, in one way or another, Marlow's feelings: Chaucer for the Pardoner, Marlowe for Dr. Faustus, Shakespeare for Macbeth, Milton for Satan, Ahab for the whale, Browning for the dark tower. But the fascination of the delectable mountains has an equally honorable history beginning with, say, Adonis; so the choice is always there. Nor is it sufficient to say that the immediate historical surroundings of our four authors conditioned their choosings. If one says that Wells and Shaw, with their elevated, Tennysonian notions of the pursuit of truth were, despite themselves, lingering Victorians, then one is presumably obligated to say that the fascination of the abomination may be found among the Victorians too—in Browning and Hardy, for example. Nor is it sufficient to blame the very differing notions of the artist's role and method that I have described; for presumably the artistry is conditioned by the feelings and impulses which produce, alternately, Kurtzes and Major Barbaras. It *does,* therefore, seem as if only a bang-up study of Shaw's relationship with his mother will do.

And yet, leaving out the mother and looking at the art I think it is at least possible to say that Ford and Conrad were the realer realists of the group. They presumably had mother troubles too, but in their art their concern for truth was like Marlow's, something they were fascinated by and propelled toward with every sentence, every character, every artifice they composed. Their act of composition may profitably be compared with psychiatric analysis, only they were their own doctors. They poured forth the dreams and then worked them out; their gloomy, Kurtzian, Heystian victories were perhaps, to the Shaws and Wellses of the world, the victories of the sick, but to them they were the ways, the only ways to health of any sort. This is not for the moment to say that the art of Conrad and Ford is therefore of a purely private reality, but that it is never, if they can help it, of a reality which their private experience cannot sustain.

In contrast Wells and Shaw, despite their insistence that they were dealing with the here and now (were not writing nuvvles), and despite Wells's assertion that novels should contain unaffected personal outbursts, seem to have been leery of private experience as the source and prop of their efforts. At the crux they think rather than look, project rather than experience. The setting is a parlor or public hall rather than a couch; the effort is to weed out the abominations or to set up a "scheme" for doing so (Wells was the greatest schemer of all time) rather than to go eight hundred miles up some cranial river to live with them. As a result the realities they proclaim have a groomed, well-tended appearance that the psychiatrist doubts, imagining that his patients thought them up to conceal something else. To draw an analogy, if the ancient mariner had, upon observing that "slimy things did crawl with legs/Upon the slimy sea," felt it his obligation to jump in with them, he would have been a good Conrad-Ford figure; but as he decided to remain on deck and managed, up there, to discover, through a process which has never been and never will be explained, that they were beautiful and lovable, he is a Wells-Shaw figure. Perhaps it is because he hates the *feel* of slimy things?—back to the mother again.

Let me end, inconclusively, on this facetious note, observing only that for better or worse Shaw and Wells have practically no modern *literary* successors. The contemporary realists of the Shaw-Wells school are, mothers and all, journalists in the modern sense: they neither write nor read literature; they regard as frivolous the activities of the artists of campus and Greenwich Village alike; for them the domain of ideas political and social is simply not a part of the domain of literature. And on this last point the literary men seem to agree with them; they take some justifiable pride in their removal from political and social affairs, and go about being alternately annoyed by the shams of journalism and fascinated by the new abominations abounding. All this of course is matter for another essay, as yet unwritten, on the dreary subject of the alienation of the artist.

The Alienated Poet Insists

I.

I have a friend, a sort of Oliver Allston character—sensitive (like me), sometimes annoyed with contemporary literary fashions (like me), poetic (like me), and so on. He is also, though, a good deal less sound and stable than I am; I regard him as one of the neglected but erratic voices of our age. Well, he has been considering giving up the Alienated Younger Poets' Association (not like me; I am the Association's Executive Secretary) on the grounds that, as a member, he has been thinking too long in selfish and sentimental terms about his cruel lot. He is tired, he says, of watching the poets and other arty types of his acquaintance sitting around in their respective dudgeons—he has one too, windowless and unheated, over his garage—complaining to themselves and each other about the world and what it has done to *them*. He wishes they would shut up, and he has frequently thought that he might set an example for the bunch of them by resigning from the Association and shutting up himself.

Not long ago he decided (the first of a series of decisions) to go into action. He would *not* resign from the Association

This essay was delivered, in slightly different form, as a lecture at the State University of Iowa in April, 1962.

(he was too old to switch; he was stuck with the poet's life; by God he was going to like it) , but on the other hand he would *not* continue to go at being a member as he had in the past, and as all his colleagues (like me) were going at it. He would *not* teach literature; he would *not* teach creative writing; he would *not* edit a little magazine; he would *not* get involved in squabbles about academic and non-academic poetry; he would *not* keep sending off poems in the mail (though he might write a few) ; he would *not* get wrought up about who was in, who was out, the prizes awarded, the appointments made (I can't imagine why he doesn't like this stuff) ; in short he would no longer conduct himself as if Art and its business were his life's program. He preferred to describe himself as being stuck with the artist's life rather than ulcerously dedicated to it.

Furthermore, he said, he was going to try to conduct himself in such a fashion publicly that nobody would think of him as discontented. He was going to transform his image, make himself into the poet as good guy.

"Golf, you mean?" I asked him.

"If necessary," Friend replied sternly.

"But what of the future of art?"

"What *of* the future of art?"

"But what will you *do?*"

"I will be a journalist," Friend said.

II.

You may remember that the old Oliver Allston, the one Van Wyck Brooks was so intimate with, had some of the same notions. He too wanted to get in the swim; and he too wanted the poet to stop complaining. A lot has happened since his time, however, and anyway the new Oliver, my Friend, is not a duplicate copy of the old: the old was "of middle height,

168

inclined to stoutness," whereas the new is very tall and thin; the old "could not stand late hours and exciting parties," whereas the new cannot stand for long to be without them; and, more important, the old had some notion that the role of art was to be, somehow, popular (as a matter of fact he was against our whole Alienated Poets' Association), whereas the new is unfortunately far past imagining such a thing, being thoroughly committed—I really can't understand why —to imagining a minor role for poetry and literature in society. Indeed, if Friend has any common thesis to which he adheres through all his various decisions (to act, or not to act, to be a poet, or to be a golfer), it is that the literary folk of most of our many denominations and shadings have generally messed up their lives by thinking constantly of how important they are, or ought to be. Thus, Friend insists, the alienated poets of one kind think they are important *even though* society ignores them, while the alienated poets of another kind—the frustrated advocates of engagement, involvement, action—think they are important because they are the unacknowledged (or even the acknowledged) legislators for society. In both camps, Friend says, the image of the literary calling has remained lofty and stern—busts of Shakespeare and Whitman all about—despite the depressing fog of our time which has rendered its loftiness invisible. Therefore, a plague on both their camps, Friend keeps saying (and I must remind you that I don't agree with him; I am the Executive Secretary of the Association).

Now—to continue with his saga—Friend decided, while wrestling with the literary egotists around him, to become a journalist. For about two months. Like so many of his erratic fellows he had been busy demonstrating for Peace, No More Tests and No More Edward Tellers, and had paraded down Fifth Avenue and had read his very best I-won't-dig-a-bomb-shelter poem in front of the offices of the A.E.C. Then the inevitable depression had set in (the A.E.C. building had not crumbled, the poem had not been mentioned in the *Times*, the general strike advocated by him and his fellow demonstrators had not visibly affected the pace or the economy of the Great City) and Friend had sat around in his dudgeon for a few days afterwards just saying to himself, "What the hell."

He had also, as it happened, been reading around in Bernard Shaw and H. G. Wells, both of whom had delighted in describing themselves as journalists. Shaw was especially vocal on the point:

Journalism is the highest form of literature; for all highest literature is journalism. The writer who aims at producing platitudes which are "not for an age, but for all time" has his reward in being unreadable in all ages . . . and so let others cultivate what they call literature: journalism for me.

That paragraph was probably the critical one in Friend's Decision for Journalism, though Wells' diatribes against the "immense artistic-preoccupations" of Conrad and Ford Madox Ford had their effect too. Reading such things he saw history repeating itself, and while he had considerable respect for both Conrad and Ford—and was not so very sure that Wells and Shaw qualified as *bona fide* journalists—he was confident that Wells and Shaw had at least analyzed the modern trouble correctly. *They* saw what was wrong with reading a delicately phrased, beautifully turned anti-bomb-shelter poem at a peace rally; *they* had a feeling for what the here-and-now of world affairs demanded; *they* knew that it made no sense, when the powers were threatening to blow all heads off, to be playing the role of poet, pruning the verbal feathers and looking off mistily toward Gambier or San Francisco for aesthetic approval. In short, said Friend, Shaw and Wells saw that for a literary man to insist upon his art—its

170

special values, its special demands—with the intensity displayed by most members of the Alienated Poets' Association, was simply to render the art ineffective. The art had to be supple, accommodating, unobtrusive. The poet orating before the A.E.C. had to take off his medals and never-sere ivy and talk turkey. If he did not he was simply, said Friend (mixing his figures freely in his enthusiasm) frosting, frosting on the cake of our culture.

I agreed vaguely—for I thought it best to humor him—and mentioned to him that I had written a rather brilliant essay on Wells, Conrad, Shaw and Ford that I would be pleased to let him read. Friend acknowledged my offer graciously but went right back to the frosting. It didn't matter, he insisted, whether the frosting was *nice* frosting—as in the case, say, of the reading of a poem by a certain elderly statesman-poet at a certain president's inauguration, or simply *foolish* frosting, as in the case of the reading of a poem before the A.E.C. Either way it was frosting, and frosting was what literature had become in the hands of its thousands of practitioners who scorned journalism. So the immediate problem, as he saw it, was not one of the importance or unimportance of literature, or its values or absurdities—but simply one of finding an honest place for it, large or small, in the going world. Such a place could only be found, he felt, by having the literary man take the Shaw-Wells line.

Trying to get Friend to look at the matter with less heat, I observed academically that the conflict between journalism and literature Friend was describing had hardly been a new one even in the time of Shaw and Wells. I reminded him of Addison's remarks in 1697 about two kinds of pastoral, one represented by Hesiod and the other by Virgil. Hesiod was the "husbandman," Virgil the poet. Hesiod, in describing the seasons, made "the whole but look like a modern almanac," while Virgil's verse abounded, said Addison, "with meta-

171

phors, Grecisms and circumlocutions, to give his verse the greater pomp and preserve it from sinking into a plebeian style."

Yes, said Friend, Addison was a snob like Ford and Conrad, and now like Eliot and Shapiro and all those.

I insisted that that was not so, or that if it was so—if it was true that Addison was a snob—still, such a private characteristic of his being had nothing to do with his philosophy of literature and poetry. I brought forth a copy of an Addison essay entitled "Virgil's Georgics" (to be found in *18th Century Essays,* edited by Scott Elledge) and read the following:

> I think nothing which is a phrase or saying in common talk should be admitted into a serious poem, because it takes off from the solemnity of the expression and gives it too great a turn of familiarity; much less ought the low phrases and terms of art that are adapted to husbandry have any place in such a work as the georgic, which is not to appear in the natural simplicity and nakedness of its subject, but in the pleasantest dress that poetry can bestow on it.

That passage, I pointed out, represented a view of the nature of poetry—not just georgics—that has persisted in various forms right up to our own time, despite the changes in the character of the society for which poetry has been written, and despite the frequent cries that poetry should be written in the language of ordinary speech. The view was therefore too deeply imbedded, I thought, in the character of the art itself to be ascribed to any personal frailty like snobbery.

Maybe so, said Friend, but all of its adherents have been snobs nonetheless, and they still are. He added that he felt that the artistic snobbery of our own day was breathtaking in its range and virulence, since it included not only the academic poets but also the anti-academic poets, and since it was being paraded before the world with less provocation than ever before in the history of art.

I told Friend that he seemed to be operating from a breath-taking definition of snobbery—that, for example, by such a definition even I was a snob—and he disappeared from my view for several weeks.

III.

When he came back he had, of course, just made a new decision. He had just had four pieces that he regarded as journalistic in the very best sense rejected by four worthy journalistic organs, one piece on the horrors implicit in James Reston analyzing the state of Kennedy's political nerves all the time (Friend said that the whole defunct, yet reigning, balance-of-power concept had now been refined to the point where the pundits felt it necessary to study minutely the physical properties, day-to-day and week-to-week, of the two leaders of the two nations), another piece on the failure of the *New York Times* to print an advertisement for a general peace strike, and a couple of other pieces of an equally belligerent nature on subjects I forget—all rejected.

Friend was furious, of course, and I could not amuse him by joking about his odd notions of how to play golf with the opposition. Nor did I console him when I pointed out that journalism had become in our time a profession that an outsider could hardly be expected to crack right off the bat. He was excessively righteous about his pieces, and he had nothing but contempt for my moderateness. He observed that journalism had indeed become a profession, a profession with great influence and greater pretensions, a profession of just the exclusive, clannish kind that its members abhorred among the literary people, a profession that had effectively stopped the Shaws and Wellses of the world from crossing over into it even when they wanted to. Not only, he asserted, did its members practice their mysteries in a special part of

173

our campuses when they were getting their training, and in special publications when they were grown up; not only did they make it difficult for a poet or other "creative writer" to get a job on a newspaper or newsmagazine, or, having got it, to practice the journalistic act according to his own conscience; but they also made it difficult for the literary man to get a hearing *anywhere* about the matters journalism had appropriated. Not just the institutions of professional journalism, but the rhetoric of professional journalism and its climate of thinking were pervasive, he asserted, in the world of "contemporary affairs," so that anyone who didn't come at those affairs the way, say, James Reston would come at them was simply regarded as too naive or ill-informed to deal with them at all.

I asked Friend not to go so fast. I was prepared to grant that the journalistic situation had deteriorated since the time of Shaw and Wells, reminding him that it had been he, not I, who had just been on a journalistic kick. And I was prepared to agree with him on a number of points he had made; for example, in the past, I said, it had always been reasonable and proper for the literary man to descend and espouse journalism if he chose to; and if he did so journalism applauded, journalism was grateful, journalism was honored by the visit. But now it was not like this; the journalists had gotten uppity and were using literature when it pleased them (running a poem a day on the editorial page, printing a bad review section for tone and cultural subscriptions, serializing a popular novel) while denying literature when it did not please them by insisting, with the new powers at their command and their shiny new journalistic ethic, that the main business of journalism be conducted by proper journalists. But I said that I was *not* prepared to grant that the fault lay entirely with the journalists. I felt that . . .

But Friend interrupted me. He wished to pile a few more curses on journalistic heads, to add that the journalists had done a good deal more than simply take over journalism. They had also, he pointed out, moved in with their new powers on literature itself. They were the ones who had "made" the big literary figures of recent years, not the nasty power cliques in the English Departments. It seemed to Friend that all the powerful English professors in the world could have plumped for Eliot and Faulkner and Hemingway and Salinger and a few others until doomsday, and those authors would still have been circulating mostly in upper-class English courses and in houses subscribing to the *Kenyon Review* if it had not been for the journalists. Who was it, Friend asked, who had got 16,000 persons crammed into a basketball auditorium to listen to Ole Possum?—not the University of Minnesota, not Allen Tate, not even Harcourt Brace, but the *Minneapolis Tribune*. Who was it who had put Hemingway *really* on the map?—not Pound, not Stein, not Scribner's, but *Life*. And so on. It was not, Friend insisted, that the English professors and their kind were powerless, but that the journalists were powerful where the big audiences, and the big money, were; and it was not that the English professors had God and the Right on their side, but that the journalists exerted their power without at the same time sharing with the professors any responsibility for literary affairs. For the journalists, Friend concluded grandly, literature was just news, whereas for the professors it was a way of life.

I asked Friend, then, if he had newly decided to return wholeheartedly to the way of life of the Alienated Poets' Association.

I confess that I was surprised, and disappointed; for he said no. He said that that way of life was a dead way of life maintained against the living facts of our time, maintained by the Association and its affiliates, maintained by topheavy English departments and narrowly specialized writing schools, maintained by a variety of gimmicks and appeals from Sex to the

175

Great Tradition, maintained by convention and religiosity, maintained by *dumkopfs,* maintained . . .

"Stop," I shouted, "Where, then, wilt thou turn now?"

"To the places of power," he sneered, evilly.

IV.

I think you can now see that Friend's saga is a complicated one. Friend is a determined man, and a not unintelligent man. Above all he is very jumpy, like a shaved cat. His next period—that of his attempt to gain publishing power—was a brief, ludicrous episode during which he schemed at creating, with the help of a few rich friends, a financial combine which would buy out the always faltering *New York Herald-Tribune* and set it up with literary journalists in control. He went so far as to declare its basic editorial premise, "Peace before Pride and the Pit," and to sketch out a model table of organization for the paper. (By this I mean a platonic model, which the earthly counterpart on 34th Street would then struggle to emulate. The table of organization included Jonathan Swift as managing editor, Mark Twain as society editor, James Thurber as chief Washington correspondent, Samuel Johnson as director of advertising, and so on.) But the details of the project, as well as those of the money to perpetrate it, had hardly been touched upon before his good sense reasserted itself and he went off on a sloop to the Bahamas to mope. There he wrote mostly poems, poems on the follies of statesmen and publishers, poems on how ridiculous it is to write poems in an age such as ours, poems on the end of the world. On his return, which was not long ago, I asked him if he *still* felt that the Association, the English Departments and the Writing Schools were off base.

He was tan, seemed robust. He had a three-weeks beard and the easy, relaxed, dissipated look of assurance that successful failures pick up in the tropics. He said yes, they were all off base as much as they ever were, but that he did not at the moment have any plans for getting them on base. He said that he thought that he would continue to stick with them, that he would give up journalism, give up golf, and that he wished I would go away. He fell asleep.

I left, disconcerted by his new indolence, his apparent apathy to all the issues which had been tormenting him for so long, and of course his annoyance at me. What had I done, after all, except sympathize and try to keep him in the Association? The next day I contemplated calling him, and had just decided not to, hoping that instead he would call me, when I was pleased to receive a special delivery letter from him, one that he must have spent the whole previous evening writing. I will read only the pertinent passages here:

Dear Reed:

I'm sorry about last night. Like some of my most celebrated contemporaries I've been on a heavy mixture of sedative and sauce, and I've also been pretty depressed, not wanting to talk very much about all the things that until recently I have wanted very much to talk about. I still don't want to talk about them in fact, and I'd just as soon we didn't see each other for a while—I'm going out to my farm near Sleepy Eye —but I do think I should write you, partly to apologize, though I know that isn't necessary, and partly to get myself straight on a couple of points.

All my recent foolishness has had its rewards for me; I feel even wise now in an insane sort of way, wise from doing the stupid and finding out that it's stupid so that I can do it again. Which I may or may not do when I get back from the farm. I've decided that I make a pretty good live Hamlet or Dr. Stockton, one of those dumb-bright rebels for audiences to be titillated by and go home and ignore; and I've decided also that now is the time, as there never before was a time, when it is simply insane to be anything else. I'm talking about the Bomb of course, and I know the Bomb is tiresome, and maybe that's why I have to do this by letter rather than over a drink. I'm really embarrassed to insist on it, but here it is: there never *was* before a time when there wasn't any way out, or any way of at least postulating an out, a 50-50 chance, say, of managing not to be caught *wholly* by the lunacy. And now the time has come, and I read the morning papers, and I walk up and down on the earth, and I know that this time I can't avoid the lunacy that has been there ever since I was born and thousands of years before but never there this way; can't avoid it, can't exile myself from it, close a door, sit on the Riviera, teach school in a town with the slogan Cows Colleges & Contentment, write my own sonnets, review other people's, and think that somehow or other it too will pass. I know in other words that those institutions of men to whom I have in the past paid passing allegiance by driving on their roads, paying their dues, serving in their armies and voting for their officers, but have also insisted on my separateness from, on the grounds that I had my own life to live and other allegiances to live up to (such as the Poets' Association) —I know that those institutions now give me *no* options, *no* separateness, though they think they still do, because they have the Bomb. And they don't even know that they have it! They sit in their in-and-out baskets and think they have something else, something that just has to do with *their* military, political and diplomatic institutions.

This is their lunacy. Now there would be, as I say, nothing remarkable about their lunacy if it were just the usual political lunacy that people have lived with for thousands of years —*lived* with, I say; not lived with well necessarily, and not lived with unanimously, but lived with mostly and lived with through war, famine, depression, all that. But as this lunacy is *not* the usual thing, and as there seems to be only the smallest chance that we can live with it or through it at all, for even a generation, then I say this is not anything we have known before; it simply cannot be looked at the way we have looked at institutional lunacy for all these years. Therefore, to go back, I say it is insane not to stand against it. Somehow.

I've had the curiously exhilarating feeling all these last difficult months that now at last, after years of repressions that I didn't recognize as such, I could do nothing wrong, no matter what. I could do no wrong because all possible wrong was already being done by those with the wherewithal really to do it. To put it differently I discovered that I could only keep what I regarded as my sanity by being a perfect lunatic according to my previous standards, that is, only by running my head lunatically against the stone walls of the powers, running it against their walls again and again and again as the only *demonstrably* sane act—act of resistance—left.

Demonstrably? The demonstration must be syllogistic:

1) All persons who are willing to try to preserve their institutions by blowing their institutions and themselves up are lunatics.

2) The majority of persons in institutions having blowing-up powers are persons who are willing to preserve their institutions by blowing the institutions and themselves up.

3) Therefore, the majority of persons in institutions having blowing-up powers are lunatics.

[Let me cut in here. Friend then devoted five dense pages to a defense of the curious premises in this syllogism, mainly to the problem of what being "willing" meant. He in effect defined willingness negatively by saying that until there was evidence of any institutional disposition in, say, Washington or Moscow to give up institutional sovereignty rather than drop bombs, a willingness to be blown up had been demonstrated. Then he had two other syllogisms in sequence purporting to prove that sane men had some obligations to do something about lunatics when lunatics were doing something about them. Then he broke into another tirade against the Poets' Association.]

The poets have, I grant [the letter continued], little in common with the lunatics in Washington and Moscow, mostly because the poets have no power. But they share with them one lunacy, and that is the conviction that the affairs of their world can continue to be conducted as they were before 1945. The governmental lunatics are still guided in their actions by the assumption that it is their first duty to retain their respective national sovereignties since, without those, all the rest of their general inherited cultures will go by the board. And the poets are still guided by the assumption that they must preserve the inherited sovereignty of their art in the affairs of the human spirit. In other words the two groups are both living, as it were, in bathyspheres sealed against the post-1945 fact that their sovereignties no longer exist. Now in the governmental bathysphere the actions undertaken to preserve the already non-existent sovereignty are the very actions which threaten to make the loss of sovereignty only too dismally clear. But in the poets' bathysphere the actions are not dangerous, they are simply trivial and stupid in a rather charmingly human way. The poets keep turning their knobs, taking readings on their dials and interpreting the readings which, they think, indicate where their bathysphere is and how it is doing. Some of them find that we are on the threshhold of a great new age for poetry (a remarkable reading, that is!) ; some of them think times are bad because somebody they don't like has been turning the dials; and some of them think it is "too early to decide" whether the times are good or bad, though not too early to decide that they are "exciting times to live in." But all of them, or anyway twice too many of them think, in good pre-1945 fashion, that because Literature has in the past been a major means of preserving and nourishing certain human assets like the soul and the word it will continue to be a means so long as we can find the right *literary* formula—Henry Miller's, Cleanth Brooks', somebody's, somebody's formula *inside* the bathysphere for setting the human spirit straight *outside.*

Now it is one thing to be *resigned* to bathysphere living (maybe the best of our poets are) and another thing to be deceived by it; and what I am saying is that the institution of literature (and particularly of poetry) as now constituted in the Association, the English Departments and so on, is deceived; that is, if we can think of the institution as having a mind, a collective mind, that mind is a bloody mixed-up mind full of pretensions picked up out of a dead past, full of plans for a doubtful future, and full—worst of all—of elaborate hierarchical formulae for a cultural here-and-now that doesn't in fact exist.

[I will interrupt the letter here again, for perhaps obvious reasons. Friend devotes three pages to the literary and publishing politics of our time, naming individuals, foundations, schools, cliques and magazines, and generally, I regret to say, disgracing himself. I have a tough skin and am not easily offended, but I am the executive secretary of the Association, and I do have a stake in these affairs, a not-unimportant one; and so I was frankly a bit shocked to see how extreme Friend's views had become. But just as I was about to put down the letter unfinished, and was thinking with some sadness of what had happened to that fine mind, that delicate talent, Friend suddenly broke off, rather pathetically I thought, with a complaint about his own incapacity as a writer, to say, and to say right, what he meant to say about this fool business. I return to the letter.]

. . . To say what one means, to say it so that you know you have *said* it and it is *there,* this is the kind of satisfaction that I suppose a writer is a writer for, the kind of satisfaction he is looking for when, as Rilke says, he would die if it were denied him that he write. And so there is a sense, I suppose, in which I have made this bloody bomb business my own private writing problem in the last months, and have thrashed around like a fish in its net, knowing all the time how ridiculous I was being in *having* the problem at all (so the poet should be Napoleon or Ghandi when he has an audience of a hundred and ten?) , and knowing also that I couldn't solve the problem anyway even for my own satisfaction, couldn't master it, couldn't write it down so that it looked right, for the simple reason that the only way I *can* write it down it always comes out with me in my solitary righteousness standing against what looks like a billion lunatics. And when I discover my isolation—as I do, every time—I say no, Friend, you've got to revise that sentence, scratch that paragraph; it can't be right *even though it is.*

Which is all simply to say, I suppose, what we all know, that real alienation isn't worth much. The impulse to achieve it may be one of the good impulses, and any poet who doesn't have the impulse, doesn't want to be saintly a few hours a week is probably not a poet at all. But after that, no. He has to join the lunacy—at least some lunacy other than his own— do *something*, something communal or institutional, something *un*alienated no matter how mad it may be, or he just can't live. In short, you may count on me, you and your unalienated alienated poets' association. I apologize for my many failures in the past, and I hope you will put me down for an omnibus review or something in your magazine in the near future. Meanwhile I'll send you some poems.

Yours for more institutional alienation,
Friend

Well, you can imagine that I was terribly pleased, after all, to receive this note from Friend. It is good to see that he is getting his feet back on the ground, and I have high hopes that the poems he will turn in to the Association magazine (it's called *Alienation First*) will be, like those in his first volume, among his best. His best, I should add, are very good. They have a fine clear music to them, a real melodic flow, and a kind of purity, a kind of detachment from mundane things that marks him, I think, as a lyricist of the first water. Indeed, if I have any complaint about his work, it is that too frequently he indulges himself in the kind of plagued-by-furies roughness and irony that you saw him demonstrating earlier. I think that if he can master this roughness and pay more attention to his true lyric tone he will shortly emerge as one of the best of our young-to-middle-aged alienated poets (that is, thirty to sixty-five). As for his feelings about the Bomb, well, looking at the end of his letter I would say that here too he seems to be calming down. You remember the sentence where he said that he couldn't stand being alone in his righteousness, and that when he found himself there he had to rethink and rewrite what he had written. Well, that's a good sign, isn't it?

I *am* a little worried, though, about some of the things he said about our Association. Also, as I write this the new bomb tests in the Pacific have just begun and I am worrying about them too—that is, I am worrying about how they will affect Friend. I don't know that he will be able to put them out of his mind and live again the fruitful artistic life he proposes. I still fear, in other words, for the tragic waste of a fine talent.

REED WHITTEMORE

Robert Browning

No more of the past! I'll look within no more.
I have too trusted my own lawless wants,
Too trusted my vain self, vague intuition—
Draining soul's wine alone in the still night.

Pauline

With these lines, and a thousand others, Browning at the age of twenty decided not to be an adolescent any more. Then he immediately undid the decision by getting the poem in which they appear published. Thereafter his feelings toward *Pauline* were only of repentance; thirty-five years later he included it in his collected works with, he said, "extreme repugnance."

What was the source of his annoyance? Serious students of Browning continue to read *Pauline* to find out, and continue to be disappointed. It is unquestionably a bad poem (though a copy of it is reported by Dean DeVane to have sold, fairly recently, for $16,000) , for it is almost unreadably disconnected and vague. But it is not bad in the way that the student might hope it to be bad: it is not racy. It purports to be a confession, a letting of cats out of the bag; but the "I" of the poem (who is Browning, despite Browning's later denials) is really remarkably reticent. He gives us no details, no private incidents, no positive revelations. He tells us merely that he likes Shelley, finds his own passions (whatever they were) disgusting, and is very, very young. He speaks for many pages in murky euphemisms dependent, primarily, upon the word "soul," and intermittently advises us that he is, by so doing, exposing his wicked past. No modern reader is likely to be impressed.

The next poem, *Paracelsus,* was published two years later. It also may be regarded as a poem of confession; read properly it seems to tell us something about Browning's relations with his parents. But it too is a disappointment as exposée. We learn in the first part that Paracelsus the poet, while most beholden to his friends Festus and Michal, has come to feel that they are holding him back, "as though [*sic*] a mother hoped/To stay the lusty manhood of the child/Once weak upon her knees." And what is it that Paracelsus is being held back from?—knowledge, power and eternal life. He needs to get out; he needs to travel, to wander over the face of the earth and pick up the "sacred knowledge" that will enable him to "beat" God's angels at their own game:

We ask
To put forth just our strength, our human strength,
All starting fairly, all equipped alike,
Gifted alike, all eagle-eyed, true-hearted—
See if we cannot beat thine angels yet!
Such is my task. I go to gather this
The sacred knowledge, here and there dispersed
About the world, long lost or never found.

And so he does go gathering, leaving the old folks at home. The results, which take four miserable books, are uneven. Like Dr. Faustus, Paracelsus succeeds in dazzling the world as a sort of doctor-astrologist-chemist; but at the end he is demonstrably a failure. He has discovered that man cannot compete with the angels, and dies admonishing Festus to remember the importance of love and God.

The differences between *Pauline* and *Paracelsus* are not

important. In the latter Browning succeeded in "distancing" himself from his narrator to a degree by basing his character upon a medieval physician. He did not, however, manage fully to commit himself to the activities of his original, who, despite Browning's researches, remains a nineteenth century introvert convinced that it is possible to talk abstractly and yet intelligently about knowledge, power and love so long as he comes to the job well equipped with exclamation points. The faint humanism emerging at the end when Paracelsus confesses that he "gazed on power" till he "grew blind," and that "hope and fear and love" had been "hid" from him, is unconvincing, since at no time have we seen either his powers or his blindness applied to a single event or situation; Paracelsus has merely talked our ears off *about* all this.

Disappointingly, in the next long poem, *Sordello,* and in several dramas written somewhat later (and actually conceived for stage production), the incessant abstract talk continues, though the verse changes somewhat in character. Browning had not learned his lesson. At the age of thirty, if judged by his most ambitious works, he appeared as an artist who had deliberately cultivated an art for which he was not suited. Probably no more undramatic poems than *Paracelsus* and *Sordello* have ever been written; probably no worse play than *A Blot in the 'Scutcheon* has ever been staged. And yet by this time in his career Browning had clearly persuaded himself that the drama was to be, even if offstage, his dish of tea. Why? Why did he want to write what he could not write? Why could he not settle for lyrics, for meditations, for straightforward expressions of his own feelings? He had precedents in Wordsworth, Keats, Shelley—particularly Shelley— and he could not seem to open his mouth without narcissistically discussing problems near and dear to himself: the problems of an artist, the problems of a "mother's boy." Why then did he not obey what seem to have been his natural impulses?

These are difficult questions, and they may be answered in

a number of ways. But before considering them I think it is necessary to point out that Browning's persistence in writing dramatically produced, ultimately, the poems for which he is now best known. In other words Browning seems to have been right about his talent after all; he could see in *Paracelsus* and *Sordello* the beginnings of a poetic procedure that in time he could master and make his own. In his struggles he was like a man who sets out to build a boat by building an airplane. He laboriously constructs the wings and the fuselage and the propeller while his audience stands around giggling; then he takes the machine down to the water and launches it, and lo! it *is* a boat after all, and a good one.

He was the son of a senior clerk of the Bank of England, and a pious lady with a square head. It has been common to make the father the chief influence in Robert's upbringing. The father had a big library; the father encouraged Robert to read Homer, Pope, Heine; the father encouraged Robert to write; the father understood. Recent studies of Browning have, however, taken the line that the father's role has been overrated and that, indeed, Robert was brought up in a matriarchy. Robert himself suggested as much in letters to his future wife Elizabeth Barrett, noting that his father had "the perpetual juvenility of a blessed child" and was as "gentle as a gentle woman." His most perceptive recent biographer, Betty Miller, finds in the son the same gentleness and juvenility, and makes an impressive case for regarding both of them as subjects, and willing subjects, rather than rulers in their households.*

It is not necessary to sustain such a thesis biographically to find, in the poetry of the son, a continuing preoccupation

---

* Prof. Elvan Kintner reports, as a frivolous instance of Mrs. Browning's ascendancy, that "the Browning family bulldog objected to overt tenderness by the Senior Browning toward his wife, and though intractable generally behaved like a lamb for her."

with the problems of being dependent. Looking at just a few of the most famous poems one discovers that the chief characters are caught, almost uniformly, in some sort of social situation that they do not control; further, that they are in varying degrees held down or repressed by that situation. Fra Lippo Lippi is a monk who ought not to have been a monk, and who accordingly has to break loose occasionally; Andrea del Sarto is a painter saddled with a wife who has effectively restrained him from doing his best work; Pompilia (the heroine of *The Ring and the Book*) is married to a man more than thirty years her senior who would have preferred to have her never leave the house; even Caliban of "Caliban upon Setebos" is an unhappy slave in the hands of a higher power than himself. All these various dependents have characteristics of their own, and it is not fair to the integrity of the individual poems to assert that they are *merely* projections of Browning's own problems. Yet dependency as a subject crops up so much in both his life and his art that it would seem to be equally unfair to accept unquestioningly his frequently repeated avowal that his work was "dramatic in principle, and so many utterances of so many imaginary persons, not mine." Browning indeed protested too much on this point; he is a fine example of a kind of artistic personality not uncommon in literature, one who resorts to literature to give his underground (his id) air, and then lets his above-ground (his ego) go about stormily denying what he has done.

For a detailed history of his dependency I recommend Miss Miller's book. Briefly, Browning was supported by his family until he reached the ripe age of thirty-four. His education was conducted very largely at home. His first books of verse were printed, and his first two trips abroad were financed, by his father and aunt. Furthermore, he lived at home, except for excursions, during this period. For a man born into the solid, work-respecting middle class, his failure to set out on his own was certainly unusual; and his idleness did not, therefore, escape notice. It particularly annoyed his future father-in-law who, Miss Miller reports, regarded his as "that man." And as the poems indicate, Browning himself was far from contented with his predicament. He would have liked to have broken away as Paracelsus did from Michal and Festus. He was thus unhappy in dependency and, at the same time, unprepared to change it, to follow Paracelsus's lead. Perversely he seems to have enjoyed what he sometimes found insufferable. And even when the great moment of breaking away and setting forth on his own finally arrived, he faced it hesitatingly, with all the vigor of a Casper Milquetoast.

This great moment was his elopement with Elizabeth Barrett. Miss Barrett was six years older than he, a semi-invalid, a poet, and a prisoner of her father:

. . . it was the tyranny of her father that kept her an invalid. The peculiar psychology which made Edward Barrett what he was had as its main constituent the religious, patriarchal conception of the family carried to the point of mania—a conception not unique among latter-day Puritans. He had scripture for it that the Lord was a jealous God and Barrett was made in his image. The family was not to be broken by marriage, and therefore the children, who at last had to be named Septimus and Octavius from the sheer scarcity of names, never dared mention the subject though they were approaching forty.

—*A Browning Handbook,* William Clyde DeVane

It was Miss Barrett's hope that a man as strong as her father would come along and carry her off to health and adulthood, but it was Robert who came along instead. The pages in Betty Miller's biography that describe Robert's evasion of his proper role make interesting reading: he expected Elizabeth to take the initiative, he insisted that "women were as strong as men," and he wanted to be "operated on." Miss Miller's conclusion, which seems thoroughly justified, is that neither of them had the willpower to get their elopement under way;

it was in effect forced on them by an unexpected attempt of Elizabeth's father to keep them apart. Under such conditions one can only wonder that the marriage succeeded at all.

But it did. They went off to Italy, leaving their respective prisons behind them, and lived there in relative amity and love for fifteen years. Elizabeth then died and Robert returned to London to live, having by then written most of his best work except *The Ring and the Book*. None of his books had, it is true, gone into a second edition; at the age of fifty he was only on the threshold of his subsequent worldly success. But he had at least mastered—or had mastered for him— the problem of being his own man. Furthermore he had done so without the unpleasantness that accompanied Elizabeth's breaking away. Mr. Barrett had disowned her when she left, and had died ten years later without ever forgiving her. Robert on the other hand had managed to enter upon and conduct his marriage without losing either his sense of obligation to his parents, or their affection. The tie went deep, it was never broken, and it had a permanent effect upon the character of his writings.

Because of Browning's excessive dependency upon his parents it is easy, and rather good sport, to look in the poems for references to it. In general critics have limited their search to the earlier poems, but the search, as I have suggested, need not stop there. Andrea del Sarto's failure to break away from a woman who had no interest in his art may, for example, be discovered to be a projection of Browning's own failure to convince his mother that poetry was better than Congregationalism. I am personally inclined to believe that such connections are reasonable, though Browning may not have been conscious of them; but I also think that such speculation is misleading. In the first place it suggests that Browning may be completely explained by describing his relationship with his family. In the second it suggests that his vision of life was

190

personal, eccentric, unworldly. The facts are otherwise. Browning's mind ranged widely, and many of the theses of his poems were commonplaces of his time.

He was a good Victorian. As such he was perhaps fortunate in being encouraged to cultivate, at home, a few solid repressions; they helped to make him a part of his age. For surely at the center of any definition of Victorianism must appear the word "respectability." Or perhaps "gentility." Cynics discoursing upon the Victorians note that Victorian morality did not go deep. They point out that politically and economically the last half of the nineteenth century was a great age for cut-throats; the lace curtains and inoffensive portraits lining a Victorian parlor were paid for by ivory from the heart of darkness or coal dug by England's own depressed proletariat. Similarly the literature of the time has been criticized for its duplicity or hypocrisy; much of it seems inappropriately ecstatic and idealistic for the sedentary age it catered to. There is, for example, an amusing sketch of Tennyson reading his famous poem, *In Memoriam,* to Queen Victoria, a sketch that represents the anomaly of a "poet of feeling" being encouraged, sponsored, patronized by upright stodginess: Lord Alfred is seated in a tremendous room on a frail wooden chair shouting his verses and waving his long arms as if leading a battalion into battle, while Queen Victoria is seated, about a hundred yards off, looking like a comfortable turnip. One might venture to put Browning in Tennyson's place, and Browning's mother in Queen Victoria's. Any artist, or any sensitive plant, born of the middle class at this time was likely to have some comfortable, and also moral, turnip to contend with.

The contention was necessarily aggravated among poets by the poetic tradition they grew up with. Shelley, for example, was Browning's childhood hero, and Shelley stood for breaking out, breaking away, breaking loose. How could one do all *that* and be a Victorian too? Shelley preached revolution, but

191

Browning was not up to revolution. Shelley preached atheism, but Browning tried out atheism briefly and abandoned it (because of his mother?) at length. Shelley preached the emotional and esthetic posturings that Browning put into *Pauline*, but Browning came quickly to reject *Pauline*. And yet, for all Browning's incapacity to be like Shelley, he never really abandoned Shelley. The Shelley in him went, as it were, underground; some of the least offensive elements of Shelley's romanticism became common elements in Browning's verse.

The "search for the infinite," for example. The phrase is Irving Babbitt's. He was describing with asperity a common romantic impulse or yearning to move onward or outward or upward toward a goal that is not only unattainable but also unimaginable, except in the vaguest terms. Shelley was a prime source, for Babbitt, of instances of this fruitless search. Shelley was always climbing or admiring climbers: he described Keats as one who "to that bright station [among the "sons of light"] dared to climb" and one who has "outsoared the shadow of our night;" and he asked the West Wind to "lift" him (that is, Shelley himself) "as a wave, a leaf, a cloud." He was probably most explicit about the purpose of his own climbing in *Queen Mab,* of which the following passage is characteristic:

> Soul of Ianthe! thou,
> Judged alone worthy of the envied boon,
> That waits the good and the sincere; that waits
> Those who have struggled, and with resolute will
> Vanquished earth's pride and meanness, burst the chains,
> The icy chains of custom, and have shone
> The day-stars of their age;—Soul of Ianthe!
> Awake! arise!
>
> Sudden arose
> Ianthe's Soul; it stood

All beautiful in naked purity,
The perfect semblance of its bodily frame.

Browning was not one to burst the icy chains of custom, but he admired from a distance those who did, and he emulated Shelley in his praise for soaring, climbing, reaching:

> For higher still and higher . . .
>> Up, the pinnacled glory reached, and the pride of
>> my soul was in sight.
>>> —"Abt Vogler"

> Ah, but a man's reach should exceed his grasp.
>> —"Andrea del Sarto"

>> No. I yearn upward, touch you close,
>> Then stand away. I kiss your cheek,
>> Catch your Soul's warmth . . . .
>>> —"Two in the Compagna"

> Yet the strong man must go:
> For the journey is done and the summit attained,
>> And the barriers fall,
> Though a battle's to fight ere the guerdon be gained,
>> The reward of it all
>>> —"Prospice"

Innumerable instances could be found to illustrate the point, but perhaps the best is from "Pauline," where Browning described Shelley (as Shelley described Keats) as a model soarer, in fact a "sun-treader." Of such yearnings upward Babbitt observed that the form the goal may take may be heaven, or a beautiful woman, or some vaguely earthly arcadia, but that the form is ultimately meaningless: "we think we see the Rousseauist prostrate before the ideal woman or before nature or before God himself, but when we look more closely we see that he is only (as Saint Beuve said of Alfred de Vigny) 'in perpetual adoration before the holy sacrament of himself.' "

The applicability of Babbitt's point to Shelley is hard to deny; Shelley was busy getting his soul airborne most of the time, and did not question the propriety of such an activity. But for Browning the display of his own passions (or, as a psychiatrist might say, the sublimating of them by the writing of climbing verse) was offensive, and so he attributed the passions to others. By doing this he modified and subdued them considerably; or perhaps it would be better to say that at his best he donated them to people on whom they were becoming, more becoming at any rate than on an incurable Victorian. This procedure, which may be found throughout the major works of the middle part of his career, is first clearly demonstrated in a little poem, "Porphyria's Lover" (1836), where the narrator-hero is presented as a madman. One can hardly imagine Robert seriously identifying himself with a madman, and yet the thesis with which this "lover" is entrusted is straight out of Shelley: the "lover" tells us that he has successfully broken the chains that have kept him and his loved one apart; he has made the jump (by killing the poor girl), with the result that their two souls have arisen like Shelley's Ianthe's, leaving behind "earth's pride and meanness."

The irony of entrusting a favorite thesis to a madman seems, from this distance, rather heavy. Was Browning *trying* to be ironic here, and telling us in effect that here was one thesis that had to be scrapped if the author of it were to be at home "in England, now?" Or was he—it seems unlikely— siding with the madman and advocating love-killings? The poem is fragmentary and irresolute on this point, which is perhaps as it should be. Clearly there is no satisfactory resolution for breaking the chains and at the same time being chained by them, and in my opinion it is to Browning's credit that he attempted none. There are, however, other opinions. In modern times there have been similar instances of romantics preaching what they have been unprepared to practice, and Browning might readily be classified with them. Yvor Winters, an American critic, in a well-known essay entitled "What are we to think of Professor X?" has, for example, sallied forth against certain teachers of American Literature who, from the security of their own social conformism, preach the anarchic doctrines of Emerson and Whitman. He compares them with a true romantic, Hart Crane (who committed suicide), and asserts that the chief difference between Crane and Professor X is that "Crane was absolutely serious and Professor X is not serious." The position of Professor X "is that of the dilettante: the nearest thing he has to a positive philosophy is something to which he would never dare commit himself; that which keeps him in order is a set of social proprieties which he neither understands nor approves." On the other hand Crane "had the absolute seriousness which goes with genius and sanctity; one might describe him as a saint of the wrong religion. He had not the critical intelligence to see what was wrong with this doctrine, but he had the courage of his convictions, the virtue of integrity, and he deserves our respect."

These are solemn words, and they may readily be applied to Shelley (equivalent to Crane) and Browning (equivalent to Professor X). But in defense of Browning it should be pointed out, first, that Browning seldom applied his romanticism as nakedly as he did in "Porphyria's Lover," and, second, that there are other ways of being "serious" than by having a considered, thought-through philosophy that one is prepared to act upon. It is the privilege of only a few to see things plain, and Browning was not among that elect. Instead he was one who had both to live and to cope intellectually with the world's contradictions and loose ends. From "Porphyria's Lover" with its loose end of what the hero-murderer will think when the dawn comes up, to *The Ring and the Book,* with its multiple and essentially unresolved analysis of the rights and wrongs of another murder, Browning was as seriously concerned with the defects and limitations of some of his era's pet theses as he was with advocating them. At his worst he was perhaps like Professor X, an unearnest preacher. But at his best he was something that a narrow moralist like Yvor Winters cannot understand.

Probably the best indication of how seriously Browning felt the contradictions in his life and writings is to be found in the poems that deal with hypocrisy, duplicity or downright fraud. The most celebrated Browning hypocrite is the Bishop in "The Bishop Orders His Tomb." Here is a man who seems to have been guilty of nearly all the sins, but who is at the same time a high-toned old Christian dignitary. Are we meant to disapprove of him? To read the poem properly, I think, is to put aside that moral decision and let the Bishop be what he had to be. And by what morality may the moral decision be omitted?—very simply, "whose house is of glass must not throw stones at another." Browning's house was of glass, and he knew it, and his way of facing (seriously) the fact of it was to write about it. He did. Among the poems selected for this volume the chief documents attesting to glass housery are, aside from the "Bishop" poem, "The Soliloquy of the Spanish Cloister," "Fra Lippo Lippi," "Bishop Blougram's Apology" and "Mr. Sludge, 'the Medium.'" In any of these poems it is possible, I think, to find analogues to Browning's own predicament as Victorian-Romantic affirmer, and in all of them Browning is surely at the top of his bent. On the other hand he is least persuasive, least clearly involved in what he is writing of, when he has created no contradictory character, like himself, to contend with. Then his work becomes placid, unruffled moralizing, as in "Prospice."

196

Modern critics of Browning have frequently been scornful of Browning's professed interest in character, declaring that at best the characters are thin disguises for Browning. This, as I have tried to indicate, is partly true, but the truth of it is deceptive, since the Browning in "Love Among the Ruins" is very different from the Browning in "The Bishop Orders His Tomb." In the former the lover is not only describing an impossibly ideal romance, but he has a romantic setting for it, an easy and maybe vulgar pastoral wasteland whose connection with any kind of life, much less Victorian London, has been effectively erased by a couple of thousand years of wind and rain. In the latter, however, the problems of Victorian London persist even though they have been transferred to Renaissance Italy. How to be pious and yet worldly, how to sail for the stars (Shelley's constant profession) and yet keep one's job in the Bank of England (Browning's father's constant profession) —these are matters that both cultures had to reckon with. It is therefore hardly a coincidence that Browning found so many fit subjects for poetry in Renaissance Italy; nor is it coincidence that his best poems have their settings there. It might be said that for Browning Renaissance Italy was a *fervent* London. It was more fervently virtuous, more fervently arty and more fervently worldly than London, but these differences, while great, did not outweigh the likenesses he found between them. Thus he could retreat to Renaissance Italy without feeling that he had retreated; he could put the distance that was so important to him between himself and his characters, and at the same time feel that he had not gone away.

This ambiguous relationship to the past may be profitably compared with his relationship with the art of poetry itself, where also he appeared as the servant of two masters. As I have said, he thought of himself as a dramatist, but not merely a dramatist. He was a poet-dramatist, which is a rather special

197

breed, and he was also a poet of the long poem, a poet in the "great" tradition of poetry. These rather obvious facts may not at first seem meaningful; but if it be considered that Browning and Tennyson (and perhaps Arnold) were among the last poets to *be* poets in this grand manner, and that accordingly they mark, in literary histories, the end of an era, then perhaps Browning's difficulties in trying to look up-to-date, to appear as a confronter of "reality," may be imagined.

Long poems *have* been written since Browning and Tennyson; so have verse plays. Even in the last twenty or thirty years a few long narrative poems have been awarded big literary prizes, and a few dramas in verse have made Broadway. It may, therefore, be a mistake to think of Browning and Tennyson as the last practitioners of a now dead art. But I don't think so. Qualifications must be made, but the qualifications do not eliminate the truth they qualify: our culture is no longer the possessor of two distinct rhetorics of consequence. A book-length narrative in verse or an undramatic verse drama is in our time a novelty, a phenomenon, as is the related conception of the poet as prophet or archbishop. But Browning and Tennyson were not novelties, even though they wrote in these now eccentric forms, and even though they set themselves up, in their latter years, as prophets and archbishops.

We are apt to forget the grandiose images they must have had of themselves. We go back to them now for their shorter and less pontifical works. We take Tennyson as a songbird, Browning as a one-act dramatic monologuist, and let them go at that. In doing so we are unquestionably doing them a favor, for we are letting the good live after them, the bad die; but we are also misrepresenting them; we are neglecting those works that make them most obviously Victorians, and therefore neglecting something about poetry, or at least poetry's past, that Browning and Tennyson can teach us. What this something is is hard to describe, but it has to do with the status of poetry in the world.

198

Status? The modern beginner with poetry—he who, for example, finds himself trapped in a sophomore survey course in English Literature—has a hard time understanding why his teacher makes such a fuss about poetry when for the most part that art is represented, in its later stages, by tiny selections of stanzas dealing with nightingales, cloistered monks, lotos eaters and golden insects in Byzantium. Not that there is anything wrong with lotos eaters. Not that there is anything wrong with tiny selections. But when one is as good as told that Western Culture hangs by these thin threads, then there is perhaps something wrong. And yet the student is frequently told this. He is told it by a teacher who, whether he knows it or not, has been conditioned to think of poetry as the Victorians did. The Victorians were the last people to have *evidence* to substantiate the great claims for poetry which are still being made. The evidence was poems, not quartos of them but bookshelves of them. Each of the most respected Victorian poets seems to have conceived it his goal to write a few epics in a lifetime, to fill out a ten- or twenty-volume uniform set. Furthermore, each of these respected poets conceived it his duty to write poetry that was clearly poetry, that is, poetry in verse. His training in verse began early and went forward relentlessly: he learned to rhyme and to write in regular cadences at about the time that the modern student is learning the components of a sentence; and he came of age convinced, if only by his upbringing, that poetry in verse was a wholly different dimension than prose. Thus it is no mere oddity that Tennyson wrote an epic of six thousand verse lines at the age of twelve, and that Browning's first published work (which appeared when he was twenty-one) was also in verse and was also, quantitatively, epic. Surely no modern schoolboy would make his first assaults upon literature in such a manner. If he were epically inclined he would start a novel, not a poem, in the nursery. Such a schoolboy has trouble, therefore, understanding why it is poetry, and not literature, that is described by his Victorian teacher as the greatest of the arts and our chief stay in a world of flux. He is accordingly gratified to discover that the word "poetry" is nowadays frequently defined without reference to verse, is defined simply as something of the imagination and vaguely "high."

Because of his dedication to verse Browning (like Tennyson and many others) developed for himself what now seems an odd philosophy of rhetoric. We want our language for any occasion to be simple, straightforward, clear and logical—and if it happens to be elegant too, well and good. Browning respected these qualities—like us he had been subjected to the call of "nature" in rhetoric—but he also had respect for, and training in, the qualities of that other, now nearly alien rhetoric which prescribed that sounds be repeated at certain intervals and that sentences be divided into feet. As a result his rhetorical headaches were frequently brought on by matters that seem to us to be largely irrelevant to the major problems of expression; and his sentences were frequently rendered devious, unclear and illogical by his commitment to such irrelevancies. He was indeed more guilty of these irrelevancies than Tennyson or his other contemporaries. He was a master of the bad verse line, the line that seems to be in verse only because the poet thinks anything is better in verse than in prose:

> Pray, Reader, have you eaten ortolans
> Ever in Italy?
> Recall how cooks there cook them: for my plan's
> To—Lyre with Spit ally.
> > —Prologue to "Ferishtah's Fancies"

Or:

> Ah, Tresham, that a sword-stroke and a drop
> Of blood or two, should bring all this about!
> Why, 'twas my very fear of you, my love

Of you— (what passion's like a boy's for one
Like you?) —that ruined me!
—*A Blot in the 'Scutcheon*

The first example may perhaps be justified as comic rhyming
and inversion, though Browning was capable of comic rhymes
and inversions when he was quite serious. But the second
example, drawn from what purports to be a drama, is inex-
cusable: the line divisions are meaningless, and yet insisted
upon by the meter; and the parenthetical remark is not only
nonsense but also impossibly literary and academic just at a
point when feeling should presumably be flowing freely and
without grammatical complication. How could Browning
have imagined that such lines would persuade any audience
that the character speaking is, as the story would have it,
dying? It is more reasonable for us to picture him as a wit
parodying rant. Browning never wholly mastered this weakness; he loved verbal ornamentation; he refused to worry
about the relevance of a description, an aside, a qualification;
and he could jumble completely the normal syntactical order
of a statement without a qualm.

Unquestionably he must be made personally responsible
for such vices; the climate in which he lived cannot be
blamed for everything. At the same time the climate encouraged him; it gave him a faith—which we have not got—in the
eternal efficacy of the most rudimentary properties of verse; it
enabled him to indulge his vices with confidence. And if he
had been a lesser poet than he was, or even less sensitive to
the demands and virtues of that other, plainer rhetoric than
he was, he probably would not have gotten beyond *Sordello*
or *A Blot in the 'Scutcheon.*

Fortunately he was a double man rhetorically as well as
thematically:

Thus much conceded, still the first fact stays—
You do despise me; your ideal of life

201

Is not the bishop's: you would not be I.
You would like better to be Goethe, now,
Or Buonoparte, or, bless me, lower still,
Count D'Orsay,—so you did what you preferred,
Spoke as you thought, and, as you cannot help,
Believed or disbelieved, no matter what,
So long as on that point, whate'er it was,
You loosed your mind, were whole and sole yourself.
—That, my ideal never can include,
Upon that element of truth and worth
Never be based! for say they make me Pope—
(They can't—suppose it for our argument!)
Why, there I'm at my tether's end, I've reached
My height, and not a height which pleases you:
An unbelieving Pope won't do, you say.
It's like those eerie stories nurses tell,
Of how some actor on a stage played Death,
With pasteboard crown, sham orb and tinselled dart,
And called himself the monarch of the world;
Then, going in the tire-room afterward,
Because the play was done, to shift himself,
Got touched upon the sleeve familiarly,
The moment he had shut the closet door,
By Death himself. Thus God might touch a Pope
At unawares, ask what his baubles mean,
And whose part he presumed to play just now.
Best be yourself, imperial, plain and true!
                              —"Bishop Blougram's Apology"

Here is a passage of mature Browning. The theme is the familiar, insistent one of how difficult it is to live two lives. The
language is, similarly, a mixture of two impulses, poetic and
prosaic. On the one hand it is removed from the world of
prose because of the iambic and because of its regular insistence upon verbal compression—for example, "at una-

wares" rather than "when he least expected it." On the other hand it is clearly prosaic in the secondary sense of the word "prosaic": its tone is matter-of-fact, reasonable, chatty rather than intense, soaring. It is also full of interjections and asides which add to its air of informality, making it seem spontaneous rather than contrived. All in all it is a fine example of how Browning could, under the proper conditions, merge his two rhetorics into a sensible whole.

But why do I find the interjections appropriate here, when I found them clumsy in the passage quoted earlier from *A Blot in the 'Scutcheon?* There are probably several reasons (one of them is that the 'Scutcheon lines *are* clumsy), but an important one is that the 'Scutcheon lines are inappropriate for the occasion: Browning had a poetic moment on his hands and was playing it as if it were a prosaic moment. In "Bishop Blougram's Apology," on the other hand, the occasion is right: the scene is a parlor; the situation is almost academic, involving merely a quiet evening of good talk over a long drink. Such a time is appropriate for the conversational, low-pitched tone Browning was best at.

Browning apparently wanted to be chatty and conversational at all times; but as he also wanted to be intense, dramatic and poetic on occasion, he was frequently chatty when he should not have been. Thus, although his dramatic qualities are those to which a teacher inevitably refers to first and most frequently, and although students will continue to classify the poor man, until the end of the world, by saying, "Browning? He wrote dramatic monologues," his capacities for the dramatic were very limited in scope. "Bishop Blougram's Apology" has perhaps too sedentary a situation; it is *merely* discussion. "Childe Roland" is perhaps not sedentary enough. But between these two poems, both of which have great merit, lies the domain in which Browning could write most comfortably.

This is the domain of "My Last Duchess," "The Bishop

Orders His Tomb," "Andrea del Sarto," "Fra Lippo Lippi," "Caliban upon Setebos," "A Toccata of Galuppi's" and *The Ring and the Book* (I regret that *The Ring and the Book* cannot be represented in an anthology of this size). In these Browning had plenty of drama to draw upon, to talk about, to refer to; yet he managed to keep all action offstage, and in fact reduce the action to simple parlor discussions.

Here he found his natural element. Here he could indulge his soaring spirit and at the same time remain comfortably seated in an overstuffed chair. Shelley would have disapproved. Yvor Winters has disapproved. Sometimes Browning himself seems to have disapproved. But it is to his credit that he recognized the doubleness of his impulses and strove to make the best of them. He did so by modeling himself and his work after some of his own most attractive characters. To like his Bishops, his Fra Lippo Lippi and his Andrea is to like him. Though different, they all seem to be from the same contrarious family.

The Virtues of Vulgarity—Russian and American Views

(Dostoevsky, Scott Fitzgerald, Marlon Brando, Norman Mailer, Beats and Buffoons)

In America the word "vulgar" has become, except in the etiquette books, a meaningless political word like "fascist," and is therefore used largely as an epithet to describe the opposition, whoever it may be. English teachers like me normally bemoan the fate of such words, their loss of meaning; but I think that in this case the fate is so natural and reasonable that I will shed no tears. After all, the word *does* mean "low" or "common," and what are one's enemies but (though not always common) low? Thus the middle classes may think of the lower classes as vulgar, but the lower classes may return the insult. Similarly our literary scholars may find our popular literature vulgar, our bourgeoisie may find our beat literature vulgar, and the beats may find *all* their enemies vulgar —though the beats in fact, and with some justice, think of the word "vulgar" as itself vulgar, and favor instead "square," which is equally an epithet and, equally also, a term describing something low. Lastly any of these groups, or representatives thereof, may undertake to describe *themselves* as vulgar, though only in a favorable sense—that is, virtuous-vulgar. I will go into this common inversion at some length, but the image I would have you retain of it is of a lad with a rough exterior and a heart of gold.

Despite this sad state of "vulgarity," I wish to resurrect it here—or at least talk around it—to make a point about American literature and its relation to manners, literary and social. I was led to my enterprise by Dostoevsky. I reread *The Brothers Karamazov* recently and was struck by the amount of energy expended by its characters, and by Dostoevsky himself, in worrying about what is vulgar, and why, and how. I was also struck by the un-American uses of the word. Unlike us, Dostoevsky thinks "big" about vulgarity, as about anything else; and in doing so he is, he insists, being merely Russian. One of his characters, Ivan Karamazov, describes this Russian disease of bigness; he says that when Russians, even the simplest of Russians, meet in a tavern they talk "of the existence of God and immortality" or of "socialism or anarchism, of the transformation of all humanity on a new pattern, so that it all comes out the same." Vulgarity comes out the same too. The vulgarity of the Karamazovs is tremendous, but it is not produced by a lack of a sense of good form, etiquette, decorum—indeed they are always tremendously sensitive to their own social or intellectual *faux pas*. It is produced instead, if we are to believe them, by the spirit of Karamazovism itself, which hurries them all to their respective ends. Thus one may say of a Dostoevskan character that he finds a continuously intimate connection between proper conduct and true virtue—or, more frequently, improper conduct and true vice. Vulgarity tends to be equated with sin and frailty.

Dmitri Karamazov will serve well to introduce this spirit, with which he is obsessed. At one point he has just received a letter from the rich lady Katerina, in which she has said, "I want to save you from yourself." Dmitri describes the letter to Alyosha, and when he repeats Katerina's words he says, "Alyosha, I am not worthy to repeat those lines in my vulgar words and in my vulgar tone, my everlastingly vulgar tone, that I can never cure myself of." Now here, clearly, vulgarity has jumped its familiar (American) borders. In the first place Dmitri is not speaking in a drawing room, where his manners might be imagined to matter, but to his brother. And in the second place Dmitri is just not a man to worry at length about his drawing room conduct except as that conduct reflects something deeper in himself. Like the other Karamazovs, and indeed like all the other characters in the book, he bears no resemblance to the virtuous-vulgar American lad I mentioned. Vulgarity, for Dmitri, is equivalent to moral depravity. Dmitri is saying that such fine sentiments are tainted by his speaking them. They are sentiments he could never have himself, and can only speak sneeringly of; but they are nonetheless high sentiments (not merely decorous statements) , and they deserve better treatment in and out of drawing rooms than he can give them.

The opposite attitude toward vulgarity or impropriety can readily be found in much of our popular literature, and a fairly recent Marlon Brando movie about Japan provides a good example. In it the very issues that Dmitri would have been obsessed by are sidetracked and left completely undiscussed in any Karamazovian sense, even though the occasion for discussion has been set up at length and with care. Marlon, an Air Force pilot with seven enemy planes to his credit, is given the opportunity to "lacerate" (a Dostoevskan word) himself endlessly, if he should so choose, about whether or not to marry a Japanese girl. He is a gentleman of the Old South, the son of a well-starred general, and the fiancé of a high-bred Virginian beauty who shows up in Japan early in the film to make things hard for him. Everybody, including Marlon, wrestles politely for a couple of hours with the color line, military regulations and doing the "right thing," and then Marlon decides that love is best, at which point two subordinates commit suicide for love, and Marlon and his

Japanese girl prepare to face the upholders of tradition and decorum together. Finis. Superficially the story resembles the story of Dmitri's difficulties with, on the one hand, the Lady Katerina and, on the other, the postitute Grushenka; Dmitri also decides against the "right" girl, and he also has to face a certain amount of social disapproval (though it is mostly ridicule) for his choice. But there the similarity ends, and it ends, I would say, because Marlon's relationship to the proprieties of the situation are so much simpler than Dmitri's.

Dmitri's troubles begin where Marlon's leave off. Dmitri must examine himself and all his motives; he must investigate the nature of his love and discover the dark truth that there is nothing in the least admirable about it; he must then decide for love *anyway* because, ultimately, he is beyond decision, hopelessly base, hopelessly given over to his lusts and his "vulgar tone," in short a Karamazov. But as for Marlon, I cannot even remember where he personally decided that love was best. It was clear to the audience from the beginning that love was *to be* discovered best, and since the film made no effort to blur that conventional clarity, Marlon's decision, and all his thoughts preceding his decision, were unimportant. The film's mission was one of proving the already proved; Marlon did not have to lacerate himself at all about his vulgar tone since, in the mind of the character he was playing, it just wasn't vulgar.

To put this another way Marlon's rebellion against army regulations and the Old South is not a rebellion at all, as the film would have us believe, but merely a switching of allegiance from one set of proprieties to another, a switching which does not for a moment do what it is supposed to do for our hero—that is, allow him to find himself (or at least start looking). To use Scott Fitzgerald's word he is as *paralyzed* after the switch as he was before. He and we have learned nothing by espousing Browning rather than Emily Post.

Paralyzed. According to Edmund Wilson, Fitzgerald was

once all fired up about the paralyzing effects on a man of trying to observe the social amenities, whatever they might be. Fitzgerald was inspired by a reading of Emily Post to think about writing a play "in which all the motivations should consist of trying to do the right thing." As he conceived it the characters would be "set at cross-purposes through stalemates of good form, from which the only possible rescue would be through the intervention of some bounder as *deus ex machina* to put an end to the suffering of the gentlefolk who had been paralyzed by Mrs. Post's principles." But *what sort* of an end, I wonder. Were they to be released to Abraham's bosom, or simply let out of the stuffy and paralyzing parlor? I assume the latter; I assume the play would have been a farce built upon the tired thesis, usually attributed to Rousseau, that man is good, civilization is bad; hence all that needs to be done to save man is to remove him from the source of vice, in this case the parlor.

It is quite remarkable how the Rousseau thesis, like an indigent relative, hangs on in our literature. Time and Freud don't seem to budge it. As a result we still produce an incredible number of heroes who are above manners and make virtue of being indecorous, like Lt. Henry or any character that Gary Cooper ever played. Also as a result we produce a number of characters who are well-mannered, but distraught *underneath*. Their "presence" is always perfect; they never bat an eye or drop a teacup even when they are lacerated to the teeth. Now sometimes the results are fine. I would be the last to deny that the whole of a serious character can be expressed by presenting his parlor being, or to affirm that a character who is tight-lipped in public simply has no character. But all too frequently the results are poverty and famine for the characters involved; they become thin advertisements for that literary device known as understatement, which in their cases might better be called insufficient statement. Their authors, in denying that manners are a clue to character, lose a lot of important evidence which they cannot readily replace.

The Karamazovs on the other hand are never paralyzed by "good form." Instead they are inspired by it to new heights and depths. Indeed, "good form"—and all the immense difficulties attendant upon displaying it—is precisely what *produces* their character for Dostoevsky. Dostoevsky has been called a novelist of ideas, and a novelist of the faith, and a novelist of the inner man—and I would not wish to deny him these titles. But he earns these titles, these other titles, partly by also being a novelist, though indecorous, of manners. The manners of Dmitri—and by this I mean his "vulgar tone"—are if you will the medium through which his ideas, his convictions and his inner torments are expressed. This is also true of Ivan and Alyosha, his two brothers. And even the lesser figures of the book are characterized as much by *how* they say and do things as by what they say and do. They are never, as in Shaw, mouthpieces for a position or an attitude. They are all lacerated inside, and their lacerations are made evident, not concealed, by their manners. This is particularly true of that relatively large group of curiosities whom Dostoevsky describes as buffoons.

Buffoonery, like vulgarity, to which it is closely related, is a big word for Dostoevsky and does not mean simply "the business of amusing others by tricks, antic gestures, etc." If it is a business at all, it is apt to be a dark business, a business undertaken by somebody whose antic spirit is a mask for a lost spirit. As Alyosha puts it, "There are people of deep feeling who have been somehow crushed. Buffoonery in them is a form of resentful irony against those to whom they daren't speak the truth, from having been for years humiliated and intimidated by them. Believe me, Kolya, that sort of buffoonery is tragic." These crushed people can clearly be related to Fitzgerald's paralyzed people, and we might expect of them therefore that they would be unable to act, move, talk or even drink; they would be the Caspar Milquetoasts of the Volga. In fact, however, the typical Dostoevskan buffoon emerges as just the opposite: he is a bull in a china shop, a drawing-room wrecker, a burlesque villain in an Emily Post skit about The Man Who Spoiled the Party.

The father Karamazov, Fyodor, is a spectacular example of this curious breed. Fyodor is even more self-conscious about his own grossness than Dmitri, but his self-consciousness exhibits itself differently. For one thing he must be vulgar in public; there he turns handsprings to show everybody what an idiot he is, and, having shown them, must continue to show them:

. . . as soon as he had delivered his tirade, he felt he had been talking absurd nonsense, and at once longed to prove to his audience and above all to himself, that he had not been talking nonsense. And, although he knew perfectly well that with each word he would be adding more and more absurdity, he could not restrain himself, and plunged forward blindly.

"How shocking," cried Miusov.

For another thing he is, unlike Dmitri, sentimental about his vices. He loves them; they are all he has; tears more of joy than sorrow come stagily to his eyes when he contemplates what a wicked old man he is. Here is an instance, from one of his conversations with Alyosha:

The wenches won't come to me of their own accord, so I will need money. So I am saving up more and more, simply for myself, my dear son. You may as well know. For I mean to go on in my sins to the end, let me tell you.

My dear son, indeed. And yet it *is* his dear son he is addressing. It is Alyosha, his favorite; and one can imagine how pitiful a figure Fyodor would like to think of himself as being, as he informs Alyosha of his bad, not his good intentions. This is buffoonery if you will, but buffoonery of the soul. As with Dmitri's "vulgar tone" it cannot be dismissed as a superficial characteristic of his being.

Another buffoon, for whom we are expected to have more sympathy, is a certain Captain Snegiryov. He is poor; he is wholly "crushed" by the mess that his life has become; but he at the same time retains his conventional military notions of honor, thus emerging frequently as both proud and submissive. At one point Alyosha offers him 200 rubles from Lady Katerina; the offer sets him off. He first accepts the money with tears of gratitude, then suddenly crumples the money up and shouts, "So much for your money," trampling it under foot. Then he starts to run away:

> He turned quickly and began to run. But he had not run five steps before he turned completely around and threw a kiss to Alyosha. He ran another five yards and then turned around for the last time. This time his face was not contorted but quivering all over with tears. In a faltering, sobbing voice he cried: "What would I say to my boy if I took money from you for our shame?"
>
> And then he ran on without turning. Alyosha looked after him grieved. Oh, he understood that till the very last moment the captain had not known he would crumple up and fling away the notes . . .

A buffoon? A man who makes a business of amusing others by tricks, antic gestures, etc.? Obviously not—and the difficulty can not be explained away by saying that "buffoon" is a poor English equivalent for a more comprehensive Russian word. I know no Russian, but it seems to me that the word "buffoon" is an apt one in context, or at least would be if we had a less limited tradition of buffoonery.

In what sense limited? An English or American buffoon is primarily a clown. He may have his tragedies, as Lear's fool had, or as Charlie Chaplin in his various roles had; and he may therefore emerge as a character not to be dismissed as

Comic Relief. But no matter how seriously human he may become, he remains an alien in the world; he remains set apart from the other characters by his dress (a clown outfit, baggy pants, a mask) or his actions (he doesn't walk but executes a parody of walking, or runs, or dances) or his talk (he is cryptic or incoherent, or he doesn't speak at all). And so his misfortunes, though they may be formidable, can only be regarded with detachment—the misfortunes of a very distant relative, not "one of us." A Dostoevskan buffoon, on the other hand, is one of the family: for example, the traits which make father Fyodor a buffoon are not peculiar to him but are simply Karamazovian. In reverse it would not be unjust to call Dmitri, the hero, himself a buffoon; indeed he is not distinguished from his father by his actions—which are surely the actions of a thoroughgoing buffoon—but by his continuing awareness of, and sensitivity to, the social consequences of his buffoonery. The father is "way out"; he has long since given up caring what "people think" of his vulgarities, his buffooning; but the son, still committed to the affairs of the world, and still concerned with trying to live up to the social and moral demands of that world, is constantly overwhelmed by his own way-outness. He is in other words a buffoon who has not as yet given in to his buffoonery, but is struggling to hang on to social normalcy, though he knows he can't. Otherwise he has all the buffoon qualities of his father; he is, in fact, buffoon and hero all at once.

This combination is rare in our literature, though we have a few characters who come close and therefore are worth mentioning here. There is Gatsby, for example. Gatsby looks, in some respects, like an American buffoon on the Russian model. He is vulgar, inept, given to fantastic displays of his misfittedness, and at the same time a good bit more than funny or pathetic. There's a lot of Fitzgerald in Gatsby, and it's too bad we don't have more of him in the novel that goes by his name. He remains mysterious, distant and pretty much undeveloped, so that we get a whiff of him but not the whole, potentially fragrant buffoon. Instead we are shifted off to the other characters who, in their good American way, follow the Marlon Brando pattern of just not penetrating the surface of the manners complex in which they live. Unlike them Gatsby has the makings of something big, something Russian-big.

Another example is Holden Caulfield in *Catcher in the Rye*. Holden also looks at first like a fine buffoon, a wonderfully serious buffoon, and therefore a literary oddity. The first thing one ever remembers about him is his vulgarity; his vulgarity never lets down and it certainly isn't, as in the case of Gatsby, *played* down. Furthermore, his awareness of his own vulgarity is what creates all the tension in him and makes him a more complete character than Gatsby. Thus he, even more than Gatsby, seems to me to be a model for the American writer who wishes to avoid the Marlon Brando treatment of manners.

And yet both Gatsby and Holden Caulfield do partake of the Rousseau myth to a degree, and no Rousseauist can, I submit, be a buffoon. He can't because he can never believe that his social failings are, ultimately, failings. Instead the failings are society's; he is normal and society is the buffoon. As a result only a clown—that is, a half-wit—can successfully play the buffoon to the idiot image of society that the Rousseauist entertains. The Rousseauist can simply not imagine a Dmitri, for his Dmitri has to be right; his Dmitri has to be the one sane voice in an insane world, in short not Dmitri at all. Thus Gatsby may not be able to say "Oxford," but he is morally superior to his neighbors who can; and Holden's vulgarity is more than matched by the vulgarity of those around him. In both cases the pure sensitive Spirit is ultimately exalted at the expense of the culture in which it lives.

And now, the beats. The word "buffoon" is a square's word; to call a beat a buffoon is like calling a junky naughty;

but otherwise there would seem to be considerable justification for thinking of the beats as buffoons. They, like the Dostoevskan characters discussed, insist upon their vices, glory in their perversities, exhibit their faults shamelessly like Fyodor or Captain Snegiryov. I think, for example, that the following speech, which has already been quoted, could be readily converted to beatdom by changing the lingo a bit (unfortunately I'm not the man to do it):

The wenches won't come to me of their own accord, so I will need money. So I am saving up more and more, simply for myself, my dear son. You may as well know. For I mean to go on in my sins to the end, let me tell you.

But our beats, alas, lead double lives; they do not—at least the literary ones—seem to take their beatdom seriously. On the one hand they will hole up with their marijuana and on the other they will start a little magazine dedicated, with utmost moral earnestness, to the destruction of middle-class morality. Indeed their moral arrogance, their assurance of their ultimate rightness, is one of the remarkable anomalies of our time—and I can only explain it by saying lamely that it is the American Way to make a *good* thing of something, anything, while it is not the American Way to have doubts about what we can make a good thing of. Our logic is circular —we are constitutionally indisposed to contemplate the possibility that we are *really* wrong, or beat, or weak; rather than do that we will sell wrongness for rightness at $5.00 a copy and become the head of a publishing company. No Dmitris can emerge from such a fantasy; it is Rousseau's fantasy basically, and it simply does not admit any sensible consideration of human weakness. Instead the *in*human is discovered to be weak; the laws, customs, conventions and manners are wrong; the class is wrong; the era is wrong—as if somehow these entities had a capacity for, and a will for, error all their own!

215

Norman Mailer's *Advertisements for Myself* is the latest beat work that I have read, so I will mention it here though I am not sure that I think Mailer thinks he's a beat at all (see Gore Vidal's piece in *The Nation* in January, 1960). I read it when I was flat on my back with pneumonia and had just stopped smoking; I was thus ripe for revolution, and was pleased to read as follows:

> We have grown up in a world more in decay than the worst of the Roman Empire . . . America is a hurricane, and the only people who do not have the sound are those fortunate if incredibly stupid and smug white Protestants who live in the center . . . our literary gardeners, our publishers, editors, reviewers, and general flunkeys, are drunks, cowards, respectables, prose couturiers, fashion mongers, old maids, time servers, and part-time pimps on the Avenue of President Madison . . ."

These are isolated sentences, chosen from here and there, but they give the flavor, a flavor that I found just great as I lay there in bed, not smoking. Not smoking makes you aware of decay, hurricanes, timeserving, and anyway Mailer was good relaxed sickbed reading; I could skip around, reading a story here, an essay there, and then (for some real polemic) the "advertisements" themselves, which were Mailer's own Dmitrying, his own notes from underground. In my weakened condition I thought at first that Mailer was doing just fine as a beat, particularly since he was so much more literate than most of the beats I had read. It was only when I started to regain my strength, to get out of bed, to walk around in my bourgeois bathrobe and to begin to think of myself again as a responsible member of that set of "incredibly stupid and smug White Protestants," that I began to doubt Mailer's position. Not that I am much of a Protestant (though white, stupid and smug), but I live in the heart of stupid and smug white Protestant country, I teach at a stupid and smug white Protestant school, I am writing this for a sheet which I trust

216

will be financed by stupid, smug, white Protestants, and I have a stupid, smug, white Protestant family. All in all, therefore, I felt (as I regained my strength and began to *care*) that Mailer was calling me names.

I was *not* offended. I have made a profession of being nothing if not critical of my set. I was, however, struck by the virulence or intemperance—I might even say vulgarity—of Mailer's attack. Indeed intemperance was the book's guiding principle; intemperance was what had been making me content there in bed, not smoking—I had needed a little vicarious bang from outer space, and I had been getting it from Mailer's rockets, of which more:

The only one of my contemporaries who I felt had more talent than myself was James Joyce . . .
Everyone who knows the South knows that the white man fears the sexual potency of the Negro . . .
I wish to attempt an entrance into the mysteries of murder, suicide, incest, orgy, orgasm and Time. These themes are now filling my head and make me think I have a fair chance to become the first philosopher of Hip.

But where did this intemperance lead? to the self-flagellations of a Dmitri? to professions of weakness, insufficiency, buffoonery? Far from it. I emerged with an image of Mailer on a white horse ("Bolingbroking," as Vidal put it), conducting a campaign, promoting himself and his various causes with all the talents at his disposal. I should add that the talents seemed very considerable, a powerful mixture of Pegler, D. H. Lawrence and a fine old Chicago anarchist I ran into long ago who wrote: "Dynamite! of all the good stuff, this is the stuff. Stuff several pounds of this sublime stuff into an inch pipe (gas or water pipe) . . ." and so forth.

I don't know that Mailer is destined to be the penultimate beat, as he proposes to be; perhaps there are other beats who will stick to their business of *being* beat more effectively. But whether he succeeds or not his book may, I think, be put on the shelf as a fine example of the anomaly I have spoken of. Then to put *The Brothers Karamazov* beside it is to understand, I think, how little the beats have done, despite their protestations, to deal with the terrors of the underground, to cope with the tragedy of human insufficiency, which is one of literature's continuing occupations. It is to understand that the beats are basically good, virtuous-vulgar American heroes too, though our postmasters can hardly be expected to think so.

But Seriously

I.

This will not be a lecture on the general aesthetic—or perhaps I should call it mystique—of humor. I am sure that many of you know a good deal more than I about the complex history of the word "humor," as well as about those related words "wit," "comedy" and "satire." I want to get to a specific point about modern humor and don't want to have to slosh through miles and miles of *The Anatomy of Melancholy* and George Meredith and Sigmund Freud to get to it. All the same I think I must first pay at least token respects (about fifteen minutes' worth) to the scholarly principle that we should know a little bit about what we're talking about before we talk. So I'll turn right to the dictionary (the scholar's way of livening up a party):

Humorist 1) one who attributes all diseases to a depraved state of the humors; 2) a person who acts according to his humor; one easily moved by fancy, whim or caprice; a person of eccentric conduct or uncertain temper; 3) a person who possesses the faculty of humor; one who entertains by the exercise of a comical fancy; a humorous talker, writer or actor; a wag; a droll.

—Century Dictionary

We can, I think, eliminate the first meaning as no longer of

219

consequence, though it is an interesting historical source for the modern meanings. Some of you may think that we should also eliminate meaning two, since when we now talk of humorists we are not talking about their character or temper —that is, about their private being—but about their capacity to entertain us in a certain way, that is, about their public conduct as artists of a certain kind. Thus Jack Benny and Mort Sahl are humorists when they are on stage, but for all we know or care they are not, in their private world, eccentric or capricious or of uncertain temper. Our concern —our intellectual concern—is with the profession and the works of the humorist rather than his temperament—meaning simply that we intellectuals scorn private details about how many sweaters Mort Sahl buys.

I confess, however, that I am interested in the temperament of the humorist (meaning 2)—not perhaps in the private life of any particular humorist but in the disposition or frame of mind which produces humor, and particularly in the dispositions of those humorists we call satirists—for satirists are humorists of a sort: I now return you to the dictionary:

Satire 1) a species of composition originally in verse characterized by the expression of indignation, scorn or contemptuous facetiousness, denouncing vice, folly, incapacity or failure, and holding it up to reprobation or ridicule; a species of literary production cultivated by ancient Roman writers and in modern literature, and directed to the correction of corruption, abuses or absurdities in religion, politics, law, society and letters. 2) Hence, in general, the use, in either speaking or writing, of irony, sarcasm, ridicule, etc., in exposing, denouncing or deriding vice, folly, indecorum, incapacity or insincerity.

Then a fine quote from Dryden:

Satire has always shone among the rest,
And is the boldest way, if not the best,

To tell men freely of their foulest faults,
To laugh at their vain deeds and vainer thoughts.

And also a quotation (from the *Century*) from one R. Garnett which is relevant here:

without humor, satire is invective; without literary form, it is mere clownish jeering.

This should be enough to establish a relationship between humor and satire; satire normally has a moral or social purpose which humor, all by itself, does not necessarily have; and satire is also something of some literary pretensions.

Now with this word "satire"—as in the case of "humor" or "humorist"—we can also conduct a discussion without reference to the personality of the satirist, but again I prefer not to do so. It seems to me we can distinguish between satirists, we can place them and even judge them by discussing the nature and extent of their *commitment* to the business of "exposing, denouncing or deriding." First, that commitment may be merely professional, a commitment to the period between the raising and lowering of the stage curtain, or it may be, as it were, a way of life; and second, that commitment may proceed from arrogance and some tremendous personal sense of righteousness, or it may proceed out of humility and a sense of all of us being in the same leaky boat.

As to the first point, I think I can demonstrate what I mean by the *extent* of a satirist's commitment, by referring you to the title of my lecture, "But Seriously." You have all heard afterdinner speakers begin, according to prescription, with a joke which may or may not have a moral or political edge to it, and then get down to the business at hand—some praise of the American Way or the Rights of Man perhaps—with the phrase, "But seriously." For such a speaker it is quite possible to tell a joke completely opposed thematically to his "serious" thesis—we see banal examples of this in the painful banter between our highest-priced humorists: Bob Hope will spend an evening making jokes about Bing Crosby, and then say "But seriously;" and you know what follows: a few moments of sentiment about good old Bing. But for the satirist to do this is, for my money, to remove him from the ranks of "serious" practitioners of the art; it is to say in effect that the art has no relation to anything but is a rhetorical device without substance. On the other hand our great satirists from, say, Cervantes to Mark Twain have not, I think, normally displayed such schizophrenic tendencies; their satire seems to have been, as in the definition (number two, of humor), a part of their temperament, a part of their whole being.

As to the second point, the source of their commitment to this curious activity, some of you doubtless know Freud's famous essay on wit and its relation to the subconscious in which he points out that one of the major kinds of wit or humor, what he calls tendentious wit, proceeds out of an impulse to aggress against someone who is, for many possible reasons, unassailable with more conventional weapons. Thus if I tell a joke at the expense of poor Dr._____sitting innocently here, I am careful to do so with all of you for an audience; for me to tell the joke to Dr._____in person would not be aggressive enough; just to have *him* laugh (at his own expense) if he chose to would have none of the delightful rewards for my malicious soul of hearing all of *you* laugh at him. Well, in a larger sense I suppose that a good deal of our social and political satire is motivated at least in part by private desires to aggress upon some opposing party or faction or person of whom we are envious or to whom we are otherwise ill-disposed for not very noble reasons. I recommend the Freud essay to you if you haven't read it, for it is not only a fascinating essay but it is also loaded with some very funny examples of this kind of wit. I think though that for my purposes it is sufficient to say here that, 1) *mere* malice or *mere* aggressiveness is not apt to be the source of good satire and that, 2) the writer who never makes himself the object of his own satire—that is, includes himself in—is probably neglecting his best subject matter.

So much for introduction. I hope you see that I have in my mind's eye an ideal satirist who is happy in his work (taking it "seriously") and who, though perhaps stuffed to the gills with subconscious aggressions, has also a sense of justice, truth, all that. I doubt, however, that many such satirists have ever lived; the trade breeds, as the definition of humor suggests, eccentrics, men governed by whim and fancy. This, I suppose, is one of the reasons why those afterdinner speakers always hasten in with their "but seriously." They do not want to be thought of as eccentric.

I can't say that I blame them. It is not nice to be thought of as eccentric, though it is always nice to be known as a chap who tells funny jokes. The afterdinner humorist who then turns serious has the best of two worlds by his action, and will therefore probably be elected president of the Junior Chamber next year. Still, I do think that the patronizing attitude he thus displays toward humor, though understandable, is a bit thick all in all. I am one of those who, when I look at history, literary and social, find that I side pretty steadily with history's eccentrics. I don't mean all the mad astrologists and mystics—the best satirists have not, I think, gravitated toward exotic ideals and idealisms—but simply the mundane eccentrics who have stood on the sidelines with the game in progress, and made frosty remarks instead of cheering. The kings and noblemen and high churchmen, the generals and senators and big-league pundits—all these responsible gentlemen who have had and continue to have the burdens of the world upon their shoulders make less of an impression upon me than the fools (like Lear's fool) and the Hamlets and the Falstaffs, the Sancho Panzas and Huck Finns and Holden Caulfields. It is in this sense, you see, that I suppose I have the disposition, the temperament of a humorist.

Now I know that such a humorous disposition may not be

attended by a real comic or satiric talent; but on the other hand, I do not think that the talent will get anywhere without the disposition either; hence my preoccupation here with these nonliterary matters. What I am saying is perhaps summed up in a rather bad poem by W. H. Auden, "Under Which Lyre," in which he divides the world up into Hermes men and Apollo men. The Apollo men are the rulers, the responsible, serious citizens I have described, and you find them in all walks of life organizing things, improving the curriculum, sending out questionnaires, talking of the challenge of the future, serving on committees. The Hermes men, on the other hand, are busy sniping around the edges, complaining about some sociologist's rhetoric, irresponsibly toasting Castro, and putting salt in the Dean's coffee. Auden, who professes to side with the Hermes men in the poem, points out that the world would be a very badly run place if it were run by the Hermes men:

> Apollo loves to rule, has always done it;
> The earth would soon, did Hermes run it,
>   Be like the Balkans.

Even so he thinks he would prefer the Balkans, and so he concludes the poem with ten commandments for Hermes men:

> Thou shalt not do as the dean pleases,
> Thou shalt not write thy doctor's thesis
>   On education,
> Thou shalt not worship objects nor
> Shalt thou or thine bow down before
>   Administration.
>
> Thou shalt not answer questionnaires
> Or quizzes upon World Affairs,
>   Nor with compliance

Take any test. Thou shalt not sit
With statisticians nor commit
    A social science.

Thou shalt not be on friendly terms
With guys in advertising firms,
    Nor speak with such
As read the Bible for its prose,
Nor, above all make love to those
    Who wash too much.

Thou shalt not live within thy means
Nor on plain water and raw greens.
    If thou must choose
Between the chances, choose the odd;
Read the New Yorker; trust in God;
    And take short views.

I said I thought this was a bad poem; but a bad poem by
Auden is better than most poems we have these days. I meant
simply that it was not one of Auden's best poems, being, I
think, rather more like a clever lecture than a poem of clear
personal commitment and involvement. Also I partly disagree
with it. Ultimately, though he sides with the Hermes men,
Auden is patronizing to them. He takes (perhaps inadvertently) the traditional view of the humorist I have been
describing, the view that emphasizes his eccentricity and general irresponsibility without taking into account why he is
this way, or in what sense he is eccentric and irresponsible.

It is here that I must deviate slightly from the traditional
view of the humorist that I have presented so far. In doing
so I am not, fortunately, alone. There is another traditional
view of the humorist or Hermes man that we carry about
with us which seems to belie the first, the image of him as

prophet, seer, truth-bringer, wise man. All those Hermes men I mentioned a few minutes ago—Lear's fool, Hamlet, Falstaff, Huck Finn, Sancho Panza, Holden Caulfield—happen to have been *right* about the world upon which they were commenting; each of them in turn demonstrated to us pretty effectively that the world *is* like the Balkans even though it is run by Apollo men. Now it is this point that Auden underplays in his poem—though I think he would agree with me —and it is this point which makes the whole world of humorous, Hermetic enterprises something more than merely pleasantly entertaining.

Surely some of the best examples of what I am getting at can be found in the works of Jonathan Swift, where consistently the real tomfoolery, the real nonsense, the real humor is perpetrated by the Apollo men, the responsible citizens, the leaders, the patriots, the organizers. One emerges from Swift with this fundamental irony pretty firmly implanted. This is not, I think, because Swift had a more Balkanlike age to live in than other satirists, or because Swift was more misanthropic than other Hermes men who have appeared among us, but simply because he was a genius: he managed to communicate more completely, more comprehensively, more vividly the basic "humorous" disposition I've been trying to characterize than any of his competitors have managed to do before or since. In doing so he emerged as one of the few great satirists, one of those few whose works cannot be readily followed up with a "but seriously." Swift is therefore probably the best instance I can give of what I mean by a serious satirist.

II.

Do we have any Swifts today? With that question I move on to part two of this little evening concert. I suppose the answer is no; and with that I might sit down; but as I rather like to hold audiences captive for more than a few minutes I'll now demonstrate my ignorance at some length. First let me mention briefly (since they are having such a run) the "sickniks," who are outside my province perhaps, being not (mostly) literary—I mean Shelley Berman, Elaine May and Mike Nichols, Mort Sahl and so on. They were written up severely recently by an English critic Kenneth Allsop, who said:

Their area of discourse is simple to define: the unspeakable. They gag about insanity and malnutrition, amputation and drug addiction, H-Bomb fall-out and nervous breakdown, perversion and disease, violence and horror.

He concluded his remarks about them in two ways. First he said, "the cruel crack is the easiest, but humor has greater power when it is informed with pity and a recognition of the fact that most of us, no matter how flippantly pessimistic we may pretend to be, have high hopes." Second, he quoted "old-hand comic Joe Adams" on the sickniks: " 'They all act like big nonconformists, but they're all aiming to get on the Ed Sullivan or Steve Allen show.' " Both these complaints seem to me to be fundamental: the best satire has to be "informed with pity" or it is inhuman; it is simply not written from the inside but is escapist. And secondly, most of the sickniks appear themselves to be motivated not by a desire to correct corruption (as the definition of satire suggested) but instead by a great big fat extraneous "but seriously"—that is, money. For these reasons the sickniks are wags—though black wags perhaps—rather than true satirists.

Where in the *literary* world should we look for our Swifts? Well, I suppose the most obvious place to look would be in *The New Yorker,* the only large magazine we have which has both comic and literary aspirations. Arthur Mizener recently asserted in the *Times Book Review* section that *The New Yorker* is the best literary magazine in the world. Maybe it is; certainly it is a literary force to be reckoned with, particularly in the world of satire. Its first team has for a long time consisted of E. B. White, James Thurber, Ogden Nash, Phyllis McGinley, J. D. Salinger and a number of others you are doubtless familiar with. Have these not given us, over a period of now decades, a pretty good body of satiric writing? —I think so, and I would pick out White and Salinger as the two in the group who come nearest to being thoroughly committed satirists, that is, writers who do not provoke a "but seriously." Unfortunately Mr. White is getting pretty old and Salinger has, with his later pieces about the Glass family, shifted gears or something so that maybe I shouldn't call him a satirist at all.

I'll come back to *The New Yorker,* but where else can we look for satire? *Esquire* is all solemn and portentous, literarily, these days. I don't really know *Playboy,* but I occasionally look at an issue and wonder what my students find so wonderful about it. *Mad* is about the same way, for my money; it is full of what that man in the dictionary called "clownish jeering." Then there's a little magazine called *Monocle* which used to describe itself as a magazine of leisurely satire and which is now threatening, I don't know how successfully, to become big. I have high hopes for this one because the editor wants me to write regularly for it—but so far, I must admit, it hasn't amounted to much. Now have I omitted any?—Probably, but I am not trying to survey our publishing world here, merely indicate that there are publishing facilities open to our young satirists before pointing out that the facilities are mostly for the kind of humor I have been frowning on, the "but seriously" kind—for several reasons.

First it is safe, as "committed" satire is not. It offends nobody and apparently pleases great numbers (even me, when it is good) .

Second (a consequence of its popularity) it is something publishers will pay a lot of money for. It is big business from Radio City to Hollywood.

Third it is, well, it is terribly American. I have been struggling for a better, more descriptive word and I can't find it. I am concerned, as I have said, with the kind of temperament it takes to produce great satire, and I've decided that it's an un-American temperament somehow. I really think that Americans in general have some curious scruples about mixing business and pleasure. Serious is serious and funny is funny, work is work and play is play; and if somebody comes along and starts to mix these neat categories, then there's trouble. The great satirist causes this kind of trouble; he would be an unsettling figure for a publisher to have in his stable. Even *The New Yorker* would probably not get along with him. As for the little literary magazines—which are, after all, indigenous American too—well, the satirist will cause them as much trouble as he will cause *The New Yorker*.

Let me take these two opposed publishing worlds up separately. First, the little magazines. Here for a change I can speak with a certain amount of authority. I have been trying to resuscitate the art of satire in the two little magazines I've edited for a great many years—first in a magazine called *Furioso* and now in *The Carleton Miscellany*—and I've found that while this has earned me a few friends and a few supporters the venture has been, as a whole, a failure. The latest severe comment upon my activities is perhaps representative of those of the serious-minded intellectuals and writers who don't like no foolin' around in the very temple of literature itself; it appeared in another little magazine, the *Minnesota Review,* and was written by one of that sheet's editors. He said in essence that we (my editors and I) lacked "seriousness and integrity" and he didn't, besides, find us very funny. We *used* to be funny, he said, when we were younger and printed *Furioso;* but now, no; now there was a certain air of

229

unhumorous sadness about our activities, "the sadness of middle-aged college boys trying to recapture the past."

Charming. You see what happens when a great satirist like me tries to make his way in this country. I am crushed, not crushed enough, however, not to reply. In the first place people said the same things about us, essentially, when my colleagues and I *were* younger. And in the second place, though he may be right about how unfunny we now are, his complaint about our lack of seriousness is just the kind of puritan literary nonsense that is apt to get good satire, if it ever should get written in these unlikely days, rejected. I will grant, for example, that *The Rape of the Lock* is probably funnier than anything I've ever written (this is big of me), but I can't see that it would fare better with this critic otherwise. Is it serious to write about a girl getting a lock of hair cut off? does Pope display literary integrity by lavishing his literary venom upon a trivial social squabble? And so on. This critic has really no room for satire on his literary stage; the medium itself lacks integrity, he thinks. This is why he may put up with *The New Yorker* (which, for such a high-serious chap is *not* a serious literary endeavor) but not the *Carleton Miscellany* which, he thinks, because it doesn't make any money, ought to be.

In all my years of little literary magazining no fact about that odd cultural activity has so impressed me as the demands for *seriousness* placed upon it, for a narrow professional seriousness that is the same thing—just the other side of the coin —as the narrow professional humorousness expected of our Bob Hopes. Now I happen to think that this kind of seriousness is itself worthy of serious satire. There is nothing, for example, inherently more ludicrous than a youthful literary editor's aspirations as he takes his first sheaf of poems and other tidbits down to the printer: those aspirations are boundless, and their chances of fulfillment zero. Nor, I think, is there anything more ludicrous than the aspirations of a contributor to that magazine as he receives his poem back first in proof and then in the earth-shaking journal itself—for at the time of the poem's appearance the contributor really thinks he's made it, made heaven or the *Golden Treasury* or something, at any rate become one of the legislators of the world that Shelley talked about, whereas in fact if anyone other than his own friends and relatives reads the poem he should feel in clover.

I hope you understand that I am not trying to exhibit contempt for that contributor's poem or that editor's magazine—I speak to you as an editor of and contributor to such affairs—I am only trying to describe the curious lack of perspective to be found in the little magazine world toward the role of "serious" literature in human affairs, especially in our time. It is not exaggerating the case to say, I think, that these somber spirits regard themselves simply as saviors of humanity, saving it from materialism and ignorance and insensitivity and conformity and a few other deadly sins, not the least of which is unseriousness. For such spirits, as I have said, the very medium of satire seems to be somehow immoral.

The case of *The New Yorker* is different. Its editors have managed, by a strenuous conditioning of its readers, to make a certain mixing of humor and seriousness, of entertainment and instruction, acceptable, a feat of really great proportions in our society. But they have had to pay for it. Not only have they been sniped at by the serious literary lights, like the editor I was just describing, for decades, but they have themselves placed certain limits upon the extent to which their two domains may intermingle. The most obvious instance of the limits of their humorousness is of course to be found in the way they manage to print the corrupt advertising that supports them and yet on occasion take pot shots at it, pot shots that are commendable but involve only a minimum commitment. Less obvious but perhaps more important are their procedures for distinguishing the serious from the comic

231

in the literary endeavors they print. Among the magazine's regular contributors only E. B. White himself has, it seems to me, consistently managed to avoid looking like *either* a funny man *or* a serious man, has in other words truly invaded that murky in-between area where the best satire operates. I haven't time here to illustrate what I mean at length, so let me just say a few words about *The New Yorker*'s poetry.

The New Yorker is the only big magazine we have, with the possible exception of the *Saturday Review,* which has any designs worth mentioning upon poetry. *The New Yorker* holds out real cash and a real audience for real poets and, as a result, gets them. The other big magazines print either practically no verse or the farm-and-home-hour kind. Furthermore, *The New Yorker* has scruples, standards about the verse it prints; it does not like bad grammar, murky statement and false rhetoric, nor does it like, except in its "funny" poets, verbal or formal eccentricity. Its ideal poem is a straightforward thing, in rhyme and stanzas, which displays the well-managed sensibility of an intelligent private individual at work on the world of his immediate neighborhood.

The critics of *The New Yorker,* and there certainly are a lot, point out that such standards, being negative, provide for nothing except safety. The admirers point out that such standards, having been neglected elsewhere, desperately need defending. I find myself on the fence here; I don't think that a clear-cut, well-turned verse line is a negative quality; nor do I see that we are in much of a position to complain about the verse inside *The New Yorker* when the verse outside it is what it is. On the other hand, as an editor I envy the editors their missed "potential" (*think* of being an editor with every bloody poet in the universe within range) ; and as a poet I've had enough well-mannered pieces accepted by them, and enough not necessarily better but certainly more wrought-up pieces rejected by them to think, I hope not in vanity, that I know *why* they've missed being better than they are. I am convinced that *if* I were to write my "Love Song of J. Alfred Prufrock" or my "Chicago" or my "Windhover," the editors of *The New Yorker* would turn it down flat. What I am saying is that the editors of *The New Yorker* favor poetry in which the poet has not really extended himself, and that the results have been mostly poor. It has satisfied itself with the minor verse of poets who have already printed their major works elsewhere (in little magazines, probably) or the verse of poets who are destined to write minor verse forever. I know that this major-minor junk is insufferable, but I'll let it stand without elaboration. *The New Yorker* has majored in the minors, and the best indication I can find of this fact is the presence of two funny poets (funny in the narrow sense, funny because you can say "but seriously" after reading them) as the *only* poets I can think of, of consequence, whose affiliation with *The New Yorker* has been an important part of their careers. I mean Phyllis McGinley and Ogden Nash.

Mind you, I like both McGinley and Nash. That, I hope it is clear by now, is not my point. I simply wish that *The New Yorker* had been more successful than it has been in its satiric endeavors, more successful in promoting and cultivating the satire of commitment of which I speak. Their failure here is like their failure with their nonfunny verse—it has produced clean minor sensible humorous verse rather than the intense, felt sort of thing that satiric verse can be. The only satiric poem I can remember printed in *The New Yorker* with these qualities was one by Edmund Wilson about Archibald Mac-Leish—and it has always seemed out of character to me for *The New Yorker* to have printed it.

Enough of *The New Yorker*. I have been circling my subject in a most unmethodical way, and I have doubtless lost a few threads en route. I think though that I can at least suggest, though not cover, most of the big issues I have been wrestling with here by reference to a recent argument about

Mark Twain. This was conducted in the Soviet *Literary Gazette* in Moscow, of all places. You may be familiar with it; for the controversy was reprinted in a pamphlet called "Mark Twain and the Russians" by Charles Neider (an American Century Special, Hill and Wang 50¢, 1960). The dispute began, Neider tells us, when a critic for the *Literary Gazette,* one Yan Bereznitsky, criticized Neider's edition of Mark Twain's autobiography for misrepresenting Twain. Bereznitsky presented this as part of a great American conspiracy (presumably ordered by our Central Cultural Committee) either to forget Mark Twain or "to crop the great writer's hair, to deflower the blazing and furious colors of his satire, to eat away the socially unmasking resonance of Twain's work, and, in the last analysis, to make him up as a benevolent and simple-minded scoffer"—that is, to reduce his work to "clownish jeering." Bereznitzky then complained specifically about Neider's omission of

Twain's famous pronouncement about American "democracy," his indignant notes about the predatory wars which the U.S. carried on half a century ago, his satirical sketches, cutting as a slap in the face, of the oil king Rockefeller, Senator Clark, General Wood, President Theodore Roosevelt, and other knights and henchmen of American expansionism.

Instead of such vital material, Bereznitsky said, Neider introduced

Twain's meditations on baldness, the value of hairwashing, on beginning writers, on phrenology, on honorary degrees, etc.,

and concluded that such a rendering of his autobiography was "exacerbating to the memory of the greatest American writer."

Mr. Neider's reply, which was printed in the Soviet periodical, pointed out that there were a good many reasons for

234

the exclusion of such material, among which was the material's presence in earlier editings of the autobiography with which Neider's edition was not trying to compete. Neider observed that it was absurd to say that the omissions were the result of an official conspiracy to silence Twain.

Now I am no Twain authority. From what I gather the complications of printing all the miscellaneous Twain autobiographical material are endless, involving pronouncements from Twain himself against the printing of some of it until A.D. 2006. I *have,* however, done a small amount of comparative work with the Neider version and the earlier versions of the autobiography, and I regret to report that I agree in part with Mr. Bereznitsky. Furthermore, I am astonished by some of Neider's incidental comments in his reply to Bereznitsky. Take first, for example, this statement:

> Mark Twain is of course primarily a humorist. If he had never possessed his humorous gift, if he had only written his social criticism, he would not now be read by millions of Russian readers and it would be useless for Soviet literary spokesmen to point to him as the great critic of democratic morals. He is also of course primarily a writer of fiction. It was through these two great gifts that he made the reputation which is so well sustained fifty years after his death.

This is a pretty high-and-mighty statement, I think. I would have you note the two "of courses" in it, for instance—"of course [he is] primarily a humorist" and "of course [he is] primarily a writer of fiction." I think somebody ought to do a Ph.D. thesis or something someday about the "of courses" of the world and how they always, of course, appear at precisely the points where an issue is in doubt. Nobody, of course, ever says that the sea of course is wet; but the Neiders of the world (and I know I can't exclude myself) are always ready to say that the sea of course is a symbol of mother or eternal flux. You know, of course, what I mean. Anyway, to get back to Neider's statement, I can't see how Twain can be primarily a humorist *and* primarily a writer of fiction, even with two "of courses." Furthermore, as I hope I indicated earlier, I object to the thinking which makes a writer necessarily serious *or* humorous; therefore I also object here to the assertion that the Russians would never have read Twain's social criticism if it had not been for his "humorous gift," since that seems to me to be a half truth of no consequence without the further remark that the Russians would not have read his humor if it had not been for his social criticism. Yet Mr. Neider persists in his half truth when he adds,

> I like to think that most Russian readers have the same common sense, that they read him basically *not* for the lessons he teaches of the inherent "evils" of the nation across the Iron Curtain *but* because he enlarges their lives imaginatively through a flow of pleasure.
>
> (my italics)

Here it is the "not for this" and "but for that" construction which bears the burden of the falsehood—the natural Russian response here, and one with which I would agree, would seem to be that they could read Twain for *both*.

Mr. Neider compounds the difficulty a bit later when he tries to describe more grandly the bases for his judgments about what to include in Twain's autobiography. Here he takes the familiar *serious* literary man's line that has bothered me so long as a little magazine editor, the line that there is yet another primary element to be considered (how many primaries can we have?). He says:

> ... the aesthetic element for me is a primary one when it comes to literature. I am content to believe that it is the first function and value of the artist to perceive and create works of beauty— that is what he specializes in, from my point of view. There are few first-rate scientists who are also first-rate political thinkers or eco-

236

nomists; and I believe there are few literary artists who are such. I do not think the less of Mark Twain for his didactic works; I admire him for them. But just as his didactic works do not heighten for me the greatness of a book like *Huckleberry Finn,* so it is that the didactic parts of his *Autobiography* do not for me heighten the more psychological and nostalgic parts.

I find this a massively confused statement, and can't begin to face up to all its difficulties. Suffice it to say here that with this remark we move well beyond the boundaries of the humorous-serious split I have been worrying about into the solemn inner sanctum of aesthetics itself, and find there also, in the thinking of Mr. Neider, the same kind of pigeonholing, the same kind of either/or logic that seems to me so wrong and so characteristic of modern American literary taste. Note, just for example, that he separates *Huck Finn* from the didactic works of Twain. I suppose he will point to Twain's comic little preface in defense, where Twain says,

> Persons attempting to find a motive in this narrative will be prosecuted; persons attempting to find a moral in it will be banished; persons attempting to find a plot in it will be shot.

I sympathize with that preface mightily and would, if I were Twain, object to those who would extract its theme and message bodily and put them in some College Outline for students who wish to copy it out on themes and tests. On the other hand I have too much respect for the book to deny it its rightful place as a great commentary upon our society, which is exactly what Mr. Neider, in the sentence I have quoted, does.

It is this quality in Neider's editing of Twain to which the Russian critic objects, and to which I am trying to object here too. It is also this quality that the Russian critic finds characteristic of American literary thinking, and I do too, not, however, sharing with the Russian the notion that this is all a premeditated bureaucratic "line." I hope you will understand that I have also a great many reservations about the Russian critic's comments, which are nationalistic in a way that Twain himself would have found most amusing. Indeed I am positive that Twain would have found more matters to satirize in the Soviet Union's concept of democracy than ours, for I'm afraid that Mr. Bereznitsky and all Communists are incurable Apollo men. But all this is beside the point; furthermore, I think it wrong to start beating the Russians over the head at the slightest provocation, as we tend to do these days, rather than looking to see first if we need to have our own heads beaten; and I confess that I think that the Russian critic in question here deserves less head-beating than we do. Whatever Twain's merits as a satirist may be, we misrepresent his character and his life's purpose, it seems to me, when we insist on talking about him in Neider's terms. I think the Russian critic would announce grandly at this point that Mr. Neider doesn't want literature, ultimately, to deal with life—and with that too, though with reservations, I would agree.

To conclude, let me give one perhaps frivolous instance of how our literary cubbyholing affects not the *literary* thinking of our time but the thinking on the other side, the thinking among the great unwashed about what literature does or is about. If you drive through Sauk Centre in my state these days you will see that the Chamber of Commerce of that pretty famous town has erected a sign at the town's approaches announcing boldly that *this* is the town about which Sinclair Lewis's *Main Street* was written. You will also see inside the town that the main street has been renamed "Main Street" and you will hear from the local residents about the big pageant they held last year celebrating an anniversary of that book's publication. Now I think an argument can be made that Sinclair Lewis is finally sympathetic with Main Street and all that he made it stand for—but this is not unusual; compassion is at least as important a quality in the satirist as the capacity for derision, and as I said earlier it seems to me that the satirist's greatest subject is probably himself and his nearest and dearest. The fact remains that there is something monstrous about the "booster" element among the Sauk Centre citizenry taking for its main publicity pitch one of the great books that this country has produced "exposing, denouncing and deriding" that particularly American vice of "boosting" (another one, of course is *Babbitt*). I can just see some member of the Junior Chamber up there in Sauk Centre, when decisions were being made for the pageant and so on, acknowledging that the book was satirical and worrying a moment about that minor fact, but then saying, "But *seriously*, now . . ."

Literature as Persuasion

I will begin with Marvell's poem, "To His Coy Mistress," because it is a fine example of persuasion, persuasion in literature. My subject is "Literature as Persuasion"—especially poetry as persuasion—so I can use Marvell's poem here to advantage to demonstrate what I am *not* talking about. You will remember that the poet in that poem is addressing, ostensibly, a lady who has been resisting his amorous advances; he points out that her "coyness" *would* be all right *if* they had world enough and time; then they could play at love for ages and ages, she refusing him regularly and he, undaunted, continuing his quest at the pace of a vegetable. Unfortunately, he then argues, they do not have world enough and time. He notes that at his back he always hears "Time's winged chariot hurrying near: and yonder all before us lye/Deserts of vast Eternity." *Therefore,* he concludes, most reasonably, "now let us sport us while we may."

He is very persuasive, is he not? He suggests that they have just two choices, to love or not to love, and that not loving is a poor choice. Therefore!—at that "therefore" the lady must realize that her side in the debate is lost; all the forces of reason have been marshalled successfully against her; she has no choice but to submit or be unreasonable. And here the poem ends. We, a third party to the affair, are left to wonder (through all eternity) what the lady did in fact do when faced with the inevitable. We are left with a fine example of persuasion *in* literature.

Another, more familiar example—in fact a worn-out example—is Antony's speech to the crowd in Shakespeare's *Julius Caesar*, the "friends, Romans, countrymen" diatribe that sends the mob roaring away to burn Brutus's house. Unlike the speech to the coy mistress Antony's speech is not chiefly memorable for its logical persistence, but rather for certain less dignified rhetorical devices such as irony ("But Brutus is an honorable man") and feigned humility ("I am no orator as Brutus is/But as you know me all, a plain blunt man"). Still, it is a masterly piece of persuasion, frequently used as a model of the public speaker's shady art. As such it is surely a natural, like "To His Coy Mistress," for my subject here.

Or is it? Is either of them? What is the difference, if any, between persuasion in literature and literature as persuasion? To get at this difference I would have you note that in both my examples we the readers are not the ones being addressed, being persuaded; in fact both Shakespeare and Marvell are at some pains to exclude us from the possible effects of their speakers' eloquence. We are to watch their respective shows, not be moved by them; we are third parties, and as third parties we are certainly not expected, for example, to go and burn Brutus's house. Shakespeare makes this quite clear to us, first, by having a good many intelligent members of his cast comment unfavorably on how easy it is to sway a fickle mob and, second, by having Antony himself say, after his great speech, "Mischief, thou art afoot." Marvell is less explicit, but my firm impression of his intentions toward us is that he too would have been delighted to have his amorous hero speak to us in an aside and say, "Mischief, thou art afoot." For both these poems are, to use a modern phrase, snow jobs, one political, one romantic. Furthermore, both Shakespeare and Marvell want us to recognize this fact and to judge their poems accordingly; they want us to be impressed by the agility of the arguers, but not to be impressed to the degree, or in the same way even, that the coy mistress and the Roman mob are to be impressed. We the audience are set apart from the persuasive action; we are observers rather than participants.

Now it would be ridiculous of me to say that all poetry and all literature follow the pattern of these examples. There are many poems, for instance, that appear to speak to us more directly than this, poems that speak to us as Whitman does when he says,

> Take my leaves America, take them South and take them
> North,
> Make welcome for them everywhere, for they are your
> own offspring.

Or as Wordsworth does:

> Behold her, single in the field,
> Yon solitary highland lass.
> Reaping and singing by herself;
> Stop here, or gently pass.

There is no coy mistress or Roman mob being addressed on the stages here. We the readers seem to be the only audience, the only persons expected to take Whitman's leaves or pass Wordsworth's lass. I say "seem to be," however, because I think there *is* somebody else being addressed. Whitman is addressing Whitman; Wordsworth is addressing Wordsworth. You may imagine them seated in their respective studies at three o'clock in the morning writing for their greatest admirers, namely themselves.

If this is so—and I think it is—it means quite simply that they, like Marvell and Shakespeare in the passages discussed, are just not concerned with the art of persuasion except hypothetically. Persuasion for them—that is, persuasion on their stages or in their secluded studies—is not the art Aristotle, Cicero and the others were talking about.

Literature, as we all know, is incurably hypothetical, but we do not all agree upon the meaning of this primary fact. To some of us its hypotheses are, at least potentially, as solemn as Einstein's; to others of us Einstein has the clear edge. But by nearly all of us the hypotheses of literature are regarded as relatable, somehow or other, to the world, to truth, to reality—and because they are they tend to get merged in our minds with the *un*hypothetical, that is, with the daily round of exposition and argument that we describe as journalism, history, criticism or, more grandly, philosophy. Thus though we may be anxious to keep literature apart from all that, and though we may even insist on its apartness, still its closeness is what we end up talking about. When we do so we are apt to talk about its rhetoric as we would talk about the rhetoric of journalism, history, criticism or philosophy; we are apt to ask if it is convincing, or valid, or reasonable, or well-founded in relevant evidence. Now I don't object to this procedure—for I don't see how one can avoid it—but I think I see some serious limitations to the practice which we should not ignore.

The persuaders of the world have Ciceronian notions; they imagine vast audiences moving to their will, responding as Dale Carnegie says they should. But a poet in his study can at best only imagine an audience that *happens* to think the way he thinks, feel the way he feels. His language, when he puts it down, is not therefore a language of strength but of weakness, not even necessarily a language of reason but of feeling. His is a language of the self, the three-o'clock-in-the-morning self with not one shoemaker, much less a Roman mob to talk to. As such it is in many respects not a language of persuasion at all.

243

At the risk of appearing to identify myself with Shakespeare, Marvell, Wordsworth and Whitman, let me illustrate this by reference to one of my own poems:

LINES

composed upon reading an announcement by Civil Defense authorities recommending that I build a bombshelter in my backyard[1]

I remember a dugout we dug in the backyard as children
And closed on top with an old door covered with dirt
And sat in hour by hour, thoroughly squashed,
But safe, with our chins on our knees, from the world's hurt.
There, as the earth trickled down on us as in an hour glass,
Our mothers called us, called us to come and be fed,
But we would not, could not hear them, possessed as we were
By our self's damp stronghold among the selfless dead.

This and a few other fantasies of my youth
I remember now as scenes in a marathon play
That plunged on for act after act with the lost hero
Preferring, to death, some brave kind of decay.
While he was still on stage I grew up
And sneaked away as he battered his hemlock cup.

Now, they say, willy nilly I must go back,
And under the new and terrible rules of romance
Dig yet another hole in which like a child
My adult soul may trifle with circumstance.
But I'll not, no, not do it, not go back
And lie there in that dark under the weight
Of all that earth on that old door for my state.
I know too much to think now that, if I creep
From the grown-up's house to the child's house, I'll keep.

---

[1] This poem was first printed in *The Sewanee Review*, and subsequently in the author's volume, *An American Takes a Walk* (Univ. of Minnesota Press, 1956).

I wrote this poem several years ago, when the announcement referred to in the title first swam into my ken. I sent it to *The New Yorker*, which returned it on the curious grounds that although they liked it they had not received it soon enough; the announcement was past; the poem was no longer timely. Personally I still regard it as, unfortunately, timely enough, but otherwise suspect. I was in doubt about putting it in my book on the grounds that I, who am as cowardly as the next man, really didn't think for a moment that I would fail to dig the bomb shelter I protested in the poem against *if* an urgent occasion arose. But then I decided to leave the poem in anyway. Why? Why did I commit myself to a poem which did not even persuade *me*? The answer is simple: I liked it. I still like it. And I am confident that I will continue to like it even as, with shovel in hand, I begin to make the prescribed mess of my backyard (perhaps I'll like it more then). For it will then still be, at least in one sense, a true poem as far as I'm concerned, true in the sense that I, a civilized human being, am being childish in the extreme when I seek salvation by digging that hole. For the poem, as I see it, is talking one level above the urgencies of the moment; it is not concerned with my saving my neck on a certain Saturday in April, but with my saving my own adult, rational, civilized soul for, say, the next couple of centuries. I can save my neck (doubtfully) by digging the hole, but to save that soul I've got to work at some less barbaric, primitive, childish solution.

To put it differently, I both do and do not believe in the poem, but my rationale for believing in it has little or nothing to do with my "politics." Politically I am as argumentative as the next man. Get me in a political situation and you will find that I am a kind of Democrat. I admit also to a very considerable contempt for most of our present foreign policy, for our handling of the atomic bomb tests, and for our persistent military nationalism by which we seem to be trying to outdo the Russians at their game. And so you can imagine me in this piece—if my subject were not what it is—endeavoring to persuade, to move you, and regretting very much that I was not programmed before some important election. And yet while writing this poem I had no such political compulsions, and after I had written it I was not, and am not, prepared to defend it politically. I would be glad to argue about it as a poem, and I would be glad to acknowledge that it expressed my feelings, more or less, at the time that I wrote it; but beyond that I could not go.

Thus, a language of weakness. What I am trying to say, I suppose, is that poetry is, frequently, above or below persuasion. It either does not descend to what the politician does when he goes about kissing babies, or it does not rise to what Milton did when he wrote his *Areopagitica*. Now the failure to descend is surely excusable—we poets can go about saying that we are *above* such-and-such; but the failure to rise is harder to defend—how does one go about explaining away a poet's persistent incapacity or unwillingness seriously to employ persuasion's greatest weapon, reason? We have all heard it said that poetry is not rational—and surely sometimes it is not—But I think this statement is too frequently made by apologists for poetry who, in the process of making out a case for poetry's dealing extensively with feeling, manage to suggest what I don't think they believe, that Reason isn't any great shakes anyway. These apologists would not argue thus in a different situation; they would not, for example, say—if they were arguing with horses—that man is superior to the horse primarily because of his feelings. It is only when they are faced with a clear case of unreason in art that they discover that man is magnificent because of his poetic, not his rational powers. I confess that I am fatigued by such arguments, and though I have managed mostly in my life to align myself with the poets rather than rationalists I do not see why I have to defend my alliance. To be always justifying, justifying, justifying my particular favorite does not appeal to me. In the first place I doubt that the other side will listen to me; in the second place I doubt that it would matter much if it did.

This is not to deny that impulse to defend poetry; its sources are clear and honorable. It has been bred into us by generations of attacks upon literature by representatives of the many and various languages of strength. Most recently we have seen a novel under fire in the Soviet Union, but we can hardly assert that such attacks are restricted to the Soviet Union. The attacks, and the treatments, mark the whole history of, for instance, English literature—a literature that has never achieved ten quiet years without some agent of strength rising to proclaim that such and such a work is immoral or irrational or irresponsible or sadistic or subversive or merely pessimistic. Now I don't wish to be heretical here (or subversive) (or etc.) but I think these unpleasantnesses arise mostly for a reason that the defenders of literature neglect; they arise simply because the agents of strength are right: the literature they criticize does display weakness; it is not clear, or it is not happy, or it is not rational, or it is not proletarian, or it is not something or other that it ought to be according to the rules of a language, a rhetoric, a philosophy of strength.

It is because, then, our position is untenable when argued from the other side that I am against arguing. I find it more sensible to give in. For me to try to defend, for instance, the analogy I draw in my poem between the hole I dug as a child and the hole I have been asked to dig as an adult is simply to ask for sneers from the logicians. They will either pick out flaws in my particular analogy, or simply and reasonably point out that *no* analogy is *ever* "valid" anyway. And so I do not choose to defend it this way; I say instead, weakly, that I "like" it or, even more weakly, that it seems to me to be true in one sense (that they won't understand) though untrue in another sense (that they will understand). When I argue thus, what do I expect?

I expect, I think, what many literary men in their optimistic moments expect. I expect not to persuade anyone but to find someone who is already persuaded. I expect, as Allen Tate puts it, someone to commune with me.

II.

Or perhaps I should say empathize. I dislike both words because they both frequently emanate from fortresses of strength, and I would not like to be caught suggesting that the communion I mean should be churchly or that the empathy I mean should be psychiatric. Otherwise, however, the words are fine, and there are perhaps no others that better describe the difference I am trying to get at between strength and weakness in language. The difference is at best relative —there are strong languages of weakness and weak languages of strength—but the difference is nonetheless with us, and those of us who are writers are constantly choosing between them. To put the nature of the choice in its simplest form let me say that when I chose to write this essay I was contracting with myself to write in a language of strength (kind of) ; I said to myself here is something I am willing to defend, though perhaps inadequately. Had I on the other hand chosen to write a poem describing the weakness of poetry—a poem on my essay's theme—I would not have expected, and would not have been prepared for, argument. I would have been saying, "Here are my 'sentiments'; take them or leave them."

To the proponents of a language of strength it is perfectly immoral for somebody to go bumbling about with sentiments that he is not prepared to defend. I sympathize with them here; I don't much like anarchic, self-generated sentiments either, and that is why I am using, and insisting upon, the word "weakness" to describe them. I might for example have chosen instead to describe poetry as the language of self, its opposite the language of no-self. These terms are meaningful: the language of the no-self (the language of strength) is the language that we are always striving to master in those various disciplines where, we feel, truth ought to be allowed to reside outside the individual; the language of the self (the language of weakness) on the other hand is never separable from its originator. Thus the world of no-self contains many theorems, many scientific laws, many ideas or mental "projections" which, though they obviously had to originate in *a* mind, float about the atmosphere of our world with no name firmly attached. But the world of the self only contains works of "character"; Shakespeare's poems are *Shakespeare's* poems (even if his name was Bacon). Furthermore the advantage of the terms "self" and "no-self" is that they are not evaluative; one language is not necessarily better, or stronger, than the other. Accordingly a defender of poetry might well favor these terms over the others.

But I favor the others. I favor them partly because, as I said, I am tired of defenses of poetry, but more because I think that only by recognizing the weaknesses of poetry can we determine what are, as it were, legitimate weaknesses. That is, when can we, when should we, when do we have to abandon the languages of strength? And in reverse, when can't we, and when shouldn't we, abandon them?

These are gigantic questions, the kind that never get answered convincingly, but they are nonetheless questions that ought to be circulating in the minds of our poets, strong or weak. When we ask, with Mr. Tate, what the function of poetry is we may not, again with Mr. Tate, be able to give an answer, and we may not think that anybody's answer, anybody's *general* answer, is worth the paper it's written on. Still we ought, I think, to be able to say in the case of a *particular* poem that it does or does not perform a function that we are happy to see a poem perform. Does this not sound like very little to ask?—it is not. If one accepts the two-world principle that there is a language of self and a language of no-self, either of which can be chosen on any occasion with equally good, though different, results, then one can without a qualm simply assert that *any* poem has a worthy function so long as it is about a self. I cannot assert this; I don't see why poets should be thus encouraged in self-indulgence; I don't like to encourage weakness, praise weakness; I merely want to deal with it intelligently since it's with us. Therefore it seems to me that the question, Does such-and-such a poem perform a worthy function? is not answered by saying that it helped the poet let off steam and saved him a trip to the couch. The question has to be answered otherwise, has to be answered somehow in relation to the world outside of the poet's self— in the world, that is, where the languages of strength usually operate. In that outside world we have to decide whether that poem should or does compete.

Each age sets up its own occasion for competition. In our time the failure of various languages of strength—from the language of our State Dept. (or Mr. Khrushchev) to the language of Billy Graham (or our Chambers of Commerce) —would seem to me to be occasions for the recognition of weakness and (thereupon) the writing of literature. But how am I, a self-centered writer, to distinguish between certain private and gruesome sentiments of despair which I entertain about the future of America as a result of eating and drinking too much, and the other kind of sentiment, the "legitimate" kind, the kind that I have said poetry should concern itself with? Obviously I will have trouble drawing the line; obviously my poems will be merely self-indulgent if I don't watch out. And yet distinctions can be made, I think. They can be made if (1) one remains as reasonable and levelheaded and generally "outgoing" as possible under the circumstances and (2) one remembers the principle of communion or empathy. To take a celebrated modern instance, what is *wrong* with Pound's cantos?—Pound has consistently written them with the false expectation that the world he writes for will be with him because, he thinks, it ought to be with him. What on the other hand is *right* about Marvell's lines to his coy mistress?—Marvell was right in hoping that the world he was writing for—say a world of incipient lovers —would be with him, with him for various reasons but with him, with him so long as he demonstrated, and demonstrated well, the marvelous unreason of reason in love. In other words Pound wrote to us from on high, telling us all to join him; Marvell wrote (even though in his three A.M. study) in the midst of us, telling us merely (though this is quite a lot) that we were where we were.

The Marvell principle is the right one for poetry, for literature. The Pound principle is wrong. In a very important sense poetry's function is to take over when the men on high fail (as they always do). But one poet in his pride can't take over; he can't be way out there in the blue like Willie Loman. Thus to my assertion that poetry is a language of weakness I think two corollaries need to be added: first, weakness *needs* company; and second, when it *has* company it can be (though it may not be) strong.

Academic Writing
and the Graces

Picture a poet (a friend of mine). His ship has come in. He has been hired by a lecture agency. His name appears on a number of campus calendars. Several airlines, motels and hotels are waiting for him. He has a typewritten schedule in triplicate of where he is to be and who is to meet him and what he is to do and when. He carries a brown leather brief-case (his first), in which are packed his complete collected works, in accordion-type lecture (for ten to fifty minutes), and a cheap anthology of other people's poems in case his own run out. He also carries a small suitcase with shirts and an emergency supply of penicillin—for he has a bronchial condition.

He is scheduled to travel on Ozark Airlines and Piedmont Airlines and North Central Airlines and Lake Central (*sic?*) Airlines, as well as some of the big ones. But especially Ozark Airlines. Ozark seems dedicated to the college scene, serving campuses all over Iowa, Illinois and Missouri, campuses that stand out like little, uniformly furnished oases amid the wheatfields and new housing developments. He has read someplace that Ozark has the oldest DC-3 now in commercial service; he gets on what appears to be it, in Chicago, and flies off south with a group of farmers, small-town businessmen and professors. He flies maybe 150 miles in two hours, landing every twenty minutes. At his destination he is met by a member of the English Department and driven to an overheated guest room opening right on to the entrance of a girls' dormitory. He washes, lies down tentatively on the bed, opens his briefcase to be sure his collected works are really there, and dozes briefly. He is awakened by a knocking, hustled off to supper without a drink, then thrust into an auditorium where he delivers his goods. He is asked what he thinks of T. S. Eliot and served coffee. The next day he flies off to repeat the performance.

After three or four such stops he observes cynically to himself that although he has been steadily on the move he seems to have been standing still, thanks partly to friendly Ozark and partly to the interchangeability of the different campuses.

And a number of other apothegms, suitable for framing.

But somewhere down or up near his bronchial condition he has stored away more than his apothegms. He also has some tawdry collegiate sentiment in stock, as well as strong memories of a past littered with DC-3's cruising Algeria, Tunisia, Sicily, Italy and Southern France with him as a passenger, bearing his two leaden olive-drab barracks bags. Continuing his new wanderings over the corn belt he follows the planes' courses closely, thinking of other courses, more remote destinations. He helps the pilots on landings and takeoffs; he studies the rivet patterns on the wings, waits for the rattle of the tail wheel in the rear hollows, is renewed in old stirrings by wind socks, single-strip runways, uninhabited ramps. At the third or fourth college the English-Department representative turns out to be a dedicated discontent, instantly describing all the failings of the president of the college, the dean, the other department chairmen; the colleges' drabness begins to diminish. At the fifth the audience for his lecture is appreciative, likes his vaudeville act when he discovers he has misplaced page six, besieges him afterwards with requests (three) for autographs, and sends him to bed ecstatic, mildly drunk, frightfully impressed with culture's penetration of the back country. He falls asleep proposing to himself to write a study of literature in places where literature is not supposed to be.

He wakes up next morning exhausted, hung over, alone, the memory of his triumph fading, the meaning of it obscure. He is driven in confusion to his placid DC-3, and thence home.

Maybe the DC-3 does it all. On a bad day it is not so much a conveyance as an insult, and flies deviously to the discovery that there is no hope for American Writing so long as the colleges have a single writer left in hand. But on a good day it is Pegasus (with rivets).

Now picture briefly a magazine (also a friend of mine). At the beginning of this year the distinguished new literary quarterly of which I happen to be editor (for a year's subscription, send $3.50 today to *The Carleton Miscellany,* Carleton College, Northfield, Minnesota) started a register of incoming mail to discover where the hell all the manuscripts were coming from. As I write this the register has been going for only a couple of weeks, so the returns are incomplete. All I can say significantly right now is that the first fifty manuscripts for the year came from twenty states, the District of Columbia and three foreign countries. New York led with six; then came California with four; then came Illinois, Texas, Oregon, Minnesota, Connecticut and Pennsylvania with three each. If we don't have all the states represented several times over before this article goes to press, it will be because we have given up the register. *What does this mean?*

It means that the writers spread themselves thin, like warm oleo, over the country; it means that writing is one of our national pastimes, not a specialty of the big cities or the universities with writers' workshops.

254

It doesn't mean, though—at least as far as *The Miscellany* is concerned—that the manuscripts are coming from all walks of life, from the shops and factories and fields and Roselands. Maybe a third of them do, but the other two-thirds come from authors with some academic connections. Surely the proportion is not so high among contributions to nonacademic magazines, but it is unquestionably high in all writing places. The colleges are packing them in.

Mostly the writers—at least the writers to *The Miscellany* —appear to be teachers. Having a writer in the barn is one way for a college to drum up trade. Aside from his merits or demerits as an educator a writer is a useful person to photograph and describe as a "creative influence" in the college's brochures; and when and if he gets published anyplace he also spreads the college's name around on his own in a small way. Colleges have become increasingly aware over the last couple of decades that they *are* business organizations, and in the process of getting firmly into the exhausting world of advertising and publicity they have complicated things for themselves immeasurably. Writers are a tiny part of the new complication.

The writers all know this; they have a good sense of their being a complication. They feel uneasy in the service, some of them devoting most of their spare time to criticizing the academic life, others writing poems and stories about it (and sending them to magazines like *The Miscellany*) and still others silently letting it gnaw at their innards. But they are apt, for all their doubts, to be businessmen too in their own small way and know a good thing when they see one. Also a few of them (though from the press they get this seems unlikely) actually *like* campus life just a bit and think that its ill effects have been overrated.

My writer-lecturer has met a few score of these writers, and he also knows the business side of college writing intimately.

255

He has become one of the country's smallest writing entre-
preneurs, having discovered that writing itself (*his* writing)
will hardly pay for the gas for his car. For his meat and po-
tatoes he teaches regularly at one institution, then arranges
at no small labor to have himself invited for appearances at
others. He, like the colleges themselves, has thus made himself into a kind of salesman: the colleges are selling the colleges (and literature) ; he is selling himself (and literature) .
The colleges are after big money, he after peanuts.

He remembers being invited to teach the first session of a
summer's writing conference at a small northern college in
the Midwest. The college was worried about its obscurity; it
was in the process of transforming itself, like a good many
academic cinderellas, from a teacher's college with a restricted
curriculum for local clientele, into a liberal arts affair of
some national consequence, and was casting about for a means
of publicly demonstrating its new allegiances. A writer's conference was conceived as a small beginning to what might become a full-blown arts festival with, presumably, symphony
orchestras and scantily dressed ballet dancers and bearded
sculptors at labor under the pines to the delight of students
and tourists from all over. Well, it didn't work that first
season; that is, my writer-lecturer was the whole arts festival
all by himself, and the throngs consisted of twenty-five very
miscellaneously qualified persons from the neighborhood.
But it didn't *not* work either; the miscellaneous persons liked
it (and he liked them) ; the program continues; the symphony
orchestras may still be expected.

Having writers on campus, he discovered in his travels, is
just one part of the colleges' literary-promotion world. The
writers in turn breed writing classes and literary magazines
and symposia (sponsored by *Esquire*) and all sorts of other
extracurricular activities. In fact so much is possible along
these lines that big colleges may, and sometimes do, get in
pretty deep. The small colleges, however, generally do not;

they restrict themselves to conducting small writing courses for regular students or bringing a writer to campus for a day or two. But in both the big and the small places the various ventures have a good deal in common, and one of the unfortunate qualities they all share is the flavor or smell of the marketplace.

For that flavor, the writer-lecturer has learned (reading Shapiro and company, and listening to perpetual campus rumblings), they catch hell from their critics. He has noted that for some obscure sociological reason writers are expected to have their rewards in large, Hollywood-type sums or in heaven. They and the colleges are frowned on for making a *business* of *culture* unless they succeed and make it a bonanza. On the one hand the country's women clubs, and their kind, tend to be offended when a writer (at least a small-time writer) refuses to appear before them for nothing, and on the other the country's most violent anti-academes see a writer's appearance on campus as a sure indication of his having sold out. Thus, he has observed, the economics of writers on campus (which is found disgraceful) and its institutionalism (which is found to destroy man's free spirit) together manage to give the business a bad name. And yet this bad name seems to be bestowed upon the business not because it is a badly run business or even because it is an unnecessary business—even the sternest critics will admit the writers and the colleges have to have wallets—but simply because it *is* a business.

Unfair, unfair, mutters my writer-lecturer, getting good whiffs of such sentiments constantly. Sometimes, though, he agrees; sometimes, when the DC-3's are especially erratic, he comes to think of the money he's making in just the way the women's clubs do. And the institutionalism? Well, that's what (he's read a hundred times) has ruined modern poetry and driven our best writers into exile and made literary dictators of small academic types like (again, of course) T. S.

Eliot. He gets these dark feelings and then finds them more than confirmed in the presence of students who can think of nothing but markets, or in the presence of roving literary wheels like himself who talk steadily about what Allen said to John and how badly Dick was treated in the *Partisan* by Alfred. Those are bad DC-3 days indeed.

But then there are the other days for him when the arguments against institutionalism seem simply antideluvian-Republican, when the particular institution he is visiting displays none of the bad qualities but looks like a real liberating force in the chain of its writers' beings—in short looks healthy, very healthy against the alternatives in the bistros, or in Paris, Mexico and/or Madison Avenue. Solid, well-financed, orderly, quiet, sociable, libraried, undemanding, the institutions are also much less cabin'd, cribb'd, confined, much less conformist than the bad DC-3 days suggest. In the high places, he discovers, the variety and excellence of the literary activity and talk are hard to match, and in the out-of-the-way places, though the talent may be skimpy and ill-trained, he finds an unpredictability as uninstitutional as a town meeting. He remembers for example meeting miscellaneous scribblers in the out-of-the-way places who seemed to have stepped straight out of a mixed-up pastoral: a fireman loose in a writer's workshop sharpening his talents for a career in a fireman's journal; an old, old dentist asking him to 'ghost' his (the dentist's) memoirs; a spinster with one eye consulting him about contest jingles; a tremendous hulk of eighteen-year-old beatnik female quizzing him about Sartre on the second floor of an unfinished gymnasium in the middle of a snowstorm in the middle of an Illinois cornfield. Indeed the very variety of his audiences or classes—such a broad assortment of Kerouacs and Eddie Guests and Dostoevskys and Alexander Woollcotts—makes it sometimes more than he's worth to find out where his audience *is* as he prattles on with his poetry. Is that bearded one in front a San Franciscan or farmer? Is that Southern belle taking notes or writing a letter? Who are those old ladies in the back and what will they say when he reads the poem blasting Christian Science off the face of the earth?—"Mr._____, I *so* enjoyed that piece about Christian Science. Do you know Edwin Dakin's book on Mrs. Eddy?" He stumbles from his podiums and out of his workshops with no sense that the academics and their institutions are taking over but, instead, that they are being taken over, taken over by everyone from "the Kentuckian walking the vale of the Elkhorn" to "prisoner, fancy-man, rowdy, lawyer, physician," in short everyone in Walt Whitman. He is not sure he's happy about this—sometimes he thinks he'd prefer a long seminar with Cleanth Brooks—but he is pretty sure that this is what is before him. He is also pretty sure that the general confusion, which certainly exists, is, whatever else, a great argument itself against many of the criticisms of writing in the colleges.

He would insist, thus, that the confusion completely erases the complaint that literature has gone academic and institutional, has been cut off from its roots in feeling and experience, and tied in instead with criticism and the thin utterances of aging potentates. He would agree that some of it is institutional and academic, but he would point to the presence of the other kind as antidote, the kind that could have six doses of Eliot's essays and six doses of simple grammar and still be wild and woolly. As for the complaint that political control of the literary country is being wielded by a certain *kind* of aging potentate hankering for a certain *kind* of poem or story, that too, he would say, is refuted by the prevailing confusion. He has seen a certain amount of uniformity and has been annoyed by automatic, dull-textbook questions thrown at him just when he has been talking to the top of his bent about blithe spirits. But all of these memories recede in importance for him when he recalls the remarkable divergence of allegiances he has found at the colleges. He has been in Ransom country (in this instance, Indiana) and found it much less Ransomy than Kilmery (at least in the section near the Student Union). And he has also been at Iowa, where one summer of the workshop there persuaded him that mad discontinuity, among both teachers and students, was much more to be expected than craven conformity. He remembers wierd juxtapositions of irreconcilable opposites in the same gaunt poets, chubby novelists. A student who spent all his days and nights at Kenney's (the local 3.2 bar), collected Henry Miller and old copies of *Neurotica,* sponsored brawls and had his driver's license taken away for more than good cause—he was the most methodical, surgeon-like New Critic on the whole Iowa River, while a plain-living, plain-speaking, bespectacled girl who should have been finishing up a dissertation on "Old-Saxon Vowels Under Weak Stress" produced a story written in intense, surging, high-octane paragraphs about fruition and the nether parts.

He has found all this most satisfying (some of the above details have been changed to confuse the innocent). And at the smaller colleges he has found conformity and predictability even more unlikely, indeed sometimes simply impossible to achieve merely because the new gospels to which conformity might be expected just haven't arrived yet. More satisfying yet. He remembers, for example, a teacher from a small college in Illinois who could do nothing but talk staunchly about his old teacher Irving Babbitt.

But not all satisfying. The bad days don't vanish just because there are good ones. When he thinks of the horrible poems and stories he has been obliged to read and confer about, and make kindly remarks about, they appear sometimes before him *en masse,* a kind of typewritten Chinese Wall between him and anything else that might ever, even in his retirement in the Virgin Islands, be good reading. One part of the wall consists of the frightening, phony beatnik things—great theorizings about experiencing life if you would render it, with intermittent comments on existentialism and status symbols and how to get out of the bourgeois rut. Another part is solidly packed with all those solid-pack poems students write after they've first learned about ambiguity, tension, indirection. And still a third part is constructed of massive fictional accounts of now impossibly dull historical situations—General Custer at home, Pericles given a heart (American) and a girl (likewise) at the Theban Gates. And so on. There are no choices here, nor does the variety stimulate. The writer-lecturer frequently wishes he were on a different circuit.

I know this writer-lecturer intimately and I can affirm what you perhaps have guessed that his fairness, his desire to find virtue in all the parties has undone him. He has been much unsettled by the variety of his DC-3 experiences, by the contradictions he has found. I have noted that his dreams and his reality are beginning to get mixed up, and that his bronchitis, which was once a pretty sensible disease, is now mostly psychosomatic. Furthermore his long sentences about the Writing Situation now tend to taper off into dots. I don't think he will ever, now, make a good contributor to my magazine.

My complaint against him—though I have a great affection for him—is chiefly that he has gotten so involved, so worked up about all these issues and forces at work in our literary places that he has begun to talk about literature merely as a bundle of issues, forces. There are always choices to be made —to be or not to be a writer at a college; to be or not to be concerned with making a living at writing; to be or not to be on the side of Bellow, Rexroth, Ciardi, Trilling, Auden, Bogan, Tate, Engle, Shapiro, Winters, Ransom, Stegner or _____ (fill in your own candidate). Now I wouldn't deny for a minute the importance of these issues; nor would I hesitate to take sides and plunge in, as he has done, if the occasion should arise. But I am a sort of sentimentalist and I remember that once *I* took a lecture trip (normally, you understand, I don't budge from the offices of my mag) to a little women's college in the South, one I'd never even heard of, and discovered something there almost unique in our writing time, certainly something that a businessman writer-lecturer like my friend would overlook ten times out of ten while traveling about in his DC-3's. I discovered that writing was being taught down there as one of the *graces!*

I don't know what all the other graces are—needlepoint, the piano, the waltz, etc.—and I couldn't begin to tell you the differences between the practice and teaching of writing as a grace and the practice and teaching of it as a profession or a means of communication or a way to dig the soul (certainly nobody at that institution *told* me they were teaching it as a grace)—I couldn't begin to describe the differences, but they were there.

The results weren't remarkable; I saw nothing but undergraduate work and it was marred by most of the usual faults of undergraduate work, and yet I found in it an interest in, and a devotion to, gesture, intonations, manner, simple elegance of form and carriage that I don't find up here in the morning mails much and can't imagine my writer-lecturer friend finding in his workshops.

They wrote sonnets mostly, sonnets that didn't say much (sonnets tend that way), sonnets that would have offended not only William Carlos Williams but also almost anybody who likes to imagine that poetry has got to be a living language, sonnets that nobody would want to print in an important public place. The only thing about these sonnets that impressed me—I keep saying they weren't very good; they weren't—was this damned elegance or finish I'm trying to get at. They had it. It was as if those girls had actually been writing sonnets for a few years—and maybe they had—as part of their training in how to be ladies.

As I say all this I recall vaguely some of H. L. Mencken's caustic remarks about Southern Writing as all decorum and flowers (he was speaking of the literature before the Fugitives and our other modern Southern celebrities) ; and I recall also the contempt which some of the Fugitives themselves— no friends of Mencken—have expressed about the empty literature of the Old South. I recognize and sympathize with these criticisms, and think that the word "empty" is the critical one here; but I think that in our various contemporary efforts to produce the opposite, that is, a literature that is in one way or another "full," we have got ourselves into a position where we tend to neglect one of the great traditional sources of strength in literature. As a result we have not even a contemporary vocabulary to deal with the qualities I am struggling to refer to. I am positively embarrassed to be talking here about "grace" and "elegance" and "finish"; I feel I should be talking instead about "technical skill" or "precision" or "a sense of structure," or perhaps not talking at all about these peripheral matters but concentrating instead on our writers' capacity really to deal with *life*. My embarrassment, I feel, is produced by a literary situation in which the academics as well as the anti-academics have played a part. Both sides keep trying to justify literature in a world where literature's power is no longer taken for granted. All is therefore purposefulness; all must be clearly directed toward some social or spiritual or emotional end. The earnest literary functionalism visible in the proliferation of our various academic writing schemes is thus just one manifestation of this. It does not matter whether the writing conference is full of talk about writing markets or, more exaltedly, "valid renditions of experience." In either case there is a puritanical sense of *mission* present—present in the teachers and the students and certainly in the administrations behind them—a sense of mission which, though admirable, has in its intensity managed practically to cancel out the archaic notion of literary grace that I found stirring in my Southern belles.

And so I think my writer-lecturer has perhaps had enough of the circuit for a while (he won't listen to me; he'll be off next year on his biggest tour yet). I'd prefer for him that he stayed home for a bit and got out of the literary swim, puttered around the garden, took up the violin, maybe sat around reading *The Miscellany*.

But no, *The Miscellany* wouldn't help either. *The Miscellany*, I do not wholly regret saying, is largely missionary too; the editors are in the swim like the writer-lecturers. I and my friend are really very close, and I don't think either one of us would like to give up what we have for a gross of Southern sonnets.

We could, though, perhaps, take a few tranquilizer pills and stop talking so much about the Literary Situation. That would at least be a way of making a start toward the rediscovery of those quaint graces.

Shakespeare, etc., at Three o'Clock in the Morning

I hope you are all wondering what on earth the connection is between Shakespeare and three o'clock in the morning. I am attracted to catchy titles and have always thought one good title was worth several poor texts. What do I mean by my title? Well, I don't mean my relations with Shakespeare at three o'clock in the morning, or your relations with him then. The title admits either possibility, but I happen to mean Shakespeare's relations with himself at three o'clock in the morning. This is a subject nobody knows anything about, so it suits my purposes admirably.

But I don't wish to be narrowly academic here and discuss merely Shakespeare. Hence, "Shakespeare, etc." I think now I can leave the title and get on.

In cartoons a Poet is frequently drawn as an emaciated, melancholy Englishman with narrow, sloping shoulders, tiny, slippered feet, and a tendency to stare vacantly out of windows. He is like the cartoon Scholar except that he does not wear glasses and seldom speaks. By day he wanders like a ghost through the parlors and formal gardens of the rich; by night he writes furiously in his garret. He lives two lives, the life of the flesh (in all those parlors) and the life of the spirit (in his garret), and he finds the latter more his dish of tea. He is in other words restrained by strange psychic forces from enjoying himself in Real Life, but he has found an Outlet in Literature.

To this caricature may be added a picture of his garret in monumental disarray. There are books and papers strewn all over the floor. There are empty coffee cups and half-smoked cigarettes surrounding his typewriter. There are perhaps even a few empty bottles lying about. All of this, added to our picture of the disheveled poet himself, suggests that at three o'clock in the morning his study is one of the town's hot spots, and his outlet in literature is quite an outlet indeed.

I hope you are all as familiar with this picture of a poet as I am, because I wish to oppose it to two other pictures, one by Brooks and Warren and one by another kind of scholar whom I shall call H. S. The Brooks and Warren picture, as a good many of you know, is of a polished poet whose emotional disturbances are always in perfect control, a kind of scientist-diplomat armed, even in the privacy of his study, with various precision instruments and a large store of delicate nuances. It is this poet who, far from writing furiously at three A.M. in his garret, carefully weighs each word he writes for three days so that you, his readers, may if you wish write a complete scholarly monograph on a single one of his immensely laboured sonnets. It is this poet who plagues you in those courses where they talk about Levels of Meaning. Do you know him now? I think you do, and assuming that you do I think you will agree with me that he somehow lacks the temperament we associate with creativity. He seems incapable of producing anything except stomach ulcers. Let us abandon him in favor of the poet presented to us by H. S.

H. S. is the Historical Scholar, and the poet he presents us with is a curious compound of forces and trends, conventions and traditions, and perhaps philosophies and superstitions, on top of which are located, like candles on a birthday cake, a few love affairs and prison sentences, trips to Rome and

Florence, and clever remarks about Life. This poet is chiefly remarkable, I think, for appearing to have no literary existence at all. He is described as a Figure of his Age, a fascinating personality, and possibly a dope fiend, but his relations with his typewriter, or fountain pen, or quill are hardly mentioned. And for good reason. The historical scholar, being a meticulously honest fellow, writes what he knows about; he does not write about what happens behind the door to the poet's study because that door is (generally) closed to him.

Now this kind of honesty, though it must earn our praise, must also, I think, be criticized just a little bit for leaving us with a lopsided picture of the writer's life, lopsided in that it leaves the writing part out. This lopsidedness is especially evident in the picture it gives of Elizabethan writers, because Elizabethans had a bad habit of not writing very much about themselves. Shakespeare was probably more remiss in this respect than any other, and as a result we carry about with us today a lopsided image of a man who was an actor and a big wheel in the Elizabethan popular theater, a man who stole plots and rewrote old speeches in such a careless way that his printers always misread him, and a man who rather oddly left, in his will, only his second-best bed to his wife. The historical scholar cannot be blamed for our not knowing more, but he can sometimes be blamed for making us think we do. Especially, I think, he can be blamed for the very common notion that great poetry and great plays came easy to Shakespeare. I do not deny that much of the historical evidence suggests this; and I do not deny that writing was probably for Shakespeare easier than for a great many other writers; but I rather resent the suggestion that this greatest man's greatest activity was as easy for him as rolling off a log. Not only does the suggestion undermine my topic here by making it doubtful that Shakespeare was ever awake at three o'clock in the morning, but it undermines my notion of what the artistic act involves.

Obviously, then, of these three pictures of the poet, I favor the first. That melancholy Englishman with his furious night life appeals to me because he seems to be taking a healthy interest in his work. That is good. I don't want the poet of my dreams either loafing on his job or being terribly efficient at it. I want him wild-eyed, with coffee nerves.

Since I don't favor the picture given us by the historical scholar, you may, then, properly wonder why I am now going to tell you about a book by a historical scholar, Alfred Harbage. The answer is that I think the historical scholar can, if inadvertently, tell us a good deal about what the three A.M. wild-eyed poet is *not* wild-eyed about. From little negatives mighty positives grow.

The book is *Shakespeare and the Rival Traditions*. The traditions in question are two rival theatrical traditions. One you are familiar with, since it is Shakespeare's popular theater. Professor Harbage describes the Elizabethan popular theater as, indeed, popular. He tells us that the number of known dramatic troupes which performed in London and the provinces between 1560 and 1642 was about 150. He tells us that the best of these troupes performed indiscriminately for royalty, nobility, substantial citizens, London throngs, and "wide-eyed villagers." And he tells us that in Shakespeare's heyday the audiences for the popular theaters in London alone came to 18,000-24,000 people weekly. This is a lot for a city of two hundred thousand—I don't know what the weekly attendance at all the movies and plays in New York is, but to equal, proportionately, this London record it would have to be close to a million.

Perhaps you don't know, however, that there was also an Elizabethan *un*popular theater. I confess that this was partly news to me too until I read Professor Harbage's book, and I am still only prepared to accept his thesis with a grain of salt. I had supposed that while the various dramatic troupes frequently performed for very select audiences, and while some of the plays were better suited for the groundlings than others, essentially the Elizabethan theater was a homogeneous industry (I am always tempted to say homogenized) characterized by a good deal of competition among theatrical companies but not containing anything so grand as the rivalry Professor Harbage suggests. This rivalry, however, if we are to believe the Professor, went very deep, and the opponents of the popular theater were contemptuous of its basic artistic and moral assumptions. These opponents were the "little eyasses" mentioned in *Hamlet*.

Hamlet and Rosencrantz were referring, as the notes tell us, to the child choristers, mainly from St. Paul's Cathedral and the Chapel Royal, who made up the acting companies for two indoor theaters, Whitefriars and Blackfriars. Hamlet and Rosencrantz were not complimentary about them; they noted that they were very fashionable, that their playwrights were overzealous in their criticism of the public theaters, and that generally they had stirred up an argument (known to us as The War of the Theaters) involving a great "throwing about of brains." Shakespeare's remarks thus suggest what Professor Harbage tries to confirm, that Blackfriars and Whitefriars were the home of a "coterie" theater whose adherents looked down their noses at the potboilers being turned out by Shakespeare and the other popular dramatists.

Unlike the popular theater, this "coterie" had academic origins. Small amateur productions, mostly in grammar schools, occasionally received public attention when a penniless schoolmaster, looking for a little pocket money, took his charges briefly out on the road. How the choristers got into the act instead of the grammar school boys is not clear to me, but at any rate they did, and the kind of plays their academic supervisors chose for them was not the popular kind, whatever that, as we shall see, may be. Things went well for them. They gathered together for their productions an audience Harbage describes as "the most *avant-garde*, the most sophisticated, the most interested in art as art . . . of all the 'publics' available in England at the time." And into their fold came play-wrights who wanted to produce *"avant-garde"* scripts: Chapman, Marston, at intervals Jonson, and others. Pretty soon their activities were sufficiently well-defined to constitute a quite different kind of theater from that at the Globe and the Fortune.

A few of the physical differences cited by Harbage are worthy of note. The coterie theaters charged several times as much for admission as the popular theaters (for the coterie theaters it was a shilling or more; for the popular theaters the base rate was a penny). Their *avant-garde* audience was therefore partly a monied as well as an intellectual audience, and it was much smaller, amounting, Professor Harbage deduces (by observing the size of the theaters and the frequency of performance), to only six or seven hundred a week. It was also primarily an urban audience; the coterie companies did not go out on the road.

These physical differences suggest what Harbage regards as the major differences in the dramas themselves. Generally, he finds the popular drama was "romantic, idealistic, positive, and often patriotic and religious," while the coterie drama was satirical and erotic. The coterie drama "sailed close to the wind of libel suits and action by the censor," while the popular companies "adopted a moral policy" that Professor Harbage compares to Hollywood's self-censorship of its movies. Then, too, the popular drama was weighted down with conventions and normally contained a clown, a chorus, a good deal of "cross-wooing of dukes and countesses," whole battles waged between four or five inept soldiers, asides that were not spoken aside, musical interludes, public soliloquies, and a good deal else of this nature, while the coterie drama made capital of ridiculing the popular theatrical conventions. All in all between the proponents of the two theaters there was, Harbage feels, a wide divergence in attitude toward "life, literature, and morality."

Thus, briefly, Professor Harbage. His book is an interesting one, I think, though I have some doubts about it, and when I came away from it, I felt as much enlightened as I ever feel now that winter is here. I felt, for example, that I knew a little more than I had known about a problem that has vexed me for some time: the very great difference between the texture of Shakespeare's and most of Jonson's plays. I felt also that I knew a good deal more about Hamlet's little eyasses. I was therefore grateful to the book for its service to my understanding, and I suspect that any future classes I may have will be subjected to quite a bit of this "rival tradition" business. But I was also suspicious that I had been brought to understand a bit too much. Let me explain.

Let us assume that all the Elizabethan dramatists also knew something about the rival traditions—more, even, than Professor Harbage. And let us assume that they are all sitting in their studies at three o'clock in the morning writing something or other. Let us even be magnanimous and say that it is raining outside—for it is of course much easier to write when it is raining. Or snowing.

The popular dramatists know that their plays should be "romantic, idealistic, positive, and often patriotic and religious," and that they should avoid smut, since the popular companies have "adopted a moral policy." The coterie dramatists on the other hand know that their plays should be erotic and satirical, for they remember what Professor Harbage told them about the coterie audience: it demands its "money's worth in a game of dangerously high flavor." And both kinds of playwrights know thoroughly the conventions of the popular theater which it will be the popular dramatists' job to exploit and the coterie dramatists' to explode. Knowing all this, can they dash off their plays in no time and hurry down to breakfast?

Obviously not—but I don't mean to be facetious. I merely wish to point out the limitations of Professor Harbage's kind of knowledge. From the dramatist's point of view it is both elementary and stale. It is elementary in that anyone remotely connected with these theaters can know as much and not faintly resemble a playwright. And it is stale in that it is a knowledge of the past—of what audiences at other plays have wanted, accepted, sanctioned, agreed to believe. It is not thereby knowledge to be scorned, but it is the knowledge that the dramatist *begins* with, just as he begins with a desk, some paper and a pencil.

Thus one of the very worst of Elizabethan playwrights, Robert Greene, began like Shakespeare himself with knowledge like this. Writing for a popular theater, he decided to turn out a romantic comedy named *Friar Bacon and Friar Bungay* with a strong moral tone. He thought it would be good theater—because it had been good theater before—to have a good deal of cross-wooing for plot, and a good deal of magic business for show—and he thought it necessary, from an ethical point of view, that in the wooing the Prince not be allowed to make mincemeat of the humble virtues of the country girl Margaret. He also thought it necessary to disown his show's greatest asset, the magic, by having his best magician turn penitent at the end and promise to spend the rest of his life "in *pure* devotion" praying to his God. I say he *began* with these thoughts, because I want to distinguish between the preliminary assumptions upon which his romantic comedy is built, and what he had to worry about, at three A.M., when he was actually writing his comedy. I have a faint suspicion that Mr. Greene was not up at three A.M. often enough, but the distinction is still valid.

The better the play the more valid the distinction becomes. That is, it is less elementary to call *Friar Bacon and Friar Bungay* "romantic, idealistic, positive, and often patriotic and religious" than it is to call *Midsummer Night's Dream* this. But the distinction should not be allowed merely in cases of exceptional merit. The distinction must be made whenever

272

we are talking about a single work of art, rather than a type or a kind of art. And in a highly conventionalized art like that of the Elizabethan dramatists the distinction is of the greatest importance. In a highly conventionalized art there are more preliminary assumptions than in a free art, and it is accordingly easier there to mistake the preliminaries for the art. If, in *Friar Bacon and Friar Bungay*, for example, we were to try to draw a line somehow through the play, putting on one side of the line the material Greene went into his study with, and on the other, the creative, the new, the untried material that he supplied at his desk at three A.M., I imagine we would find most of the material we as a modern audience find worthy of discussion to be on the "before-writing" side. And yet, to criticize Greene for what he starts with is unfair to Greene. Greene is probably a bad enough playwright to be damned for what he does rather than for what others before him have done—so let me suggest briefly part of *Friar Bacon and Friar Bungay* where we may possibly come to grips with him rather than with his tradition.

Much of the magic business is, as I have stated, in the tradition. But the presence of several magicians competing against one another is, I would guess, Greene. I suspect we are witness to late Elizabethan gothic—that is, to the Elizabethan equivalent of something like *The Return of the Wife of Frankenstein. Frankenstein* itself has already been produced several times, and now—if it is to be done effectively again—it has to be souped up. So we find Greene at three A.M. adding Bela Lugosi and Lon Chaney, Jr., to an old script that had merely poor old Boris Karloff, and we find him lavishing his attentions upon the *kinds* of tricks his magicians can perform in trying to outdo each other. This "contest" *motif* may seem ridiculous to us but it is, I am confident, pure Greene. All the details of the cumbersome machinery that must clutter up any theater producing the play is Greene's three A.M. inspiration, while the general claptrap about necromantic spells and Latin incantations, as well as the Friar's final perfunctory renunciation of his powers, is conventional. Thus Greene, at three o'clock in the morning, concerns himself, if I am correct, rather heavy-handedly with spectacle.

Now if we compare *Friar Bacon and Friar Bungay* with Shakespeare's *Tempest,* which is also a kind of Elizabethan gothic, though it is sufficiently later to complicate the problem of what is conventional, I think we can see a very great shift in emphasis. *The Tempest* is certainly a play of spectacle, and a proper production of it must require a good deal of the kind of stage "business" that we find in Greene's play. The "business," however, seems to me to be subordinated to Prospero's renunciation of the "business." Prospero the character rather than Prospero the magician is Shakespeare's three A.M. concern, with the result that Prospero's final speeches about abjuring "this rough magic" are climactic, I think, rather than perfunctory (as in Friar Bacon's case) —indeed I am foolish enough to go along with those critics who say that Shakespeare is here talking about himself and his art. Between *The Tempest,* at any rate, where the Elizabethan gothic is used to document or substantiate a statement about the flimsiness of man's greatest enterprises, and *Friar Bacon and Friar Bungay,* where the gothic is used to bring forth mainly, a few fancy stage props, I find a significant difference between Shakespeare and Greene. At three o'clock in the morning Shakespeare was struggling to find a way to make the gothic somehow real and valid, while Greene was merely struggling to make it more gothic.

Verbally Greene's gothicness emerges in ornamental displays of exotic imagery, particularly when his most gothic character, Friar Bacon, speaks. I imagine, for example, that Greene had a wild and busy three A.M. with this speech of the Friar's describing the big dinner he is going to serve up, or rather conjure up, for Emperor Frederick and King Henry:

274

Wines richer than th' Egyptian courtesan
Quaffed to Augustus' Kingly countermatch,
Shall be caroused in English Henry's feast;
Candy shall yield the richest of her canes;
Persia, down her Volga by canoes,
Send down the secrets of her spicery;
The Afric dates, mirabolans of Spain,
Conserves and suckets from Tiberias,
Cates from Judaea, choicer than the lamp
That fired Rome," etc.

I confess that the thought of such a dinner leaves me quite cold—all I can do is wonder why Greene has the Volga running, suddenly, through Persia—but I am quite confident that the extravagance here is something he worked hard on, just as Keats worked hard on that midnight lunch Porphyro served Madeline in "The Eve of St. Agnes":

". . . he from forth the closet brought a heap
Of candied apple, quince, and plum, and gourd;
With jellies soother than the creamy curd,
And lucent syrops, tinct with cinnamon;
Manna and dates, in argosy transferred
From Fez; and spiced dainties, every one,
From silken Samarcand to cedar'd Lebanon."

Both Keats and Greene have a lot of faith in what can be done with romantic listings of foreign foods, and while Keats is the more successful of the two, I doubt if he stayed up later than Greene did choosing the ingredients. Both of them, it seems to me, in this respect pay much more attention to the atmosphere of romance—or, to put it differently, take much more seriously the possibilities of romance than does Shakespeare. Shakespeare's imagery seems to me seldom to be chosen for the purpose of overpowering the audience; it is explanatory rather than ejaculatory, documentary rather than propagandistic; and on those rare occasions when he chooses to be lush, he also chooses to be more than this. One would suppose, for example, that in *Antony and Cleopatra* there was plenty of provocation, on all those gaudy nights, for a good long listing of what Antony and Cleopatra actually ate and drank—cinnamon from Lebanon, candied apples from Samarcand, gin from Holland, and so forth. But no such list (as I recall) appears. The nearest thing to the Keats or Greene kind of extravagance is found in Enobarbus's familiar description of Cleopatra herself—age cannot wither her, nor custom stale her infinite variety, etc.—which goes on for thirty or forty lines and is unquestionably one of the really great verbal extravagances in literature. The most extravagant thing about it, however, is, I think, that Shakespeare presents it to us as a kind of sample or demonstration of extravagance. In context it is the speech of a braggart boasting to the local Roman yokels about what he has seen abroad. We accept it, accordingly, as good boasting, not as gospel.

This suggests to me that at three A.M. Shakespeare's problem was not, as it would have been for Greene, thinking up what color the sails on Cleopatra's barge should be (purple), or what kind of rare metal the oars of the barge should be made of (silver)—as a matter of fact Plutarch had already thought of all these things for Shakespeare. So Shakespeare's early morning problem was how to employ the traditional extravagance of Cleopatra without sacrificing all to extravagance. It was a problem of balance, and the balance was, I hardly need add, wonderfully maintained.

Now—some of you look as if you had lost the thread of my argument as I skipped about from Professor Harbage to Greene and then to Cleopatra's barge—let me try to find it for you again. It is very simple, really. I start with the cartoonist's stock figure of the wild poet (or dramatist) in his study, and oppose it to the picture of the scientist-diplomat poet (or dramatist) given us by Brooks and Warren, and to the picture of the conventional, traditional, man-of-his-time poet (or dramatist) given us by H. S. Then I raise certain objections to the H. S. picture—chiefly that it is too elementary and general to guide us in understanding what a specific poet's or dramatist's specific problems of composition are. And finally I take the offensive and brazenly tell you what in fact Shakespeare and Greene *did* worry about. This is where I am now, and I should remind you that I have no inside track to the studies of Shakespeare and Greene and that I am really suggesting only what they *may* have worried about. All I am concerned with is indicating to you that the original picture of the wild poet surrounded by coffee cups and cigarette butts is to be preferred to the other pictures, because it emphasizes the complexity, the diversity, the uncertainty, and the intractability of the creative act.

But if this is all I am concerned with, then I have, you say, entirely too much steam up. After all, you all know the difficulties of the creative artist and do not need to be reminded of them. Quite right. But in my defense, I would like to point to the very common modern restriction upon the phrase "creative artist." The creative, or serious, artist is constantly distinguished from the hack, or popular artist. The creative artist gets a fine press in the literary journals but has a tough time with the public; the hack makes thousands of dollars a year but keeps his name hack. The distinction between these two kinds of artists is so common that, if there is any argument to be encountered at all, it is an argument about the terms to be used. A representative of the literary journals will use the terms I have, and talk glibly about serious or creative art as opposed to hackwork, potboilers, and sop for the masses. A good literary or dramatic democrat, like Professor Harbage, will on the other hand talk about popular art and coterie art, or primary and tributary art. But whatever the terms used, the distinction remains, and it is a dis-

277

tinction founded solidly upon at least one assumption common to both the highbrows and the democrats, the assumption that the popular artist or hack is not a creator so much as a caterer. He knows the pulse of the people; he is attuned to his times; he writes according to the trick; he is a student of audience responses, not of the human soul.

Because there is some truth in this assumption, it is very misleading, especially in the drama because the dramatist's audience is so much more solid and tangible an audience than the audience for poetry and fiction. Drama *is* theater, one is frequently told, and immediately to the mind comes a vision of one of those first-night audiences the movies always show us with everybody standing up at the end applauding, whistling, and crying "author." Or perhaps instead the vision is of the reverse, of a sadly neglected dramatist reading his unproduceable play to his nearest and dearest friend in somebody's closet. Subjected as we are, and properly, to the notion that drama is an art to be seen and heard, it is difficult for us to remember that the *writing* of drama, even popular drama, like the *writing* of poetry is not wholly a public catering occupation, but also a private three A.M. occupation. How it is written, and what happens to it after it is written, get mixed up in our minds with, I think, unfortunate results.

One unfortunate result is to be noted in Professor Harbage's book. There, in trying to be modest, he admits that his thesis about the rival traditions has limitations when it comes to Jonson and Shakespeare, since their genius complicated the pattern of conflict between the popular and coterie theaters. Thus he implies that genius, and only genius, complicated this pattern. This I find ridiculous. Such an implication turns most of our dramatists—all of them not complicated by genius—into objects you can slice up like sausage into traditions, conventions, and formulas. It suggests that traditions, conventions, and formulas are in effect the end product of a dramatist's activities, when actually they are what he starts with. They are what he takes into his study with him, along with his pen and ink, before he has put a word on a page.

Another unfortunate result is to be noted in that trite observation about Shakespeare that any one of us is likely to make when we think that our teacher, or student, or colleague, or roommate is reading Shakespeare too closely. We say, "Well, now, you must remember that Shakespeare was *above all* a practicing dramatist; he was not a theologian, a logician, a semanticist, or a test pilot for Brooks and Warren." What we mean of course is that we think it's possible to read more into Shakespeare than Shakespeare put into Shakespeare, and sometimes we're right. But in defending our position on the grounds that he was above all a practicing dramatist, we're saying something about practicing dramatists that cannot, I think, be said; we're saying that practicing dramatists don't have to be theologians, logicians, semanticists, and test pilots. They do. Even the hack does. Writing a play is not easy, even a bad play; it requires more, as I have tried to point out, than a knowledge of the theater.

The most unfortunate result, however, of neglecting the private nature of art in favor of its later public appearances is not to be found in our attitude toward individual artists. It is not going to hurt Shakespeare or even Greene very much if we call them hacks, and I want you to understand that I have not brought up their three A.M. revels here because I have any special biographical interest in them. But it is going to hurt the art of Greene and Shakespeare, and any other art readily subject to typing and categorization, to be talked about as if all of its exhibits were really alike, as Professor Harbage, for example, does. When he says that the Elizabethan popular drama was "romantic, idealistic, positive, and often patriotic and religious," he is as a matter of fact praising it; for he professes to like that kind of thing. For my money, however, this is faint praise. It is not that I dislike romanticism, patriotism, and so forth, but that I dislike saying *only* this—because this is saying nothing—about any work of art. Saying this does not, for example, distinguish the Elizabethan popular drama from most modern movies, which are also "romantic, idealistic, positive, and often patriotic and religious." When such broad classifications come into being, the works lamentably thus classified cease to be art and become merely specimens.

I know that none of us here is guilty of Professor Harbage's sin; in fact, he may not be as guilty of it as I suggest. I have used him as a whipping boy, and I now apologize. But I don't want merely to apologize. I would like also to propose that the next time you read a play—particularly a "conventional" play—you occasionally think of the playwright's dilemma at three o'clock in the morning. Your thoughts may not be very profound—certainly they will be inconclusive—but they should at least keep you from confusing the preliminary assumptions underlying a play, and the play itself. Then, too, in the process of trying to put yourself in the playwright's position, you will incidentally pay him and his art a compliment by facing up, vicariously, to the difficulties he had to face up to.

MISCELLANEOUS
REVIEWS

MacLeish and Democratic Pastoral

Archibald MacLeish's *Collected Poems, 1917-1952* contains perhaps eighty poems written since the publication of his earlier volume of collected poems (1924-1933). It also contains twelve poems written in the period covered by the earlier volume though not to be found in that volume, and several pre-1924 poems that, in 1933, MacLeish presumably thought of as juvenilia. Conversely only one poem, "Insomnia" (a poor poem), is to be found in the 1933 volume and not in the new one, so clearly the new volume gives a much more complete account of MacLeish's activities than the old. That it does not include his wartime radio verse plays (*Air Raid*, etc.) is a fact I can't bring myself to worry about, since his long-poem ventures are amply represented otherwise by everything, that I know of, from *The Pot of Earth* to *The Trojan Horse*.

In the old volume MacLeish asserted at the outset that "this book is not a 'collected edition' of my poems nor does it purport to trace my development as a poet." In the new volume he asserted nothing, but I think I can safely say that it is a collected edition and that it does trace his development as a poet.

---

* *Collected Poems, 1917-1952*. By Archibald MacLeish. Houghton Mifflin Co., 1952.

So much for the news.

Reading it as a prospective reviewer I was immediately depressed by the variety of materials MacLeish was presenting for review. A reviewer's lot is a hard one (though not as hard as the lot of the poet reviewed) when he is faced with thirty-five years of continuous production. Like a tourist under the guidance of Messrs. Cook, he has entirely too much at his disposal. He must choose between the tour of the Louvre and the tour of the bars. So I was, as I say, depressed; I don't like to be picky. First I considered picking the best poems and setting down a few wise words about them. Without much effort I produced the following list: "Invocation to the Social Muse," "End of the World," "You, Andrew Marvell," "Lines for a Prologue," "Critical Observations," "Eleven," "Voyage West," "Journey Home," "Where the Hayfields Were," and "Crossing." It wasn't a list I was prepared to go to court about, but it was a list of poems I would have been happy to include in the anthology of modern poetry I have not yet been asked by a publisher to edit. The real trouble with the list was that I didn't have much to say about it after I had listed it. It was a dead end; the poems represented, though good poems, did not make a thematic or rhetorical group out of which I could draw something Significantly MacLeishian. All I could do with the list was to say to myself that it was a good list and a longer list than I would be prepared to draw up for most modern poets. This was something, of course; it served to remind me of that which a good many critics these days need to be reminded of, the poetry of Mac-Leish; but it wasn't enough for the solemnities of a serious review. Was it? Anyway I gave the list up.

Secondly, I considered dividing MacLeish's poetry up into various phases. Phases were old and reliable and MacLeish had certainly had phases. He had had an Impressionist phase and a Public Speech phase and a Nationalist phase and a Riviera phase and a good many others. His present phase, perhaps the least distinct of all of them, appeared to be a phase of Uncertainty, since most of the poems composing it were tentative, slight, occasional pieces lacking both the persistence and the garrulous ease of earlier MacLeish. I thought of concentrating on this present phase.

But no. The trouble with the phases, ancient or modern, was that I didn't really believe in them. They kept vanishing or quietly merging with one another. Their integrity as units was suspect. I gave them up with regret.

Thirdly, I considered discussing MacLeish as a pastoral poet. I will admit that I was driven to this by an irrelevancy, my present surroundings, and that possibly MacLeish is not a pastoral poet at all. My present surroundings are California where, as everybody knows, versions of pastoral are constantly thrusting themselves into view. The vegetation shading my somber windows, for example, has been bred out of the desert by the watering and care of thousands of gardeners scattered liberally northward from La Jolla and Rancho Santa Fé. If it were not for these gardeners the vegetation would, I am told, rapidly be replaced by desert again; but because of them the vegetation is not merely suitable for shading my windows; it is also pretty, and the landscape which it composes satisfies completely my notion of a pastoral (a literary pastoral) scene by being both picturesque and homemade. Faced simultaneously with this landscape and MacLeish I could hardly avoid putting them together.

After putting them together for the wrong reasons I began to think there were also right reasons for doing so. MacLeish's connections with Yale, Harvard, Washington, and Farmington, Connecticut, were no deterrent, since pastorals have traditionally emerged from such places, not from places where there are shepherds and sheep. Even less discouraging was the absence in MacLeish's poetry of traditional pastoral settings or devices, since William Empson in his book, *Some Versions of Pastoral,* had opened the way—obscurely to be sure—to finding pastoral in everything and calling it Covert Pastoral. There seemed to be little to prevent a discussion of MacLeish as a pastoral poet, and a good deal to sustain one. The images to which he was most attracted, for example, and from which he expected the highest dividends appeared to be images from nature—the moon, trees, leaves, stars, wind, surf, sunlight and earth. And the theme dominating all his phases appeared to be essentially pastoral: life is richest and best in its elemental forms. Lastly, his rhetoric seemed to indicate that he was steadily, perhaps obsessively concerned with making the poet, himself, into the spittin' modern equivalent of a simple shepherd. Indeed in the mythmaking about himself he was far from content with the conventional pretense, not seriously insisted on in most pastorals, of the poet's being an uncouth swain. He felt obliged like Whitman to drive the notion home again and again. He wanted to be thought of as just a simple man with an "audience of men like other men who understand the sun on the side of a wall, and the shadow in the shade of a tree, and the feel of things, and the thinking of things, naturally and simply and with the hands and the mouth and the eyes."* His insistence upon this did not make him at all like Whitman, but it put him, with Whitman, in with that body of poets who do not wish to be thought of as Literary, the body of poets who produce much, as it seemed to me, of what Empson called Covert Pastoral. Yes, the more I looked at the California landscape, the more convinced I became that MacLeish fitted in.

It was not and is not to his discredit that he appeared to fit in, but his fitting in led me immediately into difficulty with the phrase Covert Pastoral. I didn't care what Empson meant by it, but I began to wonder what I meant. There was certainly nothing Covert about MacLeish's pastoral asser-

---

* Not from a poem but from a dissertation by MacLeish on the audience for poetry. In *Furioso,* Volume I, Number 1.

286

tions. In his Baccalaureate poem (printed in *Tower of Ivory*, 1917) he observed that, after the college learning from New Haven had gone down the drain, there would remain

> other, magic things—
> The fog that creeps in wanly from the sea,
> The rotten harbor smell, the mystery
> Of moonlit elms, the flash of pigeon wings . . .

In "Eleven" (*Streets in the Moon*, 1926) he described a child tired of things of the mind who went out of the house to find an old gardener "smelling of sun, of summer," with whom the child sat,

> Happy as though he had no name, as though
> He had been no one: like a leaf, a stem,
> Like a root growing.

In "Seafarer" (*Poems*, 1924-33) he advised voyagers in this life that the important things to learn were "to walk/The roll of earth, the pitch and fall/That swings across these trees those stars" and "to sleep against the ground." And in a recent poem, "Where the Hayfields Were," he described an old man and his daughter who, in the process of burning off a meadow, left an impression with him not unlike that left by Wordsworth's solitary reaper:

> Slightly she danced in the stillness, in the twilight,
> Dancing in the meadows where the hayfields were.

These poems, moreover, taken pretty much at random from different periods of his work, were not thematically exceptional. They were the norm, and their pastorality was positively aggressive. I began to think that Covert Pastoral was the wrong phrase.

Not entirely. Though the pastoral themes were overt, the insistence, previously mentioned, upon the poet's *being* a pastoral figure was extremely deceptive. Empson had observed that most pastoral was about the People and about the virtues of their simple, close-to-the-earth lives, but that it was not normally *by* them or *for* them. The tricky part of MacLeish's case, however, was his insistence that his verse was both by and for the elemental man. Thus he constantly framed his poems as addresses to elemental persons of one hue or another. In "Memory Green" he addressed

> . . . you at dusk along the Friedrichstrasse
> Or you in Paris on the windy quay,

"you" in this instance being the incoherent people of the world who feel things. In "Not Marble Nor the Gilded Monuments" he addressed an elemental Woman whom he said he preferred not to describe in the conventional (contrived) sonneteer's manner, since she was no contrivance but Real:

> I will [instead] say you are young and straight and your
> skin fair
> And you stood in the door and the sun was a shadow of
> leaves on your shoulders
> And a leaf on your hair.

In "Sentiments for a Dedication" he addressed the men of his own time, the *living* men:

> O living men Remember me Receive me among you.

And in "The Old Man to the Lizard" he addressed a lizard, a "natural" if there ever was one,

> tell me, lover of
> Sun, lover of noon, lizard,
> Is it because the noon is gold with
> Flame you love it so?

A different mode of address which he used frequently produced much the same effect. Instead of addressing an elemental "you," he merged the "you" with himself and talked about an elemental "us." Thus, in "America Was Promises," he said

> and we move on: we move down:
> with the first light we push forward,

thereby identifying himself with all other Americans, all of whom were taking part in an elementary evolutionary movement into the west, the future, the unknown, the what-all. And in a poem entitled simply "Men" he said,

> Our history is grave noble and tragic
> We trusted the look of the sun on the green leaves,

thereby making it understood that he too was one who trusted the sun's look. The device was a familiar one, of course; it was the device used by Antony when he said to the crowd, over Caesar's body, "I tell you that which you yourselves do know"; and it was the device used rather less effectively by Coriolanus when he attempted, only half-heartedly and under advisement, to persuade the same old crowd that he was a "man of their infirmity." Unlike Antony and Coriolanus, however, MacLeish was not a character in somebody else's drama; he was the dramatist, and he apparently wanted not merely the crowd on stage (Americans, Voyagers, Lizards and Promenaders on the Friedrichstrasse) but also his literary audience to think of him as being incapable of using an oratorical device. Or, to put it differently, he wanted to appear in the guise of the good and simple Othello who, on stage or off stage, was *really* capable of only a "round, unvarnished tale." Even to the elect he wanted to appear as common.

I say this under advisement, for it seemed to me that he never actually appeared this way. The primitive in MacLeish was outweighed in every poem by his tremendous verbal sophistication. I could not imagine a very substantial audience for his poetry other than the elect. Who among his elemental American listeners could have been expected to know that MacLeish was addressing him when using the phrase "voyagers in these leaves"? And what soldier would have realized that he was included when MacLeish said, *"we too have heard/Far off . . . the horn of Roland in the passages of Spain"*? Constantly, while professing simplicity, MacLeish indulged in the complex forms of statement of his nonpastoral poetic compatriots. Constantly he was referential and indirect when, for his announced purposes, he should have been simply reportorial, specific, straightforward. This was not, I felt, an indication that his pastorality was so much waste effort, but it was an indication of confusion, on his part, about where the effort might reasonably have been expected to have any effect. Empson's assertion that pastoral was not by or for the People could only, apparently, have served to make MacLeish mad, and yet the assertion was just as true when applied to MacLeish's pastorals as when applied to Milton's or Spenser's.

Thus, Covert Pastoral. Perhaps after all the phrase was badly chosen; perhaps Hair-on-the-chest Pastoral or Democratic Pastoral would have described MacLeish's verse more accurately. He was not trying to hide Pastoral; he was trying to deny the literary shenanigans which have traditionally enshrouded Pastoral. I was reminded of the difficulty most elemental persons, like myself, have before those elemental

290

pictures in the Museum of Modern Art. Underneath them a printed card normally announces that their creator has attempted "to regain a primitive sense of awareness" by concentrating on "essentials" and abandoning mere "representation." Something like that anyway. The statement always seemed ridiculous to me. It was all very well to abandon mere representation, but it was a mistake to regard the abandonment as a primitive action. It was a very sophisticated action; it was an action going beyond representation, an action involving abstracting the essence of something *from* the something. Similarly, in pastorals an abstracting or idealizing process was involved which was caviare to the general, nothing to the million. MacLeish was therefore misled in expecting the million to identify themselves with his voyagers in the leaves.

There remained to be considered, however, the effects of MacLeish's delusions—assuming I was correct that they were delusions—upon the poetry itself. Though fashion made it pleasant to note that MacLeish's preoccupation with extending the audience for poetry had led to a great waste of his talents, I didn't believe this. In the first place waste was what MacLeish had, I thought very properly, noted among those contemporaries of his who were contemptuous of their audiences. As an editor of a little magazine I could only agree with him that the vacuum into which most contemporary poetry set sail was fabulous. And in the second place MacLeish's preoccupation with his audience seemed to me to have had one tremendously important effect upon his writing which was not a bad effect, not wasteful. It had made him write with the intent of persuasion. What he attempted to persuade people of was not, in some cases, to my liking, but what he tried to do rhetorically when he undertook persuasion seemed to me to be elementary and admirable: he assumed he was addressing not the air but *someone;* he assumed, therefore, that he had a responsibility to that someone as well as to himself. These assumptions, far from leading to waste, served to direct the rhetoric of many of his best poems.

"Invocation to the Social Muse," for example, was addressed to a *Senora* Barinya. The girl was unimportant except as an object to address, but as such an object she served to establish immediately that the poem written to her would have to be *aimed* at her. In view of the fact that there was very little modern poetry aimed, in this sense, at anything, and in view of the fact that the aim made possible a very intelligently unacademic discussion of an academic subject, the girl seemed to me to be an important part of the poem. It didn't matter whether the aim was good or not (who cared if *she* was convinced?) and it didn't matter whether the girl was real or fictitious. What mattered was that the poet had concerned himself with more than saying what he personally found "sufficient"; he had concerned himself also with saying it in public.

There was another *senora* in "Voyage West," of less importance but useful as a point of rhetorical focus. There was Andrew Marvell himself, by implication, as the addressee in "You, Andrew Marvell." There were the dead poets in "Reproach to Dead Poets," the crew of Columbus in "Lines for a Prologue," and the lovers in "Selene Afterwards." And there were also of course all the voyagers, the People of the American Front poems. That the voyagers and dead poets addressed never, probably, received the messages didn't mean that the messages weren't addressed. They were; and because they were they were framed in the form of public, not private messages.

Allen Tate's assertion, in *The Forlorn Demon*, that the poet is primarily responsible to his own conscience, was not something I was anxious to dispute. Even less did I wish to dispute with him about the dangers attending the poet's taking on other responsibilities than this, the responsibilities,

292

for example, of persuasion. The dangers were unquestionably great. They were the dangers the teacher faced when he tried to sell Yeats to his Sophomores, the dangers the politician faced when he tried to sell himself to the People, and the simple dangers of salesmanship. They were, moreover, greater dangers for the poet than for the others because the poet was, as MacLeish himself put it, "strictly forbidden to mix in maneuvers." He was obliged constantly to remember that,

> The things of the poet are done to a man alone
> As the things of love are done—or of death
> when he hears the
> Step withdraw on the stair and the clock tick only.

What I did wish to do with Mr. Tate's assertion, however, was to suggest that perhaps MacLeish's concern with the problems of persuasion *as well as* of conscience was a healthy one and not something to be dismissed as mere "tub-thumping." "Tub-thumping" was a nasty word anyway for a potentially respectable poetic activity about which, so far as I could see, one could only be severe in severe cases. If some of MacLeish's poems were severe cases, some of them were perfectly healthy. Even some of his American Front poems were a good deal more than tub-thumping.

"America Was Promises," for example. There MacLeish had felt it necessary not simply to describe the promises America had been, but also to exhort his readers to make those promises come true. The exhortation was, I supposed, tub-thumping; the last hundred lines of the poem were the lines of a bully who just wanted his own way. But the first hundred lines were as good as any MacLeish had ever written, and it was not at all easy for me to see where persuasion ended and bullying began.

Thus, the difficulty. Against the objections to MacLeish's public pastorals, and against the objections to tub-thumping

293

included in the pastorals, there stood the first hundred lines of "America Was Promises." There stood also the lines to the *senoras* and dead poets. These had been written as public speech. These were lines of persuasion. And they were, it seemed to me, very good lines. Certainly, then, one couldn't say that MacLeish's impulse to write publicly, not merely to converse with his conscience, was in itself bad. Nor could one say that the impulse had been unproductive. Quite the contrary. It seemed to me therefore that my list of MacLeish's anthology poems—a list I was prepared to add to or otherwise adjust for my pugnacious readers—made the dangers of Democratic Pastoral and Public Speech, in MacLeish's case, worth facing.

English Bards and a Hot Reviewer*

Spender is reflective where Auden is dramatic, ponderous where Auden is shifty, and solemn where Auden is witty. But these observations have already been made about them by their critics. What have not? What observations should be made *here*, for example? None, perhaps. The temperature is 101 as I write this—so, perhaps, none. Would the *Sewanee Review* survive? Probably.

I shall be myself, however, and say something. My subject is honesty. It was brought to me by Barbara Gibbs in a review in *Poetry* of Spender's volume:

> Mr. Spender has committed many faults of taste and form. He has proclaimed *ad nauseam* that honesty (surely the most irrelevant of purposes to the artist) is his guiding principle. . . .

Though Miss Gibbs had many other things to say than this, and though this in its sad, excerpted state is not really what she said (for she happens to approve of Mr. Spender, as I guess I maybe don't), I must put it down anyway. It sticks to me like a burr, especially that parenthesis about irrelevancy. What does she mean? I suppose she means that anyone can be honest; honesty by itself produces neither poets nor poetry.

---

* *Collected Poems.* By Stephen Spender. Random House. 1955. $4.00.
The Shield of Achilles. By W. H. Auden. Random House. 1955. $3.00.

But that isn't what she says; she says that honesty has nothing to do with poets or poetry. Now *if* I take what she says to be what she means, what she says is the most ridiculous statement I've heard in at least a week. Let me explain.

A poet, even a villainous poet, a totally corrupt poet, a Iago of the little magazines, has the fundamental job of persuading his audience of Othellos that he is honest Iago. Far from being irrelevant to his artistry, his honesty or appearance of honesty is one of the most important "facts" his artistry must establish. If he does not establish it, his artistry is for naught; Cassio's drunkenness will not be blamed on Cassio; the handkerchief will not make Othello jealous.

On the other hand a nonvillainous poet, a plain, blunt chap who really wants to say what he really honestly means, is at least as much concerned with honesty as Iago is. For he must appear honest to himself as well as to Othello. Yes, Miss Gibbs? Well, then, it would seem as if honesty were the best policy for everybody. Note the word "policy," Miss Gibbs. Think of it as Shakespeare used it. To some of his characters, like Hotspur, it was primarily base; to some of them, like Coriolanus, it was primarily impossible; but to the cleverer characters policy was merely artfulness in the conduct of government and war; it might or it might not be base at heart but it was necessary and it had always to appear to be virtuous, honest. Now the problems of policy and art, Miss Gibbs, are much alike, and so I wish you had not said honesty was irrelevant to the purposes of art. It would have been more to the point if you had said that some poets, namely Mr. Spender, have the possibly mistaken notion that art and/or policy is not the best honesty. A different matter.

Have I confused you, Miss Gibbs? I hope so, for the temperature is still 101 and I would not like to think that at 101 I am entirely lucid. Certainly I am not gracious, and I apologize for picking on your one phrase about irrelevancy; it just seems to me worthy of discussion. I think I am being very

296

profound, for example, when I say that Spender thinks art is not the best honesty. He does not wholly trust his art, or at least he appears not to. Let me give some examples of this from his prosody before going on to mightier matters. His poem "Word" is a good place to begin.

> The word bites like a fish.
> Shall I throw it back free
> Arrowing to that sea
> Where thoughts lash tail and fin?
> Or shall I pull it in
> To rhyme upon a dish?

A fish upon a dish has lost not only its sea room and its wildness but also its life and true fishiness. Similarly the word "fish," caught in this rhyme scheme, trapped in the meshes of art, has lost something it apparently had before it was caught. In the poem, or on the dish, the fish is no longer the fish it was. Too bad, says Mr. Spender. And yet, despite his regrets, he does cook that fish's goose and serve it up on a dish. Why? I would suggest that what he is saying here generally about art and specifically about prosody (rhyming "fish" with "dish") is intimately connected with honesty. In the process of asserting that the fish on the dish is not the honest-to-God original fish but some modification or distortion of the original by chef or poet, he also observes that he personally is playing the role of chef or poet. He isn't sure that he likes this role (is it honest?), and so he asks, "Shall I pull it in?" But in fact he does pull it in, for we have the poem, we have the collected poems, and we have, as Auden pointed out somewhere, six feet four of Spender himself very much on the poetic scene. Dishing fishes. So far as prosody goes, then, his guiding principle would seem to be a negative one which I will phrase thus: rhyme and rhythmical regularity have something to do with poetry, so he will put up with them. How far he will put up with them varies from poem to poem, but in almost all cases he puts up with them rather than loving them. They are not wholly trustworthy, but there they are.

Examples. In "The Coward" (which, lest I forget, is a fine poem) he commits himself to a four-stress line which is predominantly iambic, and to couplets. The stresses are shifted about at will, however, and the number of unstressed syllables is changed constantly; the couplets are wide open, are marked by frequent half rhymes, and are occasionally abandoned entirely in favor of some other rhyme scheme. Again, in a less regular poem, "In 1929," the violations of the pattern dominate the pattern:

> A whim of Time, the general arbiter,
> Proclaims the love, instead of death, of friends.
> Under the domed sky and athletic sun
> Three stand naked: the new, bronzed German,
> The communist clerk, and myself, being English.

It is to be noted here that the first two lines are regular iambic pentameter; the third line is a perfectly moderate and conventional variation, but the fourth and fifth are what I can only call Busters. They indicate to me that the poet has set up the regularity of the first three lines largely so that he can knock it down. Now such Busters are not characteristic of his later poetry; there the original patterns are less emphatic and the shifts accordingly subtler. But even in the late poems I find no guiding principle other than the negative one I have described:

Sirmio's peninsula stretches out into the lake
Like one spoke thrusting to the centre
Of the mountain-circled water: where
I stand now, through brush-branched olive trees
And ragged broken arches

Ancient Romans built so long ago,
I see the water bowl's edge round me, in an almost perfect O.

This is good verse—Spender at his best metrically—but it is nonetheless frustrated iambic, an iambic unable to dominate any lines except lines five and six, but an iambic never entirely absent, never replaced by a stronger, more aggressive pattern. The objections to iambic, which Spender presumably shares with many of his contemporaries, are familiar: it is not a congenial cadence for representing modern speech; it has too few unstressed syllables; it encourages the mispronunciation (by too many equal stresses) of multisyllabic words; and it generally renders difficult any shadings of stresses. But for all this it is still a usable pattern if one will only use it. Spender does and doesn't. On the one hand he objects to it. On the other he lets it in.

He is similarly embarrassed by rhyme. He favors occasional rhyme like a drinker who, trying to taper off, avoids his evening cocktails but takes a nip whenever he happens to find himself in the kitchen:

> At dawn we rose and walked the pavement
> I your shadow you my flute
> Your voice wove a thread
> Through Paris in my head
> I followed followed
> You my sole inhabitant.

Why we should suddenly have the "thread-head" rhyme it is difficult to say. Or, to put it differently, why do we have "thread-head" and "pavement-inhabitant" but "flute-followed"? Why in such a short space do we ring all the changes: a rhyme, a sort of half-rhyme, and no rhyme? I think the answer is, again, that Spender feels an obligation or commitment to a practice of which he doesn't really approve.

The temperature has gone down to 100 now, so I'll switch over to Auden for contrast. Auden's distrust of traditional prosody may be as great as Spender's, but his early admiration for Byron, or the ham in his blood, or something, has encouraged him to be formally exhibitionistic rather than retiring. Though now in the sere and yellow leaf he still manages such rhymes as:

> When ladies ask *How much do you love me?*
> The Christian answer is *cosi cosi.*

And he can still move with grace or at least boldness from jingle to the nearly unscannable:

> "When rites and melodies begin
>   To alter modes and times,
> And timid bar-flies boast aloud
>   Of uncommitted crimes,
> And leading families are proud
>   To dine with their black sheep,
> What promises, what discipline,
>   If any, will Love keep?"
>   So roared Fire on their right:
>   But Tamino and Pamina
>   Walked past its rage
>   Sighing O, Sighing O,
>   In timeless fermatas of awe and delight
>   (Innocent? Yes. Ignorant? No.)
>   Down the grim passage.

If I may be permitted to make what may be a false distinction, let me say that when Auden does violence to rhyme or meter it is a positive rather than a negative act. Spender's is a negative act. Spender says, "I don't trust this form." Auden says, "I like this form but I want to do something new and

300

fancy with it." The results are what we see. Dudley Fitts has described them well in a review of Spender in *The New York Times* by noting that Spender, unlike Auden, is averse to "play" in his poetry. "Play, rhetorical invention, the sweet sliding and coruscation of poetry" seems unsuited to Spender's kind of high seriousness. As I understand Mr. Fitts this means that the texture of the verse of the two poets is wholly different because they have wholly different notions of what can be (honestly) done in verse. For Auden, verse is a game but an important one, and poetic honesty involves, among other things, trying to be good at the game. For Spender it is not a game, or shouldn't be, and the player spirit which pervades it is unfortunate.

Their differences are of course apparent elsewhere than in their meter and rhyme. Spender is at his best when he is relatively impersonal and reportorial, as in some of his Spanish War poems, but he is unfortunately his most characteristic self when he is rashly impressionistic and has as his reporter an obsessive and unpremeditated "I." Auden's "I" on the other hand is either unobtrusive, hardly to be distinguished from a "you" or a "one," or a distinctively dramatic poseur of an "I," an "I" being commented on or ridiculed:

> How fascinating is that class
>   Whose only member is Me!
> Sappho, Tiberius and I
>   Hold forth beside the sea.
>
> What is cosier than the shore
>   Of a lake turned inside out?
> How do all those other people
>   Dare to be about?

This difference suggests the deeper one already touched upon between their feelings about the validity or honesty of artifice. Auden will dramatize where Spender will glow. Auden will be indirect, detached, ironic where Spender, even under restraint, will indulge in heart-rant:

> To break out of the chaos of my darkness
> Into lucid day, is all my will.

In the simplest terms, indirection in all its shapes and sizes is for Spender a suspicious strategy. Strategy is itself suspicious. Let us be direct. Let us be straightforward. Let us say what we think, not what we think will work best. No wonder Miss Gibbs picked up her mistaken notions about honesty. While reviewing Spender it is difficult not to wish for dishonest or a-honest artists who will not come all over the reader with their protestations. Still, it is a mistake to think of the protestations as inartistic. Spender may wish to appear inartistic at times, and certainly succeeds, but his inartistry is in its own curious way an art of its own.

Am I confusing, Miss Gibbs? If so, Mr. Fitts is again my standard-bearer here. To his remarks about Spender's artlessness he appends the upsetting comment that Spender is really, after all, full of art. My mind runs right back to Shakespeare again and to Iago and Antony and Henry V, all those characters who professed so eloquently that they were not eloquent at all but plain blunt men like Hotspur, Coriolanus and, though he knew it not, Bottom. Thus Mr. Fitts seems to be identifying Spender with Antony, say, rather than with Hotspur. I'm unsure about this. I think it is easy to mistake Spender's apparent distrust of art for mere clumsiness, and sometimes to be entirely sure that it's mere clumsiness. But I'll agree at least that his artlessness, whether artful or not, emerges in his best poems as successful policy. Strangely it gives him sometimes an unexpected, and perhaps unfair, advantage over artful Auden.

Auden is never, conceivably, clumsy. At all times he demonstrates great proficiency, great skill, so that when a reader runs into such odd dissonances as those in the lines I quoted earlier, he is probably not prepared to be assuredly critical of them but merely to acknowledge with humility, "Ah well, Papa knows best." For when Auden grates on the ear it is knowledgeable grating. When Spender does, it may be just grating. But Auden's skill is nonetheless sometimes a handicap, bringing down on his head the accusation that he is clever, yes, just a bit too clever, together with the admonition that he try to be serious once in a while. There are characters in Shakespeare (there are always characters in Shakespeare) to illustrate this trouble: Benedick, Lucio, Ulysses. It is the trouble all wits, good and bad, serious and frivolous, have, and I bring it in merely to show the kind of advantage the nonwit, like Spender, may have over artful rivals. No Samuel Johnsons will question Spender's motives. No duke will enter to say that he does things according to the trick. But with Auden there will be Johnsons and dukes proclaiming in effect that his art is not the best honesty. Even I can't refrain from taking their position for a minute with regard to the Bucolics in his new volume. There are seven of them, covering winds, woods, mountains, lakes, islands, plains and streams. They are what I'll call (since the temperature is 99) middle Auden, neither the bright Auden of the ballads nor the solemn Auden of *Horae Canonicae* but an uncomfortable Auden struggling with uncongenial materials, not always with success. In *Plains,* for example, his tone wavers from one of mock horror at the dismalness of plains—

But I cannot see a plain without a shudder;—
"O God, please, please, don't ever make me live there!"

to a "real" distaste for them:

As it is, though, I know them [plains] personally
    Only as a landscape common to two nightmares:
Across them, spotted by spiders from afar,

I have tried to run, knowing there was no hiding and
no help . . .

Which is it? Well, he doesn't, I think, know. He's writing a
poem about plains, and he was clearly *going* to write a poem
about plains before his feelings, his honesties about plains
had any shape in his mind. The result is that the poem has
the air of an exercise and lacks the sense of genuineness
which the art of Spender seeks at all costs to cultivate. Here
clumsiness, strong feeling and large talk about agricultural
muscle, à la Sandburg, might have been the better strategy.
  Might have been. But this is one strategy Auden is not
skillful at, and I'm glad he isn't. For even in a relatively
unsuccessful poem like *Plains* he manages to demonstrate his
own kind of honesty, an honesty almost unrelated to the
plainness and bluntness of Spender but an honesty all the
same. In the last four lines he says:

I wish I weren't so silly. Though I can't pretend
  To think these flats poetic, it's as well at times
To be reminded that nothing is lovely,
  Not even in poetry, which is not the case.

Here, if I understand him, he is saying just what I have already said about the poem, only better. The subject was a
poor subject; he has been frivolous about it and now he is
depressed by his poetry more than by plains. At the same
time he recognizes that the depression is momentary and all
is not lost even though "it's as well at times" to think that
all is. Such a conclusion may not save the poem but I find it
just as convincing a demonstration of essential honesty and
integrity as the following solemn confession of a comparable
inadequacy by Spender:

To knock and enter
Knock and enter

The cloudless posthumous door
Where my guts are strung upon a harp that sings of praise
And then sit and speak
With those who knocked and entered before

In spite of everything
Be justified be justified
At last being at their side who are at my side
To know that this my quality
Of ultimate inferiority
Was on my rounded shoulders the weight of my humanity

To look down on my life
That was my life
False social puppet painted with false mouth
Yet in that mouth this voice
That is not quite all death
But its own truth witnessing its justice with living breath. . . .

Indeed, for me, the Auden passage rings more true than the
Spender. The rhetorical repetitions in the latter, the heavy
shock line about guts, and the excessive humility of the narrator seem to me to be the kind of public honesty Antony
was so good at, a pose of honesty which may or may not
reflect the "I's" true feelings. On the other hand Auden's
self-criticism emerges as a private man's critique of his own
public statements and, whether true or not, takes care of the
doubts I have about the earnestness of Spender's dramatic "I."

Is my distinction clear, Miss Gibbs? I am saying that my
opinion of both poems is partly determined by how honest
the feelings portrayed seem to me to be. I happen to find
Auden more persuasive than Spender, but whether I am right
or wrong surely honesty is a relevant factor in my judgment.
How can it be irrelevant? Even though the temperature has
dropped to 98 (Miss Gibbs), I must continue to pick on your
parenthesis.

Childe Byron

His Very Self and Voice. Collected Conversations of Lord Byron. Edited by Ernest J. Lovell, Jr. Macmillan Company. $7.50.

Byron lived to be a mere thirty-six, but in that time he both wrote more and had more written about him than a poet who lived to be four hundred and six could reasonably expect. *His Very Self and Voice* is a collection of writings about him. It consists of some six hundred dense pages of "accounts of Byron's conversations . . . extracted from one hundred and eighty-odd printed books and articles, besides unpublished sources." The collator, Ernest J. Lovell, Jr., can thus be praised for his academic diligence and at the same time warned that his proposed supplementary volume, which will contain even more extractions in God knows how many more dense pages, will not be read by this particular reader. I have had enough. I find that the present volume, together with Byron's collected works, make a complete and thoroughly satisfactory Byron kit for ordinary biographical duffers. Any supplementary volume should be brought out on 3″ x 5″ cards to indicate that it is intended only for the files of real Byron pros.

On the other hand it is possible that we are now faced with a big Byron revival, in which case the supplementary volume will be followed by several full-scale biographies and critical reevaluations. I should not like to be caught napping if this were to occur; so, though I propose personally to read no more Byron for seven years, I want to get my two bits down on him here in a hurry. My motives are therefore purely selfish, and nothing could be more irrelevant than for me to add that I happen to like Byron's poetry. That, however, I happen to do. I despise *Childe Harold, Manfred,* and most of the oriental tales, but I like the satirical Byron, particularly *A Vision of Judgement* and the early cantos of *Don Juan.* At his best he seems to me to be a very funny man.

He wasn't a very funny man, however, to his wife who, she said, had married a devil, nor to a great many of his minor social acquaintances in front of whom he preferred to play the roles of his dark heroes, being in turn mysterious, insulting, lascivious, gloomy, portentous and plain crazy. And to those who knew him better and discounted his poses he was not consistently regarded as a great wit. Some found him sparkling, some dull; some found him witty, some merely spiteful. The actual conversations recorded in Mr. Lovell's book tend to confirm the image of him which we receive from his works, a poet moving indiscriminately between tragedy and comedy, epic and burlesque, drama and melodrama, and in doing so describing primarily his own moody self. I take it, then, that even after a century and a half we have no reasonable grounds for discovering a new Byron when we revive him. He must remain the Nineteenth Century's prime prima donna no matter how we manipulate the materials of our Byron kit.

Ultimately, though, his moods reduce themselves neatly to two, serious and comic, and these two are, as he displays them, intimately opposite in the sense that, as a comic, he mocks himself as a tragedian. So perhaps he isn't such a complex after all; his motions seem no more difficult to analyze than those of a train which runs north in the morning and south in the afternoon on the same track. Nor is it hard to say which way he is, at any given moment, running. He tells us usually in the first stanzas of his poems, sometimes even in the first lines. *Childe Harold* begins grandly.

> Oh, thou! in Hellas deemed of heavenly birth,
> Muse! . . .

while *Don Juan* begins,

> I want a hero: an uncommon want,
> When every year and month sends forth a new one.

And *The Corsair* opens,

> "O'er the glad waters of the dark blue sea,
> Our thoughts as boundless, and our souls as free,
> Far as the breeze can bear, the billows foam,
> Survey our empire and behold our home!"

while *Beppo* begins,

> 'Tis known, at least it should be, that throughout
>   All countries of the Catholic persuasion,
> Some weeks before Shrove Tuesday comes about,
>   The People take their fill of recreation.

If these quotations demonstrate that Byron had a split personality, and I suppose they do, they also, and more importantly, show that he knew it. There's no confusion of intentions here; indeed, if anything, his intentions show too clearly. When he decides to be funny he becomes an utter clown. When he decides to be serious he becomes Manfred. In both mediums he depends upon grotesque exaggeration for his success—in comedy upon slapstick, bad puns and ridiculous rhymes; in tragedy upon the grandest grand manner since

Armado. Obviously no one knew better than he what Stendhal observed while discussing him: "For a man of genius, in the Nineteenth Century, there is no alternative: he is either a fool or a monster."

What Byron didn't, apparently, know, however, was how much better he was as fool than as monster. He could be importantly and seriously frivolous; he could be nothing but a ham or fraud as tragic hero. The difference in the quality of his two veins is so striking to me that I like to dream a little and imagine that he really found the production of *Beppo* and *Don Juan* and even the earlier satires a much more congenial task personally than the solemn tragedies and melodramas. I find solace in the fact that toward the end of his career the satirist in him was clearly ascendant, for this might mean that he understood himself and his true medium then as he did not when he was writing *Manfred*. But my solace is small. In the first place he apparently wrote in both veins with equal (and incredible) facility, and in the second he continued to compose in his bad vein even at the end of his career (while writing *Don Juan* he managed to turn out three monstrous dramas that I would like personally to burn page by page). Nor is there any indication that in his private life he ever lost the need to pose as monster. Only ten months before his death he put on, in a monkery, one of his greatest recorded scenes when he "burst into a paroxysm of rage, and vented his ire in a torrent of Italian execrations on the holy abbot and all his brotherhood" (E. J. Trelawney). My dreams, then, appear to be just dreams. He never really grew out of bad Byronism. For my money he never really grew up. He could eloquently criticize, as he did in *Don Juan*, all his own worst faults, but he couldn't rid himself of them.

Which brings me to my subject for today: growing up. I have been thinking of writing a short, illuminating book on the subject, featuring some select aphorisms from Polonius and Lord Chesterfield, and this essay will serve as a start.

Byron's failure to grow up may be attributed with justice to his mother, to his clubfoot, and to all the other irregularities of his private being, for there seems to be no doubt that he was a kind of "case." But I would like to suggest that his difficulty was not merely personal; he chose to be born in an age which was extremely difficult, from a literary point of view, to grow up in, an age preferring the naïveté and vigor of childishness to the wisdom and control of adulthood, an age glorifying in eloquently expressed emotional instability. He was thus encouraged by his public to be delightfully adolescent, and he was a man who needed above all else the acclaim of a public.

We live in such an age too, but the adolescent public of our time finds its Byrons mostly in Hollywood or on Broadway. There the romantic excesses persist; there also Byron's difficulty persists, and we find extremely intelligent and talented people acting, in their real lives, parts out of dime novels. In literary circles, however, there is apparently no current demand for Byrons, and so the Byron problem doesn't look like a problem. Accordingly, I can be extremely patronizing here toward Byron as I could not have been, I think, if I had lived in his time. I could have been angered or offended by him, as Leigh Hunt was, or critical of his morals, as most of England was, or generally in violent disagreement with all forms and manifestations of Byronism, as perhaps Wordsworth was, but I could not readily have merely dismissed *Manfred* as I here now do under oath and without a qualm. For I feel secure, as perhaps I should not, against the invasions of romance; the literary culture I inhabit is mature, even aged, and so I can talk about Byron's crisis as if I were conducting a course in child psychology.

For Byron, however, where was literary maturity? The kind I am talking about didn't seem to exist. The only maturity on the market was mellowed, or seasoned, or salted youth, Wordsworth grown up but hanging on desperately to his days as a bounding roe, or Southey in his forties spouting "grand heroics" with such persistence that

> The angels stopp'd their ears and plied their pinions;
> The devils ran howling, deafen'd, down to hell.
>
> ("The Vision of Judgment")

To neither of these commodities was Byron attracted, and so, after trying his hand at both romance and certain antidotes for romance, he produced *Don Juan*. *Don Juan* begins, as I have indicated, as antidote, as a kind of satire on *Childe Harold*, and to the extent that it remains satire through its seventeen cantos it is a great work, perhaps in a class with *Don Quixote* as a myth unmaker. Unfortunately it loses its bite as it progresses. It was too successful. After the first two cantos were published they were received with such enthusiasm that Byron talked grandly of writing one hundred and fifty cantos and selling them for two thousand pounds apiece. With these figures in his head he could hardly be expected to keep the edge sharp on his knife and continue to write,

> Thou shalt believe in Milton, Dryden, Pope;
> Thou shalt not set up Wordsworth, Coleridge, Southey;
> Because the first is crazed beyond hope,
> The second drunk, the third so crazed and mouthy.

That is, even in his most mature work he fell victim to his own childish inability to decide what he really wanted to say and do. The attractions of an indiscriminate public were too strong for him to persist as a real rebel against the vices of his culture. He could not govern himself and his work by any settled principles because he was himself unsettled, and his society was too. Instead, therefore, he allowed himself to be governed by whim and adulation, like all too many other writers. It is no wonder that he ended up with a fever in

311

Greece reciting deliriously *not* a battle cry for freedom in Greece (he had come to hate like poison the Greeks he was saving) or a sustained curse upon the *Edinburgh Review,* but the names of his pitifully few real friends: "Augusta—Ada—Hobhouse—Kinnaird . . . Now I have told you all."

With this solemn quotation I am about done with Byron. I wish only to add that in remaining a child he set the pattern for some twentieth century Byrons. I can think of two, Dylan Thomas and Scott Fitzgerald. Thomas had not the range of Byron, and Fitzgerald was much too interested in other people to be a great *poseur,* but both of them partook of Byron's youthful intensities even when they too were in their thirties. They could have said, as Byron said when he was thirty-five, "Few men can live faster than I did. I am, literally speaking, a young old man." And like Byron they managed to divide their time between extravagant romanticism and acidity. Byron's acidity was more productive, however; in Fitzgerald's and Thomas's work we find too little evidence—notably *The Last Tycoon* and the passages about writers in *Quite Early One Morning*—of the rebelliousness they were in real life, like Byron, noted for.

Three Reasons

Collected Poems of Edna St. Vincent Millay, edited by Norma
   Millay. Harper. $6.00.

The "definitive" collection of Edna St. Vincent Millay's
poems runs to 738 pages. This is perhaps more pages than
any lyric poet ought to leave behind; it is certainly more
pages of lyrics than any reviewer ought to unlyric. It is a lot
of pages, and I confess with shame and chagrin that the main
reason I asked to review them was that I thought the book
was one I would like to own—I had forgotten when I asked
for it that *Poetry* does not permit reviewers to keep review
copies. So I am being justly punished here for my own low,
original motive, and as penance, after finishing this review,
I propose to go right out and buy a copy (six bucks).

Even when I do this, though, my motives won't be entirely
pure. I happen to want the book, even now, after reading it.
That is, I like it. It's a good book. Perhaps my review should
end here?

No. Here come my reasons, all three of them, late but vociferous, toting their three by fives and looking offended that
I should have entertained the thought of not letting them
speak. Very well, then, they will speak. First reason?

First Reason. Good afternoon. I am not a very good reason,
I admit. I am not respectable, and respectable people gener-

313

ally fail to acknowledge me even when I'm present, as I usually am. I am a sentimental reason, bred up in tear ducts and the corners of ladies' handkerchiefs to do honor to underdogs, fallen stars, happy memories of better days, and all that. Now in Miss Millay's case, as you can perhaps imagine, I have a good deal to do honor to. I begin in the obvious manner, by honoring her dialogue between First Fig and Second Fig, where she recommends burning one's candle at both ends and building one's palace on sand. This poem has slipped into the history books; vistas of the twenties unfold before us when we hear it; and though Miss Millay might have liked to be remembered, first of all, for her other, larger accomplishments, I must insist that the Figs continue to be celebrated by the aging and maudlin.

I don't want to make too much of the Figs, though, for I want to discuss not Figs but Heart. Critics have been pouring cold water on bleeding hearts for some time now, and with success. In 1919 Irving Babbitt observed that "the disproportion between the outer incident and the emotion that the Rousseauist expends on it is often ludicrous." In 1938 Messrs. Brooks and Warren, discussing Shelley's *Indian Serenade* where he wails, "I die! I faint! I fail!" said:

> The poet tells us outright that his love is so intense that he is dying of it. But some people die very easily—they are always dying over this and that—always thinking that they are dying. Has the poet taken his lover out of this class? Has he made his audience feel that the lover's statement that he is dying is meant literally and is justified by the intensity of his love? The statement, "I die," comes with very different effect when wrung from the lips of a man of few words, cautious and well balanced, than it does when shrieked out by a flighty, hysterical sentimentalist. In the first case, it comes with tremendous effect; in the second, it merely provokes amusement or disgust.

The effect of such criticism, or of such a critical attitude toward letting hearts bleed unstaunched (or unquenched) on the pages of modern poetry, was at the least to make much of Miss Millay's kind of lyricism unfashionable, for she always —and I say this without malice—died easily; that is, she favored letting herself go emotionally; she laid herself open to the objections voiced above against Rousseau and Shelley, and she did so during an age when such objections were becoming increasingly loud and long. She had a public, of course—and a large one—which did not entertain these objections, but the objections dimmed her fame and changed her career, nonetheless. I think I can demonstrate this by reference to her last book, *Mine the Harvest.*

Mine the Harvest was printed in 1954, four years after her death. It contained a few early pieces, but most of it was mature work, written after the war and, particularly, after the unfortunate *Make Bright the Arrows,* a book Miss Millay herself described as "hastily written and hotheaded." *Mine the Harvest* has been included in its entirety in the new *Collected Poems*—and, I think, justly. I agree with Robert Hillyer who, reviewing it in *The New York Times,* found it the best of her books. And yet, if my researches are correct, this book received less attention than any of her others. It was reviewed favorably in the *Times, The Saturday Review* and the *Herald Tribune;* and it was panned by John Ciardi in the *Nation;* but in most other literary sheets it wasn't even mentioned—that is, it was not reviewed in the *New Republic, The New Yorker,* the *Sewanee Review,* the *Yale Review, Poetry,* or the *Kenyon Review* (my researches go no further). Now is this not astonishing? Why should the last and perhaps most important work of a poet as well known as Edna St. Vincent Millay be so neglected? Well, perhaps the neglect was inadvertent. I know, for example, that *Poetry* failed to review the book simply because a review that had been scheduled never got written. Perhaps some of the other magazines had good intentions too. Still, I think the neglect was too extensive to be explained by Unhappy Fortune. The real explanation is a much more unhappy one; it is that Brooks and Warren had set in. Now I think it is high time that . . .

Second Reason. Good afternoon. I hope you will pardon me for interrupting, F. R., but your argument is getting out of hand as it always does. For example, you pointed out, and I think sensibly, that Miss Millay's poetic career may have been affected by the critics, or by the critical temper of her time, especially when her time began to overlap that of the New Critics. But then you proceeded to talk about her career as if a career could only be discussed in terms of the reviews it got. Nonsense. It is possible to have a career, a fine career, in a dark hole where the *Kenyon Review* never reaches. And in Miss Millay's case this is what happened: she *had* a fine career even though she was not sponsored by the New Critics.

But I do not mean therefore that her work was unaffected by their criticism. I am interested in the work, you see, not the reviews. I too happen to like *Mine the Harvest,* but I refuse to be worried about what the *Kenyon Review* or the others didn't do for it after it was published. What is important is not the *Kenyon Review's* negligence but the influence, if any, the poetic temper of her times had upon her as she wrote the poems. Did she, for example, note her own excesses? And did she take steps in her later work to die, shall I say, less frequently? I think the answer is yes in both cases —she both noted her excesses and strove to correct them. Indeed, frequently she overcorrected them, as in this concluding stanza:

But do not for a moment believe he has forgotten Blackness:
   nor the deep
Easy swell; nor his thwarted
Design to remain for ever there;
Nor the crimson betrayal of his birth into a yellow glare.
The pictures painted on the inner eyelids of infants just
   before they sleep,
Are not in pastel.

316

Or in this (after experiencing the "shock of beauty," something she commonly found unbearable) :

I come back from the garden into the kitchen and take off
    my rubbers—the dew
Is heavy and high, wetting the sock above the shoe—but I
    cannot do
The housework yet.

In both cases above Mr. Babbitt would probably have observed that the irony is itself excessive, and that Rousseauists remain Rousseauists even when they have taken a course in understatement. He would then, I fear, have been content to go on to some other poet, neglecting all the rest of *Mine the Harvest*, for example the title poem where, it seems to me, neither Mr. Babbitt nor any New Critic could possibly complain that the matter is neglected or treated hysterically:

Those hours when happy hours were my estate,—
Entailed, as proper, for the next in line,
Yet mine the harvest, and the title mine—
Those acres, fertile, and the furrow straight,
From which the lark would rise—all of my late
Enchantments, still, in brilliant colours, shine,
But striped with black, the tulip, lawn and vine,
Like gardens looked at through an iron gate.
Yet not as one who never sojourned there
I view the lovely segments of a past
I lived with all my senses, well aware
That this was perfect, and it would not last:
I smell the flower, though vacuum-still the air;
I feel its texture, though the gate is fast.

I like this sonnet very much, but the point I want to make about it here is that it is a very different poem from anything in Miss Millay's early books. I am not thinking of the formal competence of it—for formally she nearly always had things well in hand, even at the age of nineteen; I am thinking, rather, of the conceit, if I can call it that. The details of it are plentiful and unusual; its working out seems to me to be logical and beautiful. Now in the early poems I sensed frequently an absence of interest in all but the most conventional details, the kind the New Critics say produces "stock responses"; and I sensed also a lack of interest in the workings—thus, in the following excerpt from a poem called *The Cairn* she doth, I think, protest a great deal against what children learn, without at the same time indicating much interest in, or knowledge about, what children in fact do learn:

> Come up, children! Toss your little stones gaily
> On the great cairn of Knowledge!
> (Where lies what Euclid knew, a little grey stone,
> What Plato, what Pascal, what Galileo:
> Little grey stones, little grey stones on a cairn.)
> Tell me, what is the name of the highest mountain?
> Name me a crater of fire! a peak of snow!
> Name me the mountains of the moon!
> But the name of the mountain that you climb all day,
> Ask not your teacher that.

Now why, I say to myself, in *Mine the Harvest,* was she suddenly so concerned with things the New Critics would have us concerned about? Had she simply matured? Or did she have her ear to the ground, was she listening, more than we imagine, to the voices of . . .

Third Reason. Good afternoon. I'm not even sorry to interrupt, S. R. You've gotten as far off the track as F. R. did, with your speculative departures from the text. I wish to make just two points and then shut up. First, with regard to

Miss Millay's relations with the New Critics I propose to offer up a little evidence in place of speculation. A very little. To do so I have to make F. O. Matthiesson a New Critic, but no matter. In 1950 he edited the *Oxford Anthology of American Verse,* and his selection from Miss Millay's work made her quite angry. She wrote a long letter to the publisher in which she pointed out that she didn't like to complain, that anthologists had their privileges, and that, furthermore, she had no objections to any of the Millay selections individually. But, she said, the whole selection (originally of nine poems) was preposterous in that she was mainly represented by such works as *Recuerdo,* a light piece about getting drunk, getting on a ferry, and then giving money to a woman selling flowers. To be edited down to the spirit of *Recuerdo* was, she felt, misrepresentation, and she professed with heavy irony not to understand how a serious poem, *The Return,* had crept into the anthology unless it had been chosen because it was the first poem in *Wine from These Grapes,* that is, the only poem in the volume the editor had read.

No poet, S. R., likes to discover that he is going down in history for his barroom limericks while his epics are being buried beside him, but in Miss Millay's case especially the New Critics' decision to regard her as bad when serious and good when not must have been terribly disheartening. And if she had been alive to read the Ciardi review you mentioned of *Mine the Harvest,* she would surely have been furious. Ciardi said, "When she aspires to be high serious, she is least successful." He talked of her "coy but fervent posturing" in a poem she must have put everything into. Now to the likes of this she could hardly have been, as we say, adjusted—no person with her aspirations and feelings could be; and so I say to you, S. R., that all your speculation about her knuckling under to the critical temper of the times is nonsense. I admire *Mine the Harvest* tremendously, and I do think that in it she has, as Robert Hillyer said, gone a long way toward

319

eliminating "affectation and propaganda from her work." But the point I want to make about that work is that Miss Millay is still in it; she has not merely done the voguish thing as you, alas, suggested.

My second point is more important. You must remember that we, all three of us, are Reasons for Liking Miss Millay's Poems. We are not Biographical Critics, or Psychological Critics, or even Friends. And so I must insist in the tritest possible way that the best reasons are the poems themselves. I will therefore conclude my reasoning on the whole matter by simply listing some fine poems (you may add others): *Assault, Renascence* (at least the first stanza), *Tavern, When the Year Grows Old, Spring, Elegy before Death, Mariposa, First & Second Fig, Recuerdo, Grown-up, The Philosopher,* "I know a hundred ways to die," *Cap d'Antibes,* "To whom the house of Montagu," "This is mine, and I can hold it," *The Strawberry Shrub, Armenonville, New England Spring,* "How did I bear it—how could I possibly as a child," "Sometimes, oh, often, indeed," *Rendezvous,* and Sonnets 5, 58, 59 and 159. Is that not a long list?

First Reason. Yes, but it leaves out some good ones.

Second Reason. Yes, and I think you've chosen poems that Ciardi and Mathiesson would like too.

Third Reason. Ah-ah-ah-ow-ow-ow-oo!

The Principles of Louise Bogan and Yvor Winters*

Yvor Winters has a note in the back of his *Collected Poems* in which he says:

> The title *Collected Poems* may seem too ambitious for this volume; for the volume is not a complete collection of what I have published by a very wide margin. However, the volume contains everything which I wish to keep and represents in addition a kind of definition by example of the style which I have been trying to achieve for a matter of thirty years. The poems omitted seem to me inferior in quality, and they would certainly obscure the issue which for me is the principal issue.

There is nothing, perhaps, very remarkable about this note; apologies and explanations are in order whenever a book's title is misleading. The note interests me, however, because it tells me that Mr. Winters had a double standard for selecting his own poems. He chose them partly for their "quality" and partly for something else, their competence or fitness to represent, and thus define by example, his style. Style, style, style. Whatever he meant by the word in the context, obvi-

---

* *Collected Poems.* By Yvor Winters. Alan Swallow, Publisher. 1952. $3.50. *Collected Poems: 1923-53.* By Louise Bogan. Noonday Press. 1954. $3.00.

321

ously it was the key word. It was indeed the "principal issue."

Louise Bogan has no note in the back of her *Collected Poems;* so I shall at reasonable intervals suggest that Mr. Winters' note is applicable to her volume too. I shall do this because I am reviewing the books together and it is convenient to have them share things; I shall do it also, however, because I think they do share things, and particularly one thing, an obsessive interest in Style.

Their interest in Style has been noted by several other critics. Indeed all their interests appear to have been noted by several other critics, for

> Blackmur, Cowley, Tate and Moore
> Travelled have here me before.

So have Howard Nemerov, Howard Baker and John Ciardi. So, even, have Miss Bogan and Mr. Winters, for they have reviewed each other's work. But none of these critics has been so unwary as to call either of the poets' interest in Style obsessive; on the contrary the critics generally regard it as thoroughly admirable. Thus Malcolm Cowley says of Miss Bogan's work that

> Her real subject, implicit in her manner of writing, was always poetry itself. She was saying by her example that the duty of the poet is to crowd all possible meaning into a few lines; to find the exact word, the one right image, the rhythm just awkward enough to vary the pattern without breaking it entirely.

And thus Allen Tate describes Mr. Winters as a moralist of style, a poet

> whose moral imagination takes, without didacticism, the didactic mode, striving for precision in language and, in verse, for formal elegance.

I take these remarks to mean that the two poets are modern rhetoricians in the best sense of the word "rhetorician," and that whatever their contribution to the whole art of poetry may be, certainly their verbal disciplines deserve high praise. It would seem, then, that I am overruled in objecting to their concern with Style. I am a metaphysician in the grass.

Perhaps. But I am not what I am for want of admiration for their rhetoric. I admire particularly the sense of completeness, of finish their poems give me. It indicates a long and steady dedication to their craft as a profession. Miss Bogan's volume, for example, containing the work of thirty years in one hundred and twenty pages, is not the volume of a poet for whom verse is merely a pastime, a diversion; the care with which the details have been selected and ordered in such poems as "Song" (page 69) and "Man Alone" is the care of devotion; and the balanced precision of the following quatrain from "At a Party" is a precision one does not achieve at a couple of Writing Conferences:

> Over our heads, if we but knew,
> Over our senses, as they reel,
> The planets tread, great seven, great two
> Venus, Uranus, in a wheel.

Similarly Mr. Winters is a professional craftsman toward whom, I think, no other even alien poet can reasonably be other than respectful. He is the master of his language, the captain of his quatrains; like Bogan he will not be caught out without "the exact word, the one right image." He is, furthermore, generous with his words and images, as Miss Bogan is not. He is concerned with clarity as well as rightness, fullness as well as precision, and his descriptions of landscapes and persons are accordingly thorough and substantial where Miss Bogan's are bare and skeletonic. Here, for example, are the opening lines of "California Oaks":

Spreading and low, unwatered, concentrate
Of years of growth that thickens, not expands,
With leaves like mica and with roots that grate
Upon the deep foundations of these lands,
In your brown shadow, on your heavy loam
—Leaves shrinking to the whisper of decay—
What feet have come to roam,
                              what eyes to stay?
Your motion has o'ertaken what calm hands?

All this is fine and dandy, and it may properly lead—as it has
led—to observations about the importance of cultivating a
poetry of care in a careless world. But it may also lead to
something else, something which is suggested by the critics I
have referred to above when they proceed with remarkable
unanimity to go about "placing" these poets in some other
century or culture than our own. Thus Allen Tate makes
Mr. Winters "a Renaissance humanist of the pre-Spenserian
School of metaphysical rhetoricians," while Howard Baker
finds that he's a Johnsonian who writes "not about a rose but
about *the* rose." And Miss Bogan attributes to him the
"stylistic severities of the seventeenth century," while Howard
Nemerov cagily renders him centuryless, always operating "at
some distance, so to say, from the poetry that forms and the
poetry that follows the fashion." Thus also Tate finds Miss
Bogan's best work filled with the "freshness of an Elizabethan
lyricist" and her worst rendered in "a half-lyrical, half 18th
century, satirical style." And Mr. Winters asserts that her
poems "demand—and will bear—comparison with the best
songs of the sixteenth and seventeenth centuries," while John
Ciardi, playing the Nemerov game, discovers that in her late
poems she "comes out of timelessness [her early poems] into
time." All of these placements, though contradictory, seem
to point to the conclusion that Miss Bogan and Mr. Winters
have in common the quality of being, wherever they may be,

not here. They would seem to share also the critics' approval
—except Ciardi's—for being there.

Now their otherworldliness or othercenturiness may be
scarcely worthy of note, since so many modern poets seem to
be aliens of one sort or another. But I was struck by it in
their case nonetheless, largely because, at the time when I
was gathering together the critics' remarks above, I had just
finished breezily lecturing some sophomores on the far coun-
tries of romance—the land of King Arthur, the land of the
noble savage, dreamland and any number of other remote
provinces where, I attempted to demonstrate, romantics may
and do find a home away from home. Obviously it was a bit
disconcerting for me to discover Mr. Winters and Miss Bogan
looking for a home somewhere out there too, since they were
not romantics, or at least not the kind of romantics I was
telling my sophomores about. On the contrary Mr. Winters
was, so far as I could determine, an apostle of staying put; he
was a man who could look upon the sea's exotic beckonings,
and hearing the sound of its surf describe it as "Nothing,
whispering." Similarly, Miss Bogan appeared to be a persistent negator of Romance, a lady openly suspicious of Santa
Claus:

> Now that I know
> How passion warms little
> Of flesh in the mould,
> And treasure is brittle,—
>
> I'll lie here and learn
> How, over their ground,
> Trees make a long shadow
> And a light sound.

I didn't mention my difficulty to the sophomores (I think
they should be kept in the dark about such things), but I

began to ponder the curious position of the rationalist, or anti-Romantic, or "Renaissance humanist" when he does not stay at home in his country and century. What, I wondered, is his defense for moving off into "Nothing, whispering"?

I am still wondering, but I think this is not the place for me to do so; the terms of my wondering need the kind of definition and elaboration I am not prepared to provide here. It is sufficient for this occasion to say that the removal by the critics of Mr. Winters and Miss Bogan into the sixteenth or seventeenth (or was it eighteenth?) century appears to me to be motivated by a highly romantic notion of a poet's rhetorical function in this world, the notion that a poet should choose and attempt to establish the ideal form or mode of his culture's language. Mr. Winters himself acknowledges this principle when he says that a poem is what one *should* say (in "On Teaching the Young") . The principle appears to me to be a romantic one even if what one should say turns out to be thoroughly un- or anti-romantic; the principle is romantic—in the sense in which I am using the word—because it advocates a trip to the far country of an ideal. Now the ideal in this case happens to be the "verbal disciplines" and the "formal elegance" of the sixteenth or seventeenth (or was it eighteenth?) century; but it remains an ideal nonetheless; it insists upon Santa Claus.

I have always liked Santa Claus, and I have always liked the verse of the sixteenth or seventeenth (or was it eighteenth?) century. But I am inclined to think that the verse of Mr. Winters and Miss Bogan has suffered as a result of their liking these delightful remotenesses too much. Some of the critics seem to agree with me; they have noted a coldness here, an overscrupulousness there, and a general absence of the warm rhetoric of persuasion in poems so strenuously dedicated to the "verbal disciplines" as their poems are. Mr. Blackmur has put this criticism more strongly than most by saying (of Mr. Winters) that "all the volcanic forces in his verse are extinct; no lava flows." I am inclined to disagree. It seems to me that in the work of both poets there is lava and it does flow but it is, unfortunately, a rhetorical rather than a substantive lava. To abandon Blackmur's image, their passion is rhetoric itself; rhetoric is the "principal issue."

Rhetoric appears to be the principal issue also for their admiring critics. Behind the placements of these poets is more than the scholarly impulse to place things in their proper historical surroundings. There is a political motive too, and I dislike it. Let me explain why, though it may be obvious.

An age, when one contemplates it from a distance, is not so much a temporal as a spiritual entity; it is a way of life, a set of rules, a body of principle, and therefore something one may regard and act for (or against), as one would a cause, a party, a faith. Thus most of the old New Critics act for the seventeenth century and against the nineteenth. They do it without even trying; they do it in their sleep. And they do it because the seventeenth century stands dimly for something they like, the nineteenth dimly for something they don't like. This is natural enough. I can't see why they are always saying it isn't true. Also natural enough, I suppose, is the impulse of Mr. Winters and Miss Bogan to accept the principles of another age or culture than their own for their own poetry, and the impulse of Messrs. Tate and Baker to praise them for doing this. The impulse itself can do neither the poets nor the critics any damage; they may be regarded as subversive, or reactionary, or alien in some quarters, but most of them would enjoy these tags. The difficulty arises when the campaigns for the principles take precedence over the poetry based on the principles. Then the poetry becomes campaign literature. It becomes an exercise in, or a demonstration of, principle.

This is what has become of Mr. Winters' and Miss Bogan's poetry. They have made as clear as have their critics the principles involved and their importance. They have been campaigners with their critics for the "verbal disciplines." The result is not that most of their poems are *about* poetry—though a good many of them are—but that ultimately their poems' most noteworthy element is style rather than substance. Two fine poems, Mr. Winters' "By the Road to the Airbase" and Miss Bogan's "Kept," may be cited here as examples of this.

The airbase poem is a description of the surprising and heartening seepage of man's civilizing activities into the desert of military life. After dwelling upon the barrenness of an airbase and its surroundings for three quatrains, the poet turns in his last stanza to the strange fruit:

> Yet fruit grows on the trees;
> Here scholars pause to speak;
> Through gardens bare and Greek,
> I hear my neighbor's bees.

Very neat the poem is. In sixteen short lines notably deficient in large-scale generalizations, the poet characterizes accurately the doubleness of our military and industrial society (subtropical division) and concludes, pleasantly enough, that all is not lost. I approve. I am impressed by both the observation and the conclusion. And I am attracted personally by the subject because I have lived on such airbases and found green things unexpectedly flourishing there. For all this, however, I find the subject a relatively innocent, uncontroversial and polite subject, certainly not the chief reason for my liking the poem as much as I do. I like it, instead, primarily for what has been done *with* the subject; I am particularly impressed, for instance, with the way, in context, the humble bee is made to carry so much of the burden of civilization.

Similarly, in Miss Bogan's "Kept," I turn to the technique rather than the matter for my rewards. The matter is worthy enough: as we grow older we find that we must "put away"

328

the important material possessions of our lives—described throughout as toys. We must—but how can we? they have become part of us; we have kept them until we begin

> To feel our nerves their strings,
> Their dust, our blood within.

So if they are worn out and need to be put away, perhaps we do too. Amen. Now I have nothing but sympathy for this matter, but unfortunately I remember the poem for something else, namely the lines quoted above. Look at the clever and balanced juxtaposition of nerves and strings, dust and blood. Is it not an apt construction for describing how much these possessions become a part of us? Is it not neat? Is it not Right? And so forth. With such considerations my contemplation of the problem of putting away childish things goes out the window.

This is too bad, I think. And if it be suggested that I am really quite simply objecting to things oft thought which happen to be well expressed, I'll agree with reservations, pointing out that I do not disapprove of that which is well expressed but of that in which the "principal issue" is expression. Here are two of the prominent poets of our time for whom the "principal issue" is expression. They want it known, and their critics want it known, that they stand for verbal discipline; and their success has been such that no two poets living can be said to stand for verbal discipline more firmly. Their campaign has indeed been too successful; as a result of it they may well be remembered for what they stand for and neglected as poets, much as the early Imagists are now neglected as poets and remembered as the proponents of certain Do's and Don't's.

A Letter to Karl Shapiro

In Defense of Ignorance, by Karl Shapiro.
Random House. $4.00.

Dear Mr. Shapiro:

I've made a fool of myself enough times not to wish to be patronizing about your current achievement. Anyway I haven't the fatherly eminence from which to be so. But the alternative is to be angry and argumentative, which I'd rather not be either. Here is a family crisis at which, following the hectic dinner scene of raised voices and spilled sugar, everybody had best go to different parts of the orchard and sulk. This I will now do for a few hundred words, rather than properly reviewing your book.

In the first place I don't know why you have to act as if you were the first member of the family ever to discover our frailties. As an aging member of the family myself I can remember a number of similar scenes that I surely don't need to mention to *you*; so to *me* your book sounds less like Columbus or Lindbergh than Bartlett—sour Bartlett but Bartlett.

In the second place I don't know why you have to raise your voice so, unless it is that you are not really talking to us but the neighbors—a device similar to the cheap one I am using here in pretending to write you, when really I am casting about for sympathy from the rest of the family in the face of your intemperance. We all have our dodges, I know, but I can't see that the sympathy you will get from the neighbors will amount to much. They will misunderstand you and invite you over, but you won't like it there.

And in the third place I don't know why you have to pick on our ailing elders as if they'd *made* the whole bloody mess when you know as well as I that the family was headed for isolation and penury anyway. I am not defending the elders (I'll be glad to send you a tape of some of my own dinner-table thunderings), but I resent your trying to make them out to be villains (political and literary) in a vivid melodrama. Melodrama is a discredited art form; you discredited it yourself, commenting on the Bollingen-Prize affair as rendered in the *Saturday Review* a few years back ("the methods used by the *Saturday Review* were unspeakable") —why, then, do you have to *resort* to it? And *in* the *Saturday Review,* yet? I suppose you will say that there are distinctions to be made, and will point to certain of your more judicious passages as evidence. Well, I will agree to these—your book is uneven, as certainly any book of mine of such scope would be—but your polemic drowns out your justice every time. At least the polemic is all the neighbors will hear.

Why, you may ask, am I so worried about the neighbors? Am I worried about appearances? I suppose I am, and this is cowardly of me. But I really don't think I'd be worried about appearances if the appearances and the reality were connected. They are not. What the neighbors hear from you misrepresents you (as I read you) as well as the family, and I think this is too bad; I would prefer that, if they are so disposed, they snicker at us or burn our stables for the right reasons rather than the wrong. Take, for just one example, your fulsome praise of ignorance. You are *not,* I am confident after a careful reading, suggesting that we abandon sense in favor of sensibility; you are *not* suggesting that we destroy our universities and kindergartens, or abandon our grammars and our various acquired rhetorical skills like, say, rhyme and reason—but if you think the neighbors hearing you will hear those "nots" you're sadly misled. They hear your curses, not your qualifications. You assert that you "believe in Blake's proverb that 'the road of excess leads to the palace of wisdom' "—would you not agree that this wisdom, if it is wisdom, is, like all wisdom, something to be absorbed in the closenesses, not over the back fence? Well, then, why blatantly distort it, why broadcast it loosely, why give noisy demonstrations of it so that the Huns outside (some of our neighbors, I should mention, are Huns) will put it in their Hun context and thereby rape all the children in Peoria? Or something? I mean simply that you have misrepresented "excess" as a wisdom by your rhetorical practices in your new book, and only the most sympathetic reader (that is, a member of "our" blasted family) will understand that what you are saying about the good gray Mr. Eliot, for example, is just not comparable to what you would say about Hitler or Attila, or even, for that matter, Henry Luce or J. Edgar Hoover.

And now let me return from the orchard. I know that by now you won't believe I share any of your convictions, and I am certain that we differ widely in our estimate of some of the poets you discuss. But it seems to me that these differences are local and, as I have said, familial; they are simply not discussable in the large. I think this is most evident in your relatively quiet essay, *Poets and Psychologists,* where you argued with the neighbors rather than Us, and where you were as sensitive to the differences between Them and Us as the most kinfolky member of our difficult family could well ask you to be. In that you dealt rather too glibly with the nature of the poet—as we all do, and as you apologized for doing—but at least there you had none of the desperate impulses to betray Us that is so evident elsewhere in the book. No, in that essay you were all solidarity, solidarity forever.

332

Now I think I can ridicule our solidarity as readily (though perhaps not as vividly) as you can, and I am not suggesting that we should or ever could agree on a simple party line. But I do think that you might well now come out of the orchard too, and at least be civil. There isn't much civility left in the world, even in the best places, yet we still do have, I think, one of the best places, one of the only possible places. And one of the reasons our place remains possible is that it is still civil enough to accommodate (even though you say it does not) Whitman and Eliot, Miller and Stevens and all their contemporary *literate* equivalents. The magazine that I write this for [*Poetry*] is a civil example, but so, damn it, is yours, and you know it is, and you know too that you didn't move so *very* far in moving from Chicago to Nebraska. The fight really isn't in either of these two places at all, is it?

Sincerely,

REED WHITTEMORE